PARENTS' MAGAZINE'S

CHRISTMAS
HOLIDAY
BOOK

THE STORY OF CHRISTMAS WITH A TREASURY OF FAVORITE READING, MUSIC, COOKERY, AND HOLIDAY ACTIVITIES

PARENTS' MAGAZINE'S
CHRISTMAS HOLIDAY BOOK

YORKE HENDERSON

LENORE MILLER

EILEEN GADEN

ARNOLD FREED

Illustrated by
OSCAR LIEBMAN

PARENTS' MAGAZINE PRESS·NEW YORK

Editorial Staff

Coordinating Editor	Robert H. Doherty
Copy Editor and Index	Betty W. Brinkerhoff
Special Research	Celia S. Green
Editorial Associate	Jo-ann Price Baehr
Book Design	Morton Garchik
Music Typography	Multi-art Music Corporation
Food Photography	Eileen Gaden
Cover	19th Century Winter Scene
	Painted by Marian Ebert

International Standard Book Number 0–8193–0557–X
Library of Congress Catalog Card Number 76–179337

Produced for Parents' Magazine Press by Stravon Educational Press

Manufactured in the United States of America

Contents

Color Illustrations

vii

Acknowledgments

Many of the color illustrations were provided through the courtesy of the National Gallery of Art, Washington, D.C.; The Metropolitan Museum of Art, New York; and the Print & Picture Department of The Free Library of Philadelphia. Their specific contributions are listed in the table of Color Illustrations on page vii.

Special appreciation is expressed to the following for permission to reprint copyrighted material:

American Bible Society, for the accounts of the Nativity in the Gospel of Matthew and the Gospel of Luke from the Today's English Version of the *New Testament*. Copyright © 1966 by the American Bible Society.

E. P. Dutton & Co., Inc., for *A Star for Hansi* by Marguerite Vance. Copyright © 1936 by Marguerite Vance. Reprinted in its entirety by permission of E. P. Dutton & Co., Inc.

Friendship Press, for "The Old Story in a New Land" from *We Gather Together* by Grace W. McGavran. Copyright © 1951 (sixth printing) by Friendship Press. Reprinted in its entirety by permission of Friendship Press.

The Westminster Press, for "The Small One" by Charles Tazewell, and for "Christmas Among the Animals," "Saint Francis and the Christmas Story" (originally published under the title "How Saint Francis Told the Christmas Story"), and "The Legend of Babouschka" from *Christmas Stories from Many Lands*, edited by Herbert H. Wernecke, The Westminster Press. Copyright © 1961 by W. L. Jenkins. Reprinted in their entirety by permission of The Westminster Press.

Introduction

PARENTS' MAGAZINE'S CHRISTMAS HOLIDAY BOOK is a one-volume source of Christmas lore, music, cookery, selections for reading, and family activities designed to help recreate in the home both the reverent spirit and the joyous spirit that are traditionally associated with the Christmas season but have been lost in the pandemonium of today's marketplace. Christmas is undoubtedly a good excuse (if one is needed) for a shopping spree, but first and foremost it is a time for rededication to Jesus, the *raison d'être* for the holiday.

For more than 1,900 years Christians have celebrated His birth in a variety of ways and forms—varying from country to country and from century to century. This book recounts those changes, taking us from the birth of Jesus as told by St. Matthew and St. Luke in the *New Testament* to a historical review of the development of the holiday, including the origins of Santa Claus and the Christmas tree.

Parents' Magazine's Christmas Holiday Book is more than history, however; it offers all the "time-tested ingredients" to make every Christmas a spiritually exalting experience. Of course, some of the material in the book is available elsewhere, but to find it the celebrant must resort to a variety of publications. Much of what is offered is, however, new or specifically adapted, as, for example, the music for the CAROLS chapter, which has been newly arranged to make it playable by those with only slight competence on the piano and singable by carolers who have a minimum of music-reading ability.

Because there were hundreds of Christmas tales and carols to choose from, the selections were limited to those that the editors considered "best loved" or "all-time favorites." It is the favorite Christmas tale or carol that evokes the nostalgic holiday mood and with it the sense of devotional well-being. The selections offered should help to create this mood.

Christmas feasts and merry-making are as traditional as the Midnight Mass, carol singing, Santa Claus, and the tree, so we have presented favorite recipes, each newly kitchen tested, designed to bring a full measure of cheer to the dining table.

Doing things together is probably the most satisfying aspect of a family Christmas. To help you do things together better and perhaps save you money in the process, we have included "how to" information on a variety of subjects, ranging from shopping for gifts to decorating the tree and the home.

Heeding the famous Chinese proverb, "One picture is worth more than ten thousand words," the editors have included not one but hundreds of pictures—all designed to convey the mood and spirit of Christmas. Famous religious paintings, period prints of yesteryear, earliest Christmas cards, scores of line drawings, and full-color food photographs decorate the book throughout its more than three hundred pages.

About the Contributors

Yorke Henderson, author of the first six chapters, is the editor of the London Express News and Feature Service. He has been directly responsible for the production of fifteen annual Christmas supplements dealing with historical and traditional aspects of Christmas that have been published by newspapers and magazines throughout the world.

Lenore Miller, author of the chapter FAMILY ACTIVITIES, is a free-lance writer whose assignments have included features for the NBC programs *Monitor* and *Emphasis.* She has done public relations work for the American Museum of Natural History and research writing for specialized television programs.

Arnold Freed, who arranged the music for the CAROLS chapter, is a graduate of the Juilliard School of Music and holds a Master of Music degree from New York University. Under a Fulbright scholarship, he studied composition in Italy with Luigi Dellapiccola. Upon returning to the United States, he studied piano with Paul Wittgenstein. In 1959 he was awarded a Ford Foundation grant. His published compositions have been performed in the United States and in Europe.

Eileen Gaden, who researched and tested the recipes in the chapter CHRISTMAS COOKERY, operates her own food consulting firm, creating and testing recipes for television and magazines. Her clients include leading food processors and distributors in the United States.

Oscar Liebman is a nationally known illustrator whose drawings and paintings appear regularly in important magazines, newspapers, and religious publications. His most recent major assignment, the Roman Catholic book *God's Saving Presence,* is decorated with more than thirty-five of his full-color paintings.

Betty W. Brinkerhoff, who wrote the notes to the chapter CAROLS and prepared the Index, is a free-lance writer and editor.

THE BIRTH
OF
JESUS

FROM
THE GOSPEL OF MATTHEW

FROM
THE GOSPEL OF LUKE

1 This is the birth record of Jesus Christ, who was a descendant of David, who was a descendant of Abraham.

[2] Abraham was the father of Isaac; Isaac was the father of Jacob; Jacob was the father of Judah and his brothers; [3] Judah was the father of Perez and Zerah (their mother was Tamar); Perez was the father of Hezron; Hezron was the father of Ram; [4] Ram was the father of Amminadab; Amminadab was the father of Nahshon; Nahshon was the father of Salmon; [5] Salmon was the father of Boaz (Rahab was his mother); Boaz was the father of Obed (Ruth was his mother); Obed was the father of Jesse; [6] Jesse was the father of King David.

David was the father of Solomon (his mother had been Uriah's wife); [7] Solomon was the father of Rehoboam; Rehoboam was the father of Abijah; Abijah was the father of Asa; [8] Asa was the father of Jehoshaphat; Jehoshaphat was the father of Joram; Joram was the father of Uzziah; [9] Uzziah was the father of Jotham; Jotham was the father of Ahaz; Ahaz was the father of Hezekiah; [10] Hezekiah was the father of Manasseh; Manasseh was the father of Amon; Amon was the father of Josiah; [11] Josiah was the father of Jechoniah and his brothers, at the time when the people of Israel were carried away to Babylon.

[12] After the people were carried away to Babylon: Jechoniah was the father of Shealtiel; Shealtiel was the father of Zerubbabel; [13] Zerubbabel was the father of Abiud; Abiud was the father of Eliakim; Eliakim was the father of Azor; [14] Azor was the father of Zadok; Zadok was the father of Achim; Achim was the father of Eliud; [15] Eliud was the father of Eleazar; Eleazar was the father of Matthan; Matthan was the father of Jacob; [16] Jacob was the father of Joseph, the husband of Mary, who was the mother of Jesus, called the Messiah.

[17] So then, there were fourteen sets of fathers and sons from Abraham to David, and fourteen from David to the time when the

people were carried away to Babylon, and fourteen from then to the birth of the Messiah.

THE BIRTH OF JESUS CHRIST

[18] This was the way that Jesus Christ was born. His mother Mary was engaged to Joseph, but before they were married she found out that she was going to have a baby by the Holy Spirit. [19] Joseph, to whom she was engaged, was a man who always did what was right; but he did not want to disgrace Mary publicly, so he made plans to break the engagement secretly. [20] While he was thinking about all this, an angel of the Lord appeared to him in a dream and said: "Joseph, descendant of David, do not be afraid to take Mary to be your wife. For it is by the Holy Spirit that she has conceived. [21] She will give birth to a son and you will name him Jesus—for he will save his people from their sins."

[22] Now all this happened in order to make come true what the Lord had said through the prophet: [23] "The virgin will become pregnant and give birth to a son, and he will be called Emmanuel" (which means, "God is with us").

[24] So when Joseph woke up he did what the angel of the Lord had told him to do and married Mary. [25] But he had no sexual relations with her before she gave birth to her son. And Joseph named him Jesus.

VISITORS FROM THE EAST

2 Jesus was born in the town of Bethlehem, in the land of Judea, during the time when Herod was king. Soon afterwards some men who studied the stars came from the east to Jerusalem [2] and asked: "Where is the baby born to be the king of the Jews? We saw his star when it came up in the east, and we have come to worship him." [3] When King Herod heard about this he was very upset, and so was everybody else in Jerusalem. [4] He called together all the chief priests and the teachers of the Law and asked them, "Where will the Messiah be born?" [5] "In the town of Bethlehem, in Judea," they answered. "This is what the prophet wrote:

[6] 'You, Bethlehem, in the land of Judah,
    Are not by any means the least among the rulers of Judah;
    For from you will come a leader
    Who will guide my people Israel.' "

[7] So Herod called the visitors from the east to a secret meeting and found out from them the exact time the star had appeared. [8] Then he sent them to Bethlehem with these instructions: "Go and make a careful search for the child, and when you find him let me know, so that I may go and worship him too." [9] With this they left, and on their way they saw the star—the same one they had seen in the east—and it went ahead of them until it came and stopped over the place where the child was. [10] How happy they were, what gladness they felt, when they saw the star! [11] They went into the house and saw the child with his mother Mary. They knelt down and worshiped him; then they opened their bags and offered him presents: gold, frankincense, and myrrh.

[12] God warned them in a dream not to go back to Herod; so they went back home by another road.

THE ESCAPE TO EGYPT

[13] After they had left, an angel of the Lord appeared in a dream to Joseph and said: "Get up, take the child and his mother and run away to Egypt, and stay there until I tell you to leave. Herod will be looking for the child to kill him." [14] So Joseph got up, took the child and his mother, and left during the night for Egypt, [15] where he stayed until Herod died.

This was done to make come true what the Lord had said through the prophet, "I called my Son out of Egypt."

THE KILLING OF THE CHILDREN

[16] When Herod realized that the visitors from the east had tricked him, he was furious. He gave orders to kill all the boys in Bethlehem and its neighborhood who were two years old and younger—in accordance with what he had learned from the visitors about the time when the star had appeared.

[17] In this way what the prophet Jeremiah had said came true:

[18] "A sound is heard in Ramah,
The sound of bitter crying and weeping.
Rachel weeps for her children,
She weeps and will not be comforted,
Because they are all dead."

THE RETURN FROM EGYPT

[19] After Herod had died, an angel of the Lord appeared in a dream to Joseph, in Egypt, [20] and said: "Get up, take the child and his mother, and go back to the country of Israel, because those who tried to kill the child are dead." [21] So Joseph got up, took the child and his mother, and went back to the country of Israel.

[22] When he heard that Archelaus had succeeded his father Herod as king of Judea, Joseph was afraid to settle there. He was given more instructions in a dream, and so went to the province of Galilee [23] and made his home in a town named Nazareth. He did this to make come true what the prophets had said, "He will be called a Nazarene."

FROM THE GOSPEL OF LUKE

1 Dear Theophilus:
Many have done their best to write a report of the things that have taken place among us. [2] They wrote what we have been told by those who saw these things from the beginning and proclaimed the message. [3] And so, your Excellency, because I have carefully studied all these matters from their beginning, I thought it good to write an orderly account for you. [4] I do this so that you will know the full truth of all those matters which you have been taught.

THE BIRTH OF JOHN THE BAPTIST ANNOUNCED

[5] During the time when Herod was king of Judea, there was a priest named Zechariah, who belonged to the priestly order of Abiah. His wife's name was Elizabeth; she also belonged to a priestly family. [6] They both lived good lives in God's sight, and obeyed fully all the Lord's commandments and rules. [7] They had no children because Elizabeth could not have any, and she and Zechariah were both very old.

[8] One day Zechariah was doing his work as a priest before God, taking his turn in the daily service. [9] According to the custom followed by the priests, he was chosen by lot to burn the incense on the altar. So he went into the Temple of the Lord, [10] while the crowd of people outside prayed during the hour of burning the incense. [11] An angel of the Lord appeared to him, standing at the right side of the altar where the incense was burned. [12] When Zechariah saw him he was troubled and felt afraid. [13] But the angel said to him: "Don't be afraid, Zechariah! God has heard your prayer, and your wife Elizabeth will bear you a son. You are to name him John. [14] How glad and happy you will be, and how happy many others will be when he is born! [15] For he will be a great man in the Lord's sight. He must not

Nativity with the Prophets Isaiah and Ezekiel, by Duccio di Buoninsegna

Madonna and Child with St. Peter and St. John the Evangelist, by Nardo di Cione

The Adoration of the Magi, by Sandro Botticelli

The Adoration of the Magi, by Giovanni di Paolo

drink any wine or strong drink. From his very birth he will be filled with the Holy Spirit. [16] He will bring back many of the people of Israel to the Lord their God. [17] He will go as God's messenger, strong and mighty like the prophet Elijah. He will bring fathers and children together again; he will turn the disobedient people back to the way of thinking of the righteous; he will get the Lord's people ready for him."

[18] Zechariah said to the angel, "How shall I know if this is so? I am an old man and my wife also is old." [19] "I am Gabriel," the angel answered. "I stand in the presence of God, who sent me to speak to you and tell you this good news. [20] But you have not believed my message, which will come true at the right time. Because you have not believed you will be unable to speak; you will remain silent until the day my promise to you comes true."

[21] In the meantime the people were waiting for Zechariah, wondering why he was spending such a long time in the Temple. [22] When he came out he could not speak to them—and so they knew that he had seen a vision in the Temple. Unable to say a word, he made signs to them with his hands.

[23] When his period of service in the Temple was over, Zechariah went back home. [24] Some time later his wife Elizabeth became pregnant, and did not leave the house for five months. [25] "Now at last the Lord has helped me in this way," she said. "He has taken away my public disgrace!"

THE BIRTH OF JESUS ANNOUNCED

[26] In the sixth month of Elizabeth's pregnancy God sent the angel Gabriel to a town in Galilee named Nazareth. [27] He had a message for a girl promised in marriage to a man named Joseph, who was a descendant of King David. The girl's name was Mary. [28] The angel came to her and said, "Peace be with you! The Lord is with you, and has greatly blessed you!" [29] Mary was deeply troubled by the angel's message, and she wondered what his words meant. [30] The angel said to her: "Don't be afraid, Mary, for God has been gracious to you. [31] You will become pregnant and give birth to a son, and you will name him Jesus. [32] He will be great and will be called the Son of the Most High God. The Lord God will make him a king, as his ancestor

David was, [33] and he will be the king of the descendants of Jacob for ever; his kingdom will never end!"

[34] Mary said to the angel, "I am a virgin. How, then, can this be?" [35] The angel answered: "The Holy Spirit will come on you, and God's power will rest upon you. For this reason the holy child will be called the Son of God. [36] Remember your relative Elizabeth. It is said that she cannot have children; but she herself is now six months pregnant, even though she is very old. [37] For there is not a thing that God cannot do."

[38] "I am the Lord's servant," said Mary; "may it happen to me as you have said." And the angel left her.

MARY VISITS ELIZABETH

[39] Soon afterward Mary got ready and hurried off to the hill country, to a town in Judea. [40] She went into Zechariah's house and greeted Elizabeth. [41] When Elizabeth heard Mary's greeting, the baby moved within her. Elizabeth was filled with the Holy Spirit, [42] and spoke in a loud voice: "Blessed are you among women! Blessed is the child you will bear! [43] Why should this great thing happen to me, that my Lord's mother comes to visit me? [44] For as soon as I heard your greeting, the baby within me jumped with gladness. [45] How happy are you to believe that the Lord's message to you will come true!"

MARY'S SONG OF PRAISE

[46] Mary said:
  "My heart praises the Lord,
[47] My soul is glad because of God my Savior.
[48] For he has remembered me, his lowly servant!
  And from now on all people will call me blessed,
[49] Because of the great things the Mighty God has done for me.
  His name is holy;
[50] He shows mercy to all who fear him,
  From one generation to another.
[51] He stretched out his mighty arm
  And scattered the proud people with all their plans.
[52] He brought down mighty kings from their thrones,

And lifted up the lowly.
⁵³ He filled the hungry with good things,
And sent the rich away with empty hands.
⁵⁴ He kept the promise he made to our ancestors;
He came to the help of his servant Israel,
⁵⁵ And remembered to show mercy to Abraham
And to all his descendants for ever!"
⁵⁶ Mary stayed about three months with Elizabeth, and then went back home.

THE BIRTH OF JOHN THE BAPTIST

⁵⁷ The time came for Elizabeth to have her baby, and she gave birth to a son. ⁵⁸ Her neighbors and relatives heard how wonderfully good the Lord had been to her, and they all rejoiced with her.

⁵⁹ When the baby was a week old they came to circumcise him; they were going to name him Zechariah, his father's name. ⁶⁰ But his mother said, "No! His name will be John." ⁶¹ They said to her, "But you don't have a single relative with that name!" ⁶² Then they made signs to his father, asking him what name he would like the boy to have. ⁶³ Zechariah asked for a writing pad and wrote, "His name is John." How surprised they all were! ⁶⁴ At that moment Zechariah was able to speak again, and he started praising God. ⁶⁵ The neighbors were all filled with fear, and the news about these things spread through all the hill country of Judea. ⁶⁶ All who heard of it thought about it and asked, "What is this child going to be?" For it was plain that the Lord's power was with him.

ZECHARIAH'S PROPHECY

⁶⁷ His father Zechariah was filled with the Holy Spirit, and he prophesied:
⁶⁸ "Let us praise the Lord, the God of Israel!
For he came to the help of his people and set them free.
⁶⁹ He raised up a mighty Savior for us,
One who is a descendant of his servant David.
⁷⁰ This is what he said long ago by means of his holy prophets:
⁷¹ He promised to save us from our enemies,

And from the power of all those who hate us.
⁷² He said he would show mercy to our ancestors,
And remember his sacred covenant.
⁷³⁻⁷⁴ He made a solemn promise to our ancestor Abraham,
And vowed that he would rescue us from our enemies,
And allow us to serve him without fear,
⁷⁵ To be holy and righteous before him,
All the days of our life.
⁷⁶ You, my child, will be called a prophet of the Most High God;
You will go ahead of the Lord
To prepare his road for him,
⁷⁷ To tell his people that they will be saved,
By having their sins forgiven.
⁷⁸ For our God is merciful and tender;
He will cause the bright dawn of salvation to rise on us,
⁷⁹ And shine from heaven on all those who live in the dark
shadow of death,
To guide our steps into the path of peace."
⁸⁰ The child grew and developed in body and spirit; he lived in the desert until the day when he would appear publicly to the people of Israel.

THE BIRTH OF JESUS

2 At that time Emperor Augustus sent out an order for all the citizens of the Empire to register themselves for the census. ² When this first census took place, Quirinius was the governor of Syria. ³ Everyone, then, went to register himself, each to his own town.

⁴ Joseph went from the town of Nazareth, in Galilee, to Judea, to the town named Bethlehem, where King David was born. Joseph went there because he himself was a descendant of David. ⁵ He went to register himself with Mary, who was promised in marriage to him. She was pregnant, ⁶ and while they were in Bethlehem, the time came for her to have her baby. ⁷ She gave birth to her first son, wrapped him in cloths and laid him in a manger—there was no room for them to stay in the inn.

THE SHEPHERDS AND THE ANGELS

[8] There were some shepherds in that part of the country who were spending the night in the fields, taking care of their flocks. [9] An angel of the Lord appeared to them, and the glory of the Lord shone over them. They were terribly afraid, [10] but the angel said to them: "Don't be afraid! For I am here with good news for you, which will bring great joy to all the people. [11] This very night in David's town your Savior was born—Christ the Lord! [12] This is what will prove it to you: you will find a baby wrapped in cloths and lying in a manger."

[13] Suddenly a great army of heaven's angels appeared with the angel, singing praises to God:

[14] "Glory to God in the highest heaven!

And peace on earth to men with whom he is pleased!"

[15] When the angels went away from them back into heaven, the shepherds said to one another, "Let us go to Bethlehem and see this thing that has happened, that the Lord has told us." [16] So they hurried off and found Mary and Joseph, and saw the baby lying in the manger. [17] When the shepherds saw him they told them what the angel had said about this child. [18] All who heard it were filled with wonder at what the shepherds told them. [19] Mary remembered all these things, and thought deeply about them. [20] The shepherds went back, singing praises to God for all they had heard and seen; it had been just as the angel had told them.

JESUS IS NAMED

[21] A week later, when the time came for the baby to be circumcised, he was named Jesus—the name which the angel had given him before he had been conceived.

THE FIRST CHRISTMAS

ALL THAT THE Bible tells us about the birth of Jesus is contained in two accounts in the New Testament that together would about fill a modern newspaper column. The two accounts —by St. Matthew and St. Luke—have only one fact in common: that the Holy Family was in Bethlehem when Jesus was born. St. Matthew, for instance, says nothing of his having been born in a stable, nothing about shepherds. St. Luke nowhere refers to the wise men or the star that led them to Bethlehem, nor does he mention the massacre of the innocents or the flight into Egypt. And yet, curiously, the two texts complement each other in the light of known historical facts.

At that time Emperor Augustus sent out an order for all the citizens of the Empire to register themselves for the census. When this first census took place, Quirinius was the governor of Syria. Everyone, then, went to register himself, each to his own town.

Joseph went from the town of Nazareth, in Galilee, to Judea, to the town named Bethlehem, where King David was born. Joseph went there because he himself was a descendant of David. He went to register himself with Mary, who was promised in marriage to him.

LUKE

From Nazareth to Bethlehem is about 70 miles in a straight

line. But the road between those two small Jewish communities was anything but straight, so that the journey was hard and long and could take even an able-bodied man nearly a week. To a pregnant young woman who had probably never been away from her native village, the journey must have seemed interminable and frightening.

Much of the way from Nazareth to Bethlehem led through the land of the Samaritans, between whom and the Jews there was little love lost. The Jews disapproved of the Samaritans, a racially mixed people who observed only part of the Jewish religion. In Jewish eyes, the Samaritans seemed far more concerned with obtaining a share of the prosperity that the Roman conquerors had brought to the Eastern shores of the Mediterranean than with throwing off the Roman yoke. To the Samaritans the Jews probably seemed stiff-necked, bigoted, and uncompromising. A Jew did not look for much in the way of hospitality from a Samaritan; indeed, thirty years later Jesus was to use the ill feeling between Jews and Samaritans as the basis of one of his parables, the story of a wounded Jew, ignored by his own people, who was eventually succored by one of the despised Samaritans.

But the times were troubled and violent in any case, and traveling was not undertaken lightly. It had been sixty years since the Romans under their great general Pompey had crushed Jewish resistance and added the coastal lands of the Eastern Mediterranean to their empire; and thirty years had passed since their puppet Herod had been placed on the throne in Jerusalem. Nevertheless, rebellion still simmered just below the surface. In secret places among the hills, armed men waited restlessly for the Messiah who, the old prophets had promised, would come to deliver the Jews from their oppressors. Indeed, it was from the very town of Bethlehem, toward which the Nazarene carpenter and his wife were going, that the prophet Micah seven hundred years earlier had said that the Messiah would come: "You, Bethlehem, in the land of Judah, are not by any means the least among the rulers of Judah; for from you will come a leader who will guide my people Israel."

The old prophecies also said that the deliverer would be a Nazarene. But the child who was soon to be born in Bethlehem was not the kind of leader awaited by the men of the resistance.

Their Messiah was to be another Joshua or Gideon or Judas Maccabaeus, a mighty warrior with the wrath of God in his sword arm. Such concerns, however, were not for Joseph and his young wife struggling toward Bethlehem. They were humble people who knew nothing of politics, and who would be grateful when they were done with the tiresome business of registering with the census-takers in Bethlehem. They had to travel to Bethlehem because Joseph was "a descendant of David." Under the old Jewish tribal system, he belonged to the same clan as the great warrior king who had slain Goliath, and consequently his home town was the same as David's—Bethlehem. The Roman overlords taxed their subject peoples heavily, and, being bureaucrats at heart, they liked to do that taxing in a tidy and orderly way. Thus the Roman governor had decreed that all heads of households should return to their home towns to register for taxation purposes.

Bethlehem was an odd sort of place. Even to a people with a long history, as the Jews were, Bethlehem was old. It had always been there, a triangle of stone houses on a limestone hill six miles from Jerusalem. An even more ancient people had named it Ephrata. The Jews, pouring into their promised land, called it Bethlehem, "the house of bread," probably because of the richness of the cornfields below the town. There was always bread in Bethlehem.

Somehow, the town seemed to go to the very roots of the Jewish people. It was strong on its limestone hill, dominating a main road and a wide plain. It was rich in its cornfields and in the flocks grazing on the surrounding hills. David, the mightiest of Jewish kings, had come from Bethlehem; and Ruth, the embodiment of selfless devotion and one of the best-loved women in the long history of the Jews, had lived there. Yet the town had remained small and simple while only six miles away Jerusalem grew in worldly splendor.

Normally Bethlehem was a quiet place. It was far enough from Jerusalem to feel few of the ripples emanating from Herod's court, and, at the same time, too near to be a stopover for travelers on their way to the capital. But now, as a census point for the Romans, Bethlehem was crowded and noisy. Small as it was, it cannot have had much of an inn; what little accommodation was available had doubtless been preempted by the

census officials even before the families of the house of David
had begun to arrive from all over the country.

> She was pregnant, and while they were in Bethlehem,
> the time came for her to have her baby. She gave
> birth to her first son, wrapped him in cloths and laid
> him in a manger—there was no room for them to stay
> in the inn.
>
> Luke

There is no reason to doubt St. Luke's account of Jesus'
having been born in a stable. The Roman governor had ordered
that every man report back to his own town; and when the Romans gave orders it was advisable to obey them at once. Since
many families were of the house of David, and since not all of
them had to come from as far away as Galilee, every house that
could be used as lodging must already have been pressed into
service by the time Mary and Joseph limped into Bethlehem.

Incidentally, over the centuries artists have created a tradition that Mary rode on a donkey from Nazareth to Bethlehem,
but there is no evidence to support the belief. It is unlikely
that a poor carpenter would have been able to afford a donkey,
and the chances are that Mary walked beside Joseph all those
long sore miles.

In fact, Mary and Joseph were probably lucky to get the
space in the stable. People in the Middle East in those days
were accustomed to living close to their animals. Indeed, in
many parts of the world today—even in remote parts of Europe—peasants still live in a proximity to their domestic animals that would make city dwellers of the West shudder with
distaste.

Whoever owned that stable in Bethlehem—and his name
is not known—might very well have made a few extra coins
for himself by letting it out to someone better able to pay than
a Nazarene carpenter with little more than the shabby clothes
he was wearing. But the Jews are a hospitable people. Perhaps
because for so much of their history they have been compelled
to wander, they have come to set a high value on hospitality.
Pregnant women especially have always been accorded particular consideration, partly because any woman might give

birth to a son, and to the Jews the birth of a male is an occasion for rejoicing. Any male could be the awaited Messiah; and since the days of Moses the Jewish law has said: "Every male opening the womb shall be called holy to the Lord."

Almost certainly, the stable that Mary and Joseph found would not have been a building, not even the primitive wood and thatch structure familiar in religious art. More likely, it was one of the limestone caves common to the area. It would have been warm and dry and probably, by the standards of the day, even clean. Far from feeling abandoned and unwanted, Joseph and Mary must have been both relieved and grateful for its shelter. Time might have decreed that Mary would have to give birth to the child by the roadside. But, by the grace of God, they had reached Bethlehem and had found shelter. And so it was here, according to St. Luke, in a cave stable, in a small, crowded, noisy town, that the most momentous birth in history took place.

Little more is written of Bethlehem until A.D. 127, when the Emperor Hadrian became interested in it. By that time the village had acquired a mystical significance strong enough to have reached the emperor and disturbed him. Unwittingly and quite contrary to his intentions, he helped to perpetuate that mystical significance. In the Roman destruction of the Jewish state, the dispersal of the Jewish people, and the ruthless persecution of Christians, the identity of Christ's birthplace might well have been lost. Intending to eradicate the sacred aura of the site, Hadrian actually preserved it by ordering that a grove be planted for the worship of Adonis over the cave in which Jesus had been born. The grove of Adonis marked the spot until A.D. 330, when the Emperor Constantine, who had become a Christian, decided to erase what he believed to be a grave blasphemy. He had the grove removed and a church built on the site. Other Christian churches and monasteries followed, until at present the distinguishing mark of Bethlehem is its abundance of Christian institutions.

If St. Luke was right about the shepherds being in the fields when the angel of the Lord appeared to them, we can be fairly certain that Jesus was not born in midwinter, the time of year when the Christian world celebrates Christmas. At midwinter Bethlehem is in the grip of frost, and no sheep would have been out on the hillsides in such weather, least of all at night. Indeed, the old Jewish records show that flocks were put out to pasture in March and brought in again about the end of October. But then, this discrepancy between tradition and apparent historical fact should surprise no one. It has never been seriously claimed that December 25 was the true birthday of Jesus.

Since the dawn of history, every society has held some kind of celebration at midwinter, the point in the year at which men took comfort from the fact that the days were growing longer and the sun was returning. Almost invariably it was a feast of light, fire, and rejoicing, with rebirth as the theme. Thus when the early church was substituting Christian festivals for pagan ones, it was natural that they should choose midwinter as the time to celebrate the birth of the founder of the religion.

Can we even be sure that Jesus was born in the year we regard as the beginning of the Christian era, the year zero? On the contrary, the indications are that he was born several years earlier. The evidence for this is twofold. The first clue is the reference by St. Luke to Caesar's order for enrollment, which, he tells us, was carried out when Quirinius, or Cyrinus, was the governor of Syria. We know that Quirinius was the Roman soldier and administrator P. Sulpicius Quirinius, who was highly regarded by the Emperor Augustus. We also know that Quirinius carried out a census, but that was in A.D. 6. In the other account of Jesus' birth, by St. Matthew, we are told that Jesus was born "during the time when Herod was king." Yet, from records of the time, we know that Herod died in 4 B.C. Both those dates rule out any question of Jesus' having been born in the year zero, and at first glance there seems to be no way of reconciling them. Reading the text of St. Luke more carefully, however, we find that he says: "When this first census took place, Quirinius was the governor of Syria." Why "first"? It cannot have been the first census the Romans carried out in that part of the world. They had been there for nearly sixty years, and from their records we know it was their practice to conduct a census every fourteen years. But suppose we read it: This census was the *first made by Quirinius*, the governor of Syria. In fact, we now know that Quirinius served twice in the Middle East for the Emperor, and that he established his seat of government in Syria between 10 and 7 B.C. Thus, there was a time when Quirinius was conducting a census while Herod was on the throne in Jerusalem. Further, knowing that the Romans held a census every fourteen years, and knowing also that one was held in A.D. 6, we need only count back to discover that the previous one must have been about 7 B.C.; and at that time Quirinius was the governor of Syria.

A second piece of biblical evidence confirms the date of Jesus' birth as 7 B.C.

For centuries St. Matthew's mention of a star mystified scholars. Although there is an abundance of astronomical records for the time, nowhere in them is there any mention of a new star. In 44 B.C. and in 17 B.C., brilliant comets were reported by watchers in the Mediterranean area. The next to be reported was not until A.D. 66. But around the supposed year of

Jesus' birth there was no record of any significant astronomical phenomenon. Yet St. Matthew records the arrival in Bethlehem of "men who studied the stars" and their report of having seen a star. Was he merely repeating a legend that gave to the birth of his beloved Lord some of the glory he felt it should have had? That is not really likely. In an age when men were far more astronomically concerned than is the layman today, to invent a new star that no one else had seen would have been to invite discredit as a fanciful liar; and the lot of a Christian was hard enough in those days without courting unnecessary trouble.

Then what was the star whose existence St. Matthew reported? It seems to have been the great European mathematician and astronomer Johannes Kepler who first put his finger on the explanation. One night in 1603 Kepler was watching the approach of two planets, Saturn and Jupiter. Sometimes two planets move so close to each other that they give the viewer the impression of being a single large and brilliant star. It is what astrologers call a conjunction; and on that night Saturn and Jupiter were in conjunction. The sight triggered something in Kepler's mind, and he went back to his books. He was looking for a note written by the rabbinic scholar Abarbanel. And there it was. According to Abarbanel, Jewish astrologers believed that the Messiah would appear when there was a conjunction of Saturn and Jupiter in the constellation Pisces. According to Kepler's astrological tables, there had been just such a conjunction in the year 6 B.C.

Curiously, Kepler's findings were for a long time disregarded, and not until the twentieth century were they confirmed by modern scientific research. It came about in 1925 when a German scholar named Schnabel was studying the records of an ancient academy, the School of Astrology at Sippar in Babylonia. Checking through the voluminous dates of celestial observations, Schnabel came across a note about the position of planets in the constellation Pisces. He found that Jupiter and Saturn were entered over a period of five months. By modern calendar reckoning, the year was 7 B.C. Using modern methods of calculation, astronomers determined that in 7 B.C. the two planets were in conjunction three times, in May, October, and December. So here we find not only another support

for the theory that Jesus was born in 7 B.C., but also the two quite different accounts of his birth interlocking like a jigsaw puzzle and bearing each other out. St. Luke makes no mention of the wise men and the star. St. Matthew says nothing of the census and the journey to Bethlehem. Yet modern scientific and archaeological research reconcile the two accounts in time.

How, then, did all of Christendom come to get the date of Jesus' birth wrong? Blame for the mistake is usually laid on a rather shadowy character, a monk named Dionysius Exiguus, who had gone from what is now southern Russia to Rome in the early part of the sixth century. It is said that in the year 533 Dionysius Exiguus was given the task of determining the beginning of the Christian era by working backward in time. It appears, however, that not only did he ignore the year zero that came between 1 B.C. and A.D. 1, but he also overlooked four years when the Roman Emperor Augustus reigned under his own name of Octavian.

Who were the men who came from the east seeking the new king of the Jews? To begin with, we do not know that there were three of them. St. Matthew's account neither numbers nor names them. Yet the Christian legend over the centuries has always portrayed three wise men, has given them names, and has gone so far as to suggest that they were kings. All that we know about them from St. Matthew is that they were men who studied the stars and that they came from the East.

We can start by dismissing the thought that they were kings. Remember that Palestine was a Roman colony ruled by a puppet monarch. Kings in those days traveled with retinues the size of small armies, and neither the Roman governors nor Herod himself were likely to have calmly accepted the sudden arrival of a large armed force looking for a new king of the Jews. Wars started over much less than that. Nor is it likely, as some writers have suggested, that the three "kings" left their retinues on the far side of the Jordan River and crossed unescorted into Palestine to avoid any sort of incident. Neither the Romans nor Herod would have tolerated an army camped on their borders any more than they would have permitted one actually to enter their country. Furthermore, there is no rational explanation of why three monarchs should have traveled from their own countries to see the problematical new king of a not particularly important nation. The legend of the kings probably started in the Middle Ages and was based on the richness of the gifts they brought to Jesus and Mary—the gold, frankincense, and myrrh. In fact, the traditional number of three visitors probably was derived from the itemization of three gifts.

St. Matthew calls them "men who studied the stars," and the description clearly refers to astrologers. This identification is borne out by their explanation: "We saw his star as it came up in the east." But then, curiously, they add, ". . . and we have come to worship him." Now why should foreign astrologers make a long and dangerous journey to worship a new Jewish ruler? Unless, of course, they were themselves Jews. If we start with that assumption, then several things fall into place. St. Matthew says they were from the east. Babylon is east of Palestine, and since the time of King Nebuchadnezzar many Jews had remained in Babylon. Also it is known that many of them studied at the School of Astrology in Sippar. Although they had stayed on in Babylon, those men had not ceased to be Jews, and they must have accepted the Jewish tradition that the Messiah would appear when Saturn and Jupiter were in conjunction in the constellation Pisces. What more natural than that, having seen this conjunction three times in one year, these men should have journeyed west into Palestine to see the Messiah? It is understandable, too, that they would have gone straight to Jerusalem, to the center of things, and asked there about the new king, and that Herod's spies promptly would have brought the tyrant word of the strangers and the question they were asking.

None of St. Matthew's account of the visitors with precious gifts for the Messiah is necessarily fanciful. There is, for instance, nothing strange in Herod's not knowing the prophecy that the Messiah would be born in Bethlehem. Herod was not a Jew but an Idumaean, one of a people from the province south of Judea, most of whom had been forcibly converted to Judaism. By conviction Herod was no more of a Jew than was necessary to be accepted as the Romans' puppet ruler of Palestine. At the time of Jesus' birth, Herod was an old man. He was also, by today's standards, insane. Suspicion, fear, and, more than likely, the disease that was eventually to kill him had affected his mind. He was a hideous caricature of the handsome

Idumaean prince, athlete, and hunter who, more than thirty years earlier, had been chosen by the Roman conquerors as their puppet ruler.

Herod knew that the Jews had never really accepted him as ruler. He suspected—much of the time correctly—that plots and conspiracies were constantly being hatched against him. Several times he had been compelled to put down rebellions ruthlessly. Over the years his fears had fed upon themselves and fueled his suspicions so that eventually it was not only the Pharisees and the Sadducees, the Essenes and the Zealots that he suspected and feared, but his closest courtiers and even

The Virgin with St. Inés and St. Tecla, by El Greco

The Madonna of Humility, by Fra Angelico

members of his own family. He murdered his wife and had his mother-in-law executed for treason. Fearing that his brother-in-law, who was a legitimate heir, might succeed him on the throne, he had him killed. He quarreled with his sons and exiled them to Rome, and when they returned he threw them into prison and then executed them. Even the Romans, who were ruthless by the harsh standards of the time, were appalled; the Emperor Augustus said that he would rather be Herod's swine than his son, meaning that since pork was forbidden to the Jews he would be less likely to be butchered.

Herod reached the stage at which he did not trust even his own spies; he took to disguising himself as a private citizen and wandering around Jerusalem talking to the people, trying to discover what they really thought about him.

It is not difficult, then, to surmise what went on in Herod's mind when he heard the strangers in Jerusalem were asking about a new king of the Jews. It was what he had always feared. He had never really understood the Jews, with all their mysteries and prophecies. They gave him the impression always that they were looking above and beyond him, waiting for something to happen.

In fairness to Herod, however, it should be said that few if any rulers of the time would have taken calmly reports that the successor to their throne had been born. Some kings would have had the bearers of the report tortured and killed. Most of them would have had the infant usurper sought out and slain—as Herod plainly intended.

Why, then, did Herod go to the trouble of summoning the visitors and asking them to find the child for him, on the pretext of wanting to pay his respects? Why not simply send a body of soldiers down to Bethlehem to find and destroy the child? It can only have been because Herod knew how close to the surface rebellion was simmering, and feared that it would erupt if he openly murdered the child who might be the Messiah. He cannot have doubted the Romans' ability to quell any rebellion; but he probably feared that if he precipitated such a situation he would be removed from the throne as incompetent. Better by far to have the child identified by the visitors and then quietly removed.

It is more than possible that Herod also intended to do

away with the visitors once they had served their purpose.
There would have been little point in disposing of the child
and leaving the astrologers alive to talk about what they had
seen and heard. It also seems probable that the visitors guessed
what Herod had in mind. They must have known his reputation
for suspicion and ruthlessness, and, having met him face to
face, they can have been in little doubt about how he was
likely to act.

God warned them in a dream not to go back to
Herod; so they went back home by another road.

MATTHEW

The chances are that even before they had left Herod's
palace they had decided to get out of Palestine as soon as they
had seen the child.

After they had left, an angel of the Lord appeared in
a dream to Joseph and said: "Get up, take the child
and his mother and run away to Egypt, and stay there
until I tell you to leave. Herod will be looking for the

child to kill him." So Joseph got up, took the child
and his mother, and left during the night for Egypt,
where he stayed until Herod died.

This was done to make come true what the Lord
had said through the prophet, "I called my Son out of
Egypt."

MATTHEW

Herod was acting in character when he issued the com-
mand to kill all boys two years old and younger in Bethlehem
and its vicinity. Tricked by the visitors and balked of his victim,
he abandoned all pretense of rational behavior and lashed out
in a fury born of fear and frustration. But by that time Joseph,
Mary, and Jesus were safely out of the mad king's reach.

St. Matthew's account gives no clue as to where in Egypt
the Holy Family took refuge. In such circumstances, however,
people seek out their own kind if at all possible; and there is
historical evidence that at Mataria, just north of Cairo, there
was a small community of Jewish gardeners brought from the
Jordan valley to look after the herb gardens of Cleopatra.
Legend has credited Mataria with being the Holy Family's
home in exile; and the legend sits easily with the facts.

Within three years Herod was dead. He died in an agony
of mind and body so great that he tried to take his own life.
A Jewish writer of the time said that he died like a dog.

After Herod had died, an angel of the Lord appeared
in a dream to Joseph, in Egypt, and said: "Get up,
take the child and his mother, and go back to the
country of Israel, because those who tried to kill the
child are dead." So Joseph got up, took the child and
his mother, and went back to the country of Israel.

When he heard that Archelaus had succeeded
his father Herod as king of Judea, Joseph was afraid
to settle there. He was given more instructions in a
dream, and so went to the province of Galilee and
made his home in a town named Nazareth. He did
this to make come true what the prophets had said,
"He will be called a Nazarene."

MATTHEW

CHRISTMAS TRADITIONS

"CHRISTMAS HAS BECOME a consumer festival." The complaint has been heard increasingly in recent years that commercialism has replaced worship as the reason for Christmas. Instead of being a devout thanksgiving for the birth of Christ, the Christmas season is now notable for the crowds of shoppers who pack city streets the world over, spending heavily on gifts, food, drink, and decorations. We sometimes seem to be celebrating the age of plenty rather than the Mass of Christ.

In fact, we are unknowingly reverting to a primitive human instinct: the celebration of the turn of the year, when winter begins to wane and the sun starts once more to climb in the sky, and when crops and fruits are reborn. Almost every known civilization throughout the ages has had such a festival, and all of them have celebrated it with feasting and rejoicing.

It was not until the fourth century that Christmas—literally, a Mass held for Christ—was acclaimed a public festival by the Church. Until that time, the Church fathers had been reluctant to make Christmas a festival because it so nearly coincided with Saturnalia. Early in the history of the Roman Empire, Saturnalia had become the main annual festival. Saturn was the god of farming, and his festival—observed by the astronomically skillful Romans at the accurate winter solstice, in contrast to the November feasts of the early northern races—merged with the Kalendae new-year celebrations in honor of the twin-faced deity Janus.

The result of the merger was seven uninterrupted days of

wild feasting throughout the Roman Empire, which stretched across half the world, during which masters served slaves and rules were turned inside out. The Greek Libianus wrote of it: "The impulse to spend seizes everyone. He who the whole year through has taken pleasure in saving and piling up his money becomes suddenly extravagant."

So man has not changed much, nor have those who reproach him for his indulgences.

If the Romans influenced centuries of subsequent December celebrations, the Persians anticipated to an astonishing degree the religious aspects of Christmas. When Christianity was just beginning, the Persian cult of Mithras was flourishing throughout the East. Not only was it remarkably similar to its successor in its practices—it featured baptism, the sacramental meal, observance of Sunday as holy, and the ideas of good and evil, heaven and hell, and Judgment Day—but it further celebrated the birth of its god on December 25, a date not fixed for Christmas until several centuries after Jesus' birth. Long before Saturnalia and Mithraism, primitive northern men rejoiced at midwinter—or their estimate of it—and thanked their horned gods for the new life of a coming year.

Running through these diverse celebrations of very different peoples, we find not only a common time, midwinter, and a common theme, rebirth, but also the eminently practical sentiments of peace and goodwill. For with the land temporarily dead, the squabbles and rows between farmers and peasants lay dormant, too.

So despite the reluctance of early Christian churchmen to associate their faith with what they must have considered orgiastic and pagan traditions, the midwinter anniversary of Christ's birth—as they believed it to be—fell at an opportune time of the year. It allowed conservative pagans to absorb Christianity gently, without sudden and dramatic overthrow of their own time-honored customs of solstice celebrations. And it served as comprehensible symbolism to simple folk that the birth of God's son, which they had to imagine, and the birth of the trees and grass and sunshine, which they could see around them, were concurrent.

Thus when we complain that "Christmas isn't what it used to be," with all its spending and eating and drinking, the

fact is that Christmas *is* just what it was in those early days.

An ancient Roman, an early Norseman, or a medieval Englishman would be equally amazed and confused if confronted with twentieth-century Western life: miniskirts and motorcars, skyscrapers and cinemas, telephones and transistor radios. It would seem to them a different world peopled by an alien race. Technology, along with scientific sophistication, has revolutionized man's living habits. If one of your distant ancestors were to observe you in most of your everyday activities—traveling to your office by car or train, watching television, opening a can of food to heat on your electric stove, taking off from an airport on holiday—he would be dumbfounded. But let him see you on Christmas Eve, preparing your home for Christmas, and a common chord might be struck. For at Christmas we still observe customs and rituals born centuries ago and shared by peoples of otherwise contrasting life styles ever since.

Christmas greenery is one of the ancient customs that remain largely unchanged. It is no coincidence that the holly and ivy and mistletoe with which we bedeck our homes today are among the few evergreens that bear recognizable fruit only in winter. They were seen by the ancients, shivering through bleak winters, as one of the rare signs of fertility triumphing over the elements. People took them into their homes as a sort of luck charm for a fruitful year ahead.

The decking of temples with greenery was later adopted by the Christian Church, but one traditional Christmas plant the Church has never adopted is the Kissing Bough—mistletoe. It is a peculiar plant, with its pale berries and parasitical growing habits, and it has a history to match.

A killer, and a healer; mistletoe carries both tags, though with what justification it is hard to say, since the origins are impossible to check. Balder, the Norse god of light—a Scandinavian Apollo—was said to have been slain by mistletoe. His fellow gods, realizing what a catastrophe it would be if the god of light were ever to die, laid every living thing under a vow not to harm Balder—all except the mistletoe, which they considered too puny and insignificant to do any harm. Loki, the god of evil, discovering this omission, tricked the blind god Hoder into throwing a mistletoe dart, which miraculously killed Balder. Fortunately, the sun continued to shine.

The Bretons, too, held mistletoe in contempt, for equally unprovable reasons. They believed that the mistletoe was once a tree and was used to make the cross on which Christ was crucified, after which it shrank in shame to a contorted parasitic bush.

Whatever the justification of these myths, from earliest times mistletoe has been banned from churches. But it has been welcomed into Christian homes—indeed, made an honored Christmas guest—which reflects its obverse reputation as a healer.

The Druids used mistletoe as a driver out of devils and a cure-all that could even protect houses from lightning. For centuries English countryfolk fed mistletoe to sick cattle, both to cure them and to bring good fortune to the rest of the herd.

It was also given as medicine to humans, especially for falling-sickness, as epilepsy was then called. It could not have done anybody much good, since modern pharmaceutical science has classified the berries as purgative and emetic and the whole plant as a cardiac depressant. Mistletoe was also used as a remedy for snakebite and toothache, and was supposed to be a composer of quarrels. It was even used for making flypaper, because of its stickiness. The Druids used to cut it ceremonially with a golden sickle, preferably when it was found on an oak tree, a rare straying from its normal habitat of apple, poplar, hawthorn, lime, or maple.

The popularity of mistletoe is highest in America and England (in Australia it is considered a dangerous forest weed). The tradition of kissing beneath it—possibly a symbol of peace or sacrifice—is echoed only in Austria. There the mistletoe-wreathed Sylvester figure leaps out at maidens and kisses them, but he is more a satyr figure than an expression of Christmas gaiety.

Holly, on the other hand, is well rooted in Christian lore as well as being one of the best-loved Christmas plants because of its bright red berries and sturdy, shiny leaves. With its thorns and red fruit, holly is associated with the Passion; the Scandinavian name for it is literally "Christ-thorn." It has long been held to be in opposition to the ivy—perhaps because the ivy's traditional place was Bacchanalian, the tavern, whereas holly belonged to the Church and the home; perhaps because holly's associations were resilient and male whereas ivy's were clinging and female.

Like mistletoe, holly was long held to be a medicament for ailments as diverse as measles and rheumatism. Argentinians still drink maté tea, made from holly leaves, a potion shared by early North American Indians. Holly also has many associations with good fortune. In Louisiana its berries were kept for luck and it was believed to protect both animals and humans from lightning, fire, and the evil eye.

According to English belief, holly even held prophetic properties. To induce a dream of his or her future mate, a young person would pick nine holly leaves in silence on a Friday midnight, then tie them with nine knots into a three-cornered handkerchief and place it under the pillow. If the curious one remained silent from the time of picking the leaves until the next morning, his or her future mate was supposed to appear in a dream.

Ivy, too, was supposed to be able to foretell the future, both generally and maritally. In Scotland a girl could hold an ivy leaf to her heart and recite:

> Ivy, Ivy, I love you;
> In my bosom I put you,
> The first young man who speaks to me
> My future husband shall be.

There is no record of the efficacy of this early variant of computer dating.

A traditional Christmas plant that has lost favor is the rosemary, celebrated by Shakespeare in *Hamlet:* "Rosemary, that's for remembrance." From the fourteenth until the nineteenth century it was the most prized of decorations, after which it was displaced by the introduction of the Christmas tree. Rosemary had a lovely scent and a magnificent purple flower, and it was also used as a garland for the traditional boar's head at Christmas dinner.

The rose of Jericho, a small annual rose whose dried leaves and flowers open out when moistened, was long considered a special Christmas plant and was said by generations of monks to symbolize the opening and closing of Mary's womb. Its popularity vanished with its mystery when seventeenth-century scientists explained its movements as purely botanical.

The plant with perhaps the strangest Christmas legend attached to it—at least in Britain—is the hawthorn.

The story of the Glastonbury Thorn begins in the early years of the Christian era when Glastonbury was an orchard island in the Somerset marshes—King Arthur's Isle of Avalon. To this island from Gaul sailed Joseph of Arimathaea, who, according to tradition, had taken Jesus' body from the cross and placed it in the tomb. While climbing the steep hillside known as Glastonbury Tor, Joseph sank his staff into the soft soil. The day was Christmas Eve. The next day the staff, which was hawthorn, burst into bloom. It was a miraculous sign. When Glastonbury Abbey was built nearby, the thorn was replanted within its grounds, and it continued to flower every Christmas Day. Since then it has been mentioned in chronicles throughout the centuries and has been a popular place of pilgrimage at Christmas.

In the seventeenth century, the Puritans considered belief in the Glastonbury hawthorn a sacrilege, and one of them went to chop down the twin-trunked tree. The first trunk fell easily, but as he hacked at the second, "some of the prickles flew into his eye," according to the historian James Howell, "and made him monocular." What is more, the felled trunk continued to flower for another thirty years before mysteriously disappearing.

English monarchs valued the legend—King James I paid well for a single cutting from the tree—and when during the Civil War another Puritan dug out the remaining trunk, both tree and legend were too firmly established to die. Grafts and cuttings of the original thorn had been planted in the vicinity over the ages.

When England adopted the Gregorian calendar, in 1753, the date of Christmas was moved back eleven days. And when, according to the contemporary *Gentleman's Magazine,* a crowd gathered round the hawthorn tree on the new December 25, it failed to blossom. However, on January 5, the old Christmas Day, blossom it did. Which proved, according to the magazine, how foolish it was to meddle with the calendar. Pilgrims still visit the Glastonbury Thorn, some on Christmas Day, some on January 5. And sometimes it blossoms, sometimes it doesn't.

Sadly, the explanation is a mundane one. The blossoming of the hawthorn depends on the wetness or dryness of the previous summer. Botanically the tree is known as *Crataegus monogyna biflora,* and it produces flowers twice annually, once around Christmas and once in the spring.

The Christmas tree may not equal the hawthorn in legends, but in its relatively short life it has become far more widely known. There are few major cities in the world where you would not find a decorated Christmas tree on December 25. And not only Christian countries mark the season with a decorated evergreen; the custom has been adopted in Japan, with a Christian population of less than 1 percent.

The Christmas tree, nevertheless, is very much a Western

innovation. Its origins are Germanic, and even today Germans consider it a more important part of Christmas than do Americans or British.

In the Middle Ages, the German peoples celebrated the feast of Adam and Eve, and at the center of the ritual was a dramatization of the story of the Garden of Eden. One of the props used for this was a fir tree decked with apples to represent the Fall. On the following day, Christmas, it was the custom to burn pyramid-shaped candelabra called "Lightstocks." Over the years these candles came to be added to the fir tree along with round cookies—shaped like the Host—as symbols of the Redemption. Thus the Christmas tree was born.

"At Christmas," wrote a Strasbourg merchant in 1605, "they set up fir trees in the parlor at Strasbourg and hang on them roses cut out of many-colored paper, apples, wafers, gold-foil, and sweets."

The tradition naturally spread through the fir-covered Scandinavian countries before it reached the rest of Europe and America. In fact, the Christmas tree was known in America before it became popular in much of Europe; it was introduced by German settlers in the eighteenth century and later spread by Hessian soldiers.

But the facts have to give way to legend, as in so much Christmas lore, and the traditional inventor of the Christmas tree is the Protestant reformer Martin Luther. One Christmas Eve, so goes the story, Luther was walking beneath a night sky filled with stars, while the moon lit up the surrounding snow-clad firs. Moved by the scene, he hurried home and set up a sapling in his house, laden with candles to simulate the stars. And so the Christmas tree was born—several hundred years after it had already become popular. But no one can begrudge such a charming legend a little latitude in its chronology.

Long before Luther, many parts of Germany—headed by Saxony—celebrated Christmas with a tree substitute, a pyramid made of wood and decorated with candles and fruit. In some cases these "trees" were carried from house to house with requests for money, a practice later to be adopted by carol singers. It has been suggested that the wooden replicas were an economy measure, since they could be used year after year, but this explanation does not take into account the abundance of fir trees in Germany at that time.

The first known use of Christmas trees in America was among German settlers in Pennsylvania as early as 1746. The custom did not spread from Germany to neighboring France until the early nineteenth century. And although it was known, albeit not widely, in England around that time, it was Prince Albert of Saxe-Coburg who established it as a tradition after he married Queen Victoria in 1840. As the Christmas tree grew in popularity, Britons took it to all parts of their empire, which explains its presence in some unlikely places.

Ironically, the Christmas tree was a major cause of tragedies until recent years. When Australians first tried to reproduce western Christmas with candle-lit fir trees, the candles melted and bent in the heat and became a serious fire hazard. In America and Europe, when muslin dresses and long hair were in fashion, fire brigades knew the Christmas tree as a major danger. Electric lights have removed much of the danger, but we have lost more than a hazard from those nineteenth-century years. Trees then were hung with sweetmeats and fruits, and when Twelfth Night came around and it was time to dismantle the tree, it was not a sad day for the children but a joyful one, for they ate the decorations.

Communal Christmas trees were probably common in seventeenth- and eighteenth-century Germany, but they were not found elsewhere until 1909, when the town of Pasadena, California, set up a lighted tree on Mount Wilson. Since then, the custom has become widespread.

A Christmas tree can be recognized as a Christmas tree the world over, so long as it is decked out for the occasion. But strip off the decorations and a New Zealander might walk past an American Douglas fir, for example, without associating it with December 25. For at home the New Zealander uses as his Christmas tree a pohutukawa, which has red flowers and silvery leaves in winter and is also often misshapen, like a Japanese bonsai. In Europe the spruce is generally used. At Hilton Park, in Wilmington, North Carolina, an ancient oak provides a permanent Christmas tree, trimmed with 7,000 colored lights and several tons of Spanish moss.

Whatever the type of tree we individually know and love as a Christmas tree, and whatever its ritual origins, Cecil Day-Lewis probably speaks for all of us when he writes in "The Christmas Tree":

So feast your eyes now
On mimic star and moon-cold bauble:
Worlds may wither unseen,
But the Christmas tree is a tree of fable,
A phoenix in evergreen,
And the world cannot change or chill what its mysteries mean
To your hearts and eyes now.

Sadly, the Yule log has not survived along with the Christmas tree. Indeed, it could be said that on its way down the Yule log met the Christmas tree on its way up. The meeting would have taken place in the nineteenth century, about the time when Charles Dickens was writing *A Christmas Carol.*

The Yule log is memorialized in the form of cakes or their decorations, but the burning of a huge log—a custom spread by the Vikings and other Scandinavians who lived in bitter climates—has almost died out.

Like so many Christmas customs, the Yule log can be traced back to the pagan celebration of the nativity of the sun. Very early civilizations feared that the sun was dying as the days grew shorter toward the winter solstice. So on what they judged was the shortest day of the year they tried to revitalize the sun by burning huge fires. Later, more sophisticated peoples maintained the ritual as an act of worship to the sun gods.

On the stroke of midnight on what was to become Christmas Eve, the sun-worshiping Egyptians would cease their prayers and leave their inner shrines to cry out: "The Virgin has brought forth, the light is waxing." To them the new sun was like a newborn child, yet another parallel with Christmas.

When the Church fathers in the fifth century declared December 25 to be Christ's birthday, they wisely allowed pagan fire festivals to be continued, adopting them into their own services. Thus today candlelight services are held in darkened cathedrals, and candles—real or electric—burn on Christmas trees. In many parts of the world Christmas trees are collected and burned on Twelfth Night. And, of course, the Yule log became part of Christmas.

On Christmas Eve, as the village church service began, the head of the family—having carefully washed his hands, because according to legend unwashed hands would stop the log from burning—rolled the heavy Yule log into the hearth and set it afire. His family, kneeling round the hearth, recited three "Pater nosters" and three "Aves." "Bless this log and this home, O Lord," they prayed. And when the church bells rang to signal the beginning of the sacrament of the Mass, the log was sprinkled with holy water and blessed in the name of the Holy Trinity. The Yule log was kept burning for the twelve days of Christmas, and then its charred remains were carefully put aside to kindle the Yule log the following year, and meanwhile to act as a charm to protect the house against lightning and fire. The luck and protection of the Yule log were qualified, however, by certain odd restrictions. For example, no one who squinted could enter the room where the log was burning, and barefooted—and even more important, flatfooted—women had to keep away.

France with its *bûche de Noël*, Greece with its cedar logs, and the Slavic countries all share the ancient tradition of burning a ritual log on or around December 25. The word Yule itself is thought to derive from a Scandinavian word meaning the turning of a wheel—in other words, the rotation of the seasons.

In the west of England the custom of the Ashen Faggot, similar to the Yule log, survives. Unmarried girls sit around the fire and choose one of the nine bands of ash with which the faggot is bound. The girl whose band bursts first in the heat is said to be the one who will marry first.

In Burgundy, the Fire Log brought treats for the children. After carols had been sung, the small children were sent into a corner to pray, and when they returned they found the Fire Log had rewarded them with sweets.

In Syria fire is still a Christmas essential, both in church and at home. On Christmas Eve, all the family stand round a blazing hearth, candles in hand, singing carols and watching the flames closely for signs of good luck. At midnight, each member of the family, from old women to young children, leaps over the dying embers—symbol of the dying winter sun

—and makes a wish. And before the summer sun appears on Christmas morning, a fire is kindled on the church floor to help it on its way.

To the wheat farmers of the Ukraine, sunshine and summer crops are inseparable. So on the same day that the Romans, half the globe and two thousand years away, used to celebrate Saturnalia, the feast of the god of farming, the Russian farmers bake a harvest cake of cereal, honey, raisins, and nuts and top it with the sun symbol, a Christmas candle.

The Iroquois Indians of America had their own version of a fire festival, at exactly the same time of year. Flaming coals and sticks were hurled at the head of anyone unwary enough to venture within throwing distance. And as the festival progressed and the sun grew stronger, the young braves celebrated by scattering fire in the wigwams.

The Jews also celebrate a festival of light in December. Called Hanukkah, it marks the victory in 164 B.C. of Judas Maccabaeus and his army over the Syrians, and the rededication of the Jewish temple after its defilement by the king of Syria. During the eight-day festival, candles are lighted, one more each night, in special candelabra. In modern times, Hanukkah has become an occasion of gift-giving, especially to children.

Although Christmas lights have pagan origins, the Christmas crib is unmistakably Christian. In both Roman and Egyptian times, there was a parallel antecedent to the figure of the child Jesus. The Egyptians thought of the new sun as a newborn child and had doll-like symbols of the sun specially for the December festival. The Romans gave one another gifts of dolls during Saturnalia. But these really have no bearing on the tradition of the Christmas crib.

The first recorded popularization of the crib took place at Greccio, Italy, in 1224, when St. Francis celebrated Mass at a specially constructed manger, attended by an ox and an ass. Giotto painted a famous representation of the scene. Long before St. Francis, however, there are historical references to dramatized Nativity scenes at Rome's Church of Santa Maria Maggiore, which was dedicated to the new festival of Christmas by Pope Liberius in the fourth century. But apparently it was St. Francis who popularized the use of the crib, the tradi-

Madonna and Child, by Sandro Botticelli

The Rest on the Flight into Egypt, by Gerard David

tion quickly spreading into the church on a grand scale and into the home on a smaller scale.

In Naples in the eighteenth century, the building of the model crib, or *presepio*, became a popular craft. The crib-makers were known as *figuarari,* and the figurines as *pastori.* It was a Bourbon king and a Dominican friar who brought crib-making into such fashion that it developed into a flourishing business. King Carlo III was fascinated by anything mechanical, and instead of letting his servants construct the lavish Nativity scenes for his castle, he built them himself, and the queen and her ladies-in-waiting made the elaborate costumes. Naturally, the court immediately adopted the fashion, and it soon became socially advantageous to produce ever more elaborate cribs.

Simultaneously, at the other end of the Neapolitan social scale, Fra Gregorio Rocco, a civic crusader who introduced the city's first public lighting system, launched a campaign to fight vice and crime by urging every family to build its own *presepio.*

As it spread through Italy and Germany, the custom of building Nativity scenes developed into the construction of entire models of towns, villages, or castles containing the manger. Thus the modelers displayed the everyday life of their time with Jesus at the center of it all, a pleasing means of bringing home to the people the presence of God in their midst. The custom spread to both of the Americas and to Africa, where it still flourishes.

Churches in most Christian countries today display a crib either inside or outside the building; it is common to see crib scenes in store windows at Christmas; and, of course, the crib is a popular theme for Christmas cards. But one of the prettier variations seems to have disappeared completely—the nineteenth-century Advent box, a glass-covered box containing one or two holy dolls, which was carried from house to house during the Christmas season.

Perhaps the most active custom associated with the crib is the old *Kindelwiege,* a ceremony that took place in church around a cradle containing an image of the infant Jesus. The congregation danced around the cradle to a kind of waltz tune, and one by one each person approached the cradle and rocked it in time to the music. It may seem an irreverent custom today, but it sprang from a simple and joyous concept of religion.

Being devout need not mean being joyless. And even those who complain loudest about the commercialization of Christmas could scarcely gainsay the pleasures of giving and receiving gifts at Christmas, as long as it's the thought that counts, and not the cost or impressiveness of the present.

The giving of gifts is as old as Christ's birthday itself; the Magi, after all, bore gold and frankincense and myrrh to Bethlehem. But it is just as likely that the tradition survives from the Roman Saturnalia and Kalendae celebrations, when people gave gifts or *strenae* to their poorer neighbors and received garlands in return. The gifts had symbolic as well as intrinsic value: money or precious metals to bring prosperity in the coming year, sweets and cookies to bring happiness. There are vestiges of this ancient symbolism in the Scottish custom of offerings brought by first footers—the first persons to cross the threshold of a home in the New Year.

The actual day on which gifts are exchanged varies from

country to country. Most English- and German-speaking countries favor Christmas Day, but in some countries—France, for example—New Year's Day is observed.

The motives behind modern gift-bearing also vary, not only from person to person but from country to country. There are the gifts given to children by the mythical figures of Santa Claus or Kriss Kringle—he is known by many names. There are those given out of charity to the poor and needy, which are most closely allied to the Saturnalia; those given among relatives and friends, which possibly originated in the winter festivals of northern peoples honoring St. Nicholas, St. Martin, and so on. Certainly in the United States gifts were given to the poor many years before it became customary to give them to friends, but it is arguable whether this was a tradition brought with them by northern pioneers, or merely human compassion. Finally, there is the British custom of presenting gift boxes to employees or servants on Boxing Day, the first weekday after Christmas.

The writer H. H. Munro, known as "Saki," put some very jaundiced views of Christmas gifts into the mouth of one of his characters: "There ought to be technical education classes on the science of present-giving. No one seems to have the faintest notion of what anyone else wants, and prevalent ideas on the subject are not creditable to a civilized community."

But this view is mild compared to George Bernard Shaw's bitter diatribe at Christmas in general, written in "Our Theatre in the Nineties":

"I am sorry to have to introduce the subject of Christmas in these articles. It is an indecent subject; a cruel, gluttonous subject; a drunken, disorderly subject; a wasteful, disastrous subject . . . in its own merits it would wither and shrivel in the breath of universal hatred; and anyone who looked back on it would be turned into a pillar of greasy sausages."

Strong stuff. It sounds very much like our modern complaints about Christmas—except that it was written half a century ago. And how many people really believe it? I wonder if Shaw believed it. No one who ever woke up wide-eyed long before dawn on Christmas Day to realize with a thrill of delight that Father Christmas had filled his stocking or sock or sack could despise the Christmas custom of exchanging gifts.

CHRISTMAS FESTIVITIES

THE TRADITIONAL CHRISTMAS feast has produced some very strange menus. For instance, dinner at Voisin's in Paris during the Prussian siege of 1870—provided by courtesy of the sewers and the zoo—included elephant consommé, braised kangaroo, and roast cat garnished with rats. In thirteenth-century England, Henry III observed Christmas at York with a dinner at which six hundred oxen were killed and eaten. Argentinians still enjoy their traditional "stuffed children" (*niños envueltos*) at Christmas—but it's just their name for stuffed beafsteak.

More conventionally, the traditional Christmas boar's head has long since given way to the turkey. Mince pies have shrunk and shrunk in size, and Christmas pudding is made very differently today than it was in 1848 when the *Illustrated London News* pronounced: "A kiss is round, the horizon is round, the earth is round, the sun and stars and all the host of heaven are round. And so is plum pudding."

But what has changed is less than what has remained. Come what may, in the direst of circumstances, men will find a way to feast on Christmas Day. And the feast remains in essence what it was many centuries ago.

The winter feast can be traced back almost as far as history itself. There was an element of sacrifice in the slaughter of animals for it, but there was a practical element as well. As winter set in and fodder was in short supply, it became necessary to slaughter livestock and to salt and dry the meat for use

52

toward the end of the barren season. Thus economic necessity and the spirit of sacrifice were merged. The seventh-century English historian the Venerable Bede placed the slaughtering time around November, coinciding with the old Teutonic New Year.

With the spread of Roman influence, however, the winter feasting became concentrated around the celebration of Saturnalia, which the Romans held at the astronomically correct winter solstice.

The pig rather than the ox became the customary Christmas dish, probably because few smallholders and cottagers could afford to buy and keep an ox; pigs ate acorns and beechnuts, which were available free in the woods.

In tradition, the pig soon became a boar—in particular, a boar's head. This had much to do with the fact that the hunting and killing of a wild boar was a legendary triumph; and besides, a boar's head looked far more impressive on a platter. The boar's head decked with rosemary and with an apple or an orange—representing the sun—in its mouth was a Christmas centerpiece throughout the Middle Ages. In Scandinavia, bread fashioned in the shape of a boar was eaten at Christmas.

England was long famed for literally making a meal of Christmas. *"Ha piu da fare che i forni di Natale in Inghilterra,"* ran an Italian saying about a busy person—"He has more to do than the ovens in England at Christmas." So it was a blow when eventually the boar was hunted to extinction in England. Back came the pig as the central Christmas dish, in place of the boar that had originally ousted it. But the pig nevertheless remained no more than a stand-in for the romantically inspired boar.

Later on in England, the main Christmas dish for the gentry became the peacock, skinned, roasted, and then sewn back into its feathers and gilded on beak and claws. Sometimes a wick saturated with spirits was stuck in its beak and lighted, in the tradition of solstitial fire, an association that later was transferred to the brandy-soaked Christmas pudding.

Germany also ran short of wild boars to decorate the table and adopted the goose as its Christmas dish. This large, plump bird still enjoys much popularity in England and Europe, bedecked with a string of sausages representing the boar's garland of rosemary.

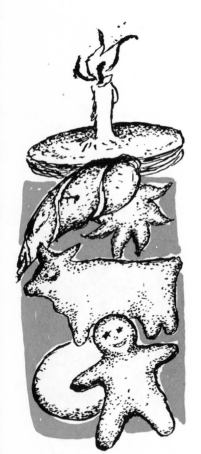

But it is the turkey—one of America's first contributions to world traditions—that has come to mean Christmas in the past hundred years or so. Despite its name in English, and in early French—*poulet d'Inde,* or Indian hen—the turkey is a native of the Americas. It was introduced in Europe as early as the sixteenth century, when Spanish ships brought the birds back from Mexico, where the Aztecs bred them. In 1555 the French naturalist Pierre Belon made an accurate drawing of a turkey, and at about the same time an Englishman, William Strickland, was granted a crest featuring a turkey-cock for bringing the first bird to England. King George II kept thousands of the birds for hunting in Richmond Park, near London; and for two hundred years Norfolk has been the center of turkey farms in England. In the eighteenth century great flocks of the fat, gobbling creatures were herded all the way from Norfolk to London with the aid of red rags tied to sticks, because turkeys, like bulls, were believed to hate the color red. In parts of Europe turkeys are still herded like sheep through village streets. By Victorian times the turkey was as much a festive dish in England and most of Europe as it had long been in America.

Mince pies, another Christmas specialty, have no particular religious significance, although their forebears—called Christmas pies and stuffed with minced meat, not fruit—were often fashioned in the shape of a crib and sometimes had a figure of Christ laid on top. For a while in England they were condemned by Puritans as "an abomination, idolatry, superstition and popish observance" and were banned by law. The Restoration saw the return of mince pies, some of them weighing as much as one hundred pounds and requiring iron bands to hold them together during cooking; but the custom of baking them crib-shaped never returned.

Europe shared one common Christmas eating habit: cakes and cookies baked sometimes in the shape of animals' horns in the pagan tradition, sometimes in the shape of a Christ figure, and occasionally in the shape of the sun and decorated with candles to represent the new year (a custom we still observe to celebrate our own birthdays). Some of these confections were gilded, but they were meant for eating as much as for decoration. One school of thought maintains that the figures represented pagan human sacrifice, just as the animal shapes stood for animal sacrifice. But however confused and intermingled the symbolism, the presence of wheat is constant, in propitiation of the elements that make the crops grow.

Of all Europeans, the Germans have retained the greatest number of their baked links with the past, in the Nuremburg spice cakes called *Lebkuchen,* the *Printen* cakes of Aix-la-Chapelle, and many other variants. The French still bake a form of Yule log called *bûche de Noël; pain d'epice* (gingerbread), which is sometimes gilded; and doll-shaped cakes called *naulets.* Italy and Spain specialize in nut-filled nougats—*torroni* or *turrones.* Sweden still produces boar-shaped loaves, one of the earliest winter customs. Estonia, too, features a Christmas boar, a long cake with turned-up ends, which stands on the main table until New Year's Day, when it is distributed among the cattle.

The Christmas pudding is the offspring of an alliance between frumenty and hackin. Frumenty was a sweetened and spiced cereal boiled in milk, which originated as a dish for religious fasting and evolved into an egg- and prune-fortified plum porridge. Hackin was a boiled meat sausage required to be cooked by dawn by the girls of the household; lateness resulted in their being forced to run around the village square. Both of these dishes disappeared two hundred years ago or more, leaving the Christmas pudding as their sole heir. Or so we might suppose. There is reason to believe, however, that hackin is thriving in Scotland under the assumed name of haggis, which has not otherwise changed much from the time when the poet Robert Burns eulogized it: "Oh what a glorious sight, warm-reekin', rich! . . . great chieften of the puddin' race."

By the nineteenth century the Christmas pudding had become an institution in England. It was prepared five weeks in advance in the great copper pot that was used the rest of the year for washing clothes. The mixing of the eggs and fruit and spices—and, of course, brandy—became a family ceremony, with everyone having a stir and a wish. This took place on the last Sunday before Advent, appropriately known as "Stir up Sunday" because of the Collect of the Mass for that day, which begins with the words, "Stir up, we beseech thee, O Lord, the wills of Thy faithful people. . . ."

The stirred pudding, to which had been added silver coins

—another remnant of Saturnalia—was then cooked in a bag or cloth. Thus Charles Dickens recorded in the Cratchit home at Christmas "a smell like washing-day."

At the turn of the century one bakery in London advertised "Teetotal plum puddings" for "dry" households. It was a battle lost from the start.

> Was-hael for knight and dame!
> O merry be their dole!
> Drink-hael! in Jesu's name
> We fill the tawny bowl; . . .

So wrote an English parson in the nineteenth century, and he was not referring to milk or tea, but to alcohol. "Wassail" was a medieval greeting that came to be associated with drinking in Anglo-Saxon times, when it was used as a toast equivalent to "Cheers" or "Good health." The greeting and the practice were integral parts of Christmas right up to this century. And if the term wassail has now lapsed into disuse, the drinking attached to it has not.

By 1190 the word had come to be synonymous with heavy drinking. Referring to English students at the University of Paris, the English monk and satirist Nigel Wireker wrote that they were "too much addicted to wessail and dringail," and Shakespeare used the word to denote heavy drinking.

Yet by the seventeenth century wassail had come to mean a specific custom, that of drinking ale or mead from a communal bowl or loving cup on Christmas Day and Twelfth Night. It was not long before the poor seized on the idea of carrying an empty wassail bowl from house to house, to have it filled at every stop. This in turn developed in some areas into a custom of wandering the streets at Christmas with a wassail bowl filled with "Lambswool," a hot punch of beer mulled with nutmeg, sugar, roast apples, and sometimes toast. Hence the expression to "toast" someone, or drink their health.

> Come, butler, come fill us a bowl of the best;
> Then we hope that your soul in heaven may rest;
> But if you do draw us a bowl of the small,
> Then down shall go butler, bowl and all.

So runs an old carol. To render this threat less necessary, wassailers introduced entertainment as leaven for their begging —the singing of Christmas songs outside the homes of potential wassail providers. Hence today's carol singers, who sometimes expect hard cash in place of hot ale.

Ever since the Romans turned their ordered world upside down once a year at Saturnalia, Christmas has been a time for games, in which even the dourest and the most earnest of souls

are expected to join. The custom of diversion at the turn of the year can be traced even farther back than the Romans. Along with the celebrations and sacrifices to mark the rebirth of the sun, primitive peoples whose everyday life was hard and unrelenting relaxed and let themselves go a little.

By the Middle Ages in most of Christendom, the fun and games of Christmas were centered around the parish church. Wrestling matches and cock-fighting were popular in England around this time, but they were no rival to dancing, which was even performed in some country churches to cries of "Yole, Yole" (an early pronunciation of Yule). Ritual games developed differently from parish to parish, let alone country to country. An indication of how arbitrarily some of these could arise is the account by Thomas Blount, published in 1679, of the origins of a custom at Stamford in Lincolnshire.

> William Earl Warren, Lord of this Town in the time of King John, standing upon the Castle Walls, saw two Bulls fighting for a cow in the Castle Meadow, till all the Butchers Doggs pursued one of the Bulls (maddened with noise and multitude) clean through the Town. This sight so pleased the Earl, that he gave the Castle Meadow, where first the Bulls duel began, for a common to the Butchers of the Town, after the first grass was mowed, on condition that they should find a madd Bull, the day six weeks before Christmas Day, for the continuance of the sport forever.

Many other men in England held land on condition that they presented food, poultry, or other tokens to the landlord on Christmas Day, and occasionally that they performed ludicrous acts such as dancing and playing the fool before the landlord, who in many cases was the king. Some of these customs appear cruel and callous to us today, but in rougher ages they were not remarkable.

Thus the Hunting of the Wren, a custom of St. Stephen's Day, seems to us at variance with the gentle spirit of the season. The wren, one of the smallest and least offensive of birds, is legendary king of the birds and strictly forbidden to the hunter. But on December 26—in the typical spirit of

Saturnalia—this rule is reversed and the wren is traditionally pursued to death and borne in triumph. Legend has it that St. Stephen was about to escape from his captors when a wren sang its disproportionately loud song and awoke his guards. So on the Saint's day the bad luck normally associated with harming a wren is waived.

In justification the hunters can recall the unprincipled method the wren used to become king of the birds. He nestled unseen on the back of an eagle, and when the eagle had flown higher than any of the other birds to prove himself their monarch, the wren emerged and flew just that bit higher to defeat him for the title. French legend has it that the killer of the first wren became king. In recent times the robin has come to be confused with the wren and to take its place, not in a hunter's sights, but on Christmas cards and decorations.

Christmas crackers or snappers, for young children an important part of the celebrations, are latecomers to Christmas traditions. In 1860 appears the first record of an exploding cracker, probably an adaptation of the French bag of bonbons that had to be pulled apart by two children. But by 1900 the manufacture of crackers, filled with miniature jewelry, crowns, harps, magic flowers, tiny books, and masks, had become a minor industry. Masks and paper hats, both still found in crackers today, are among the last physical remnants of the medieval Feast of Fools, a close cousin to Saturnalia.

The Feast of Fools was in fact an unedifying revelry initiated by the lower-ranking clergy, who were often of earthy stock. It involved the burlesquing of church services and the ridiculing of senior clergymen, sometimes with the most junior cleric sitting upon the bishop's throne— all in the topsy-turvy tradition of Saturnalia. Church reformers regularly condemned the practice, and in 1435 it was prohibited. But it proved to be too ingrained a tradition to die, and it continued in open secrecy until the late sixteenth century, when royal laymen adopted it for themselves. Universities, the nobility, and the courts themselves organized such revels all over Europe, with their own variant of the Lord of Misrule—a buffoon-like master of ceremonies—to lead them.

The Haxey Hood game, played at Haxey in Lincolnshire, is a Saturnalia-grounded derivation that survives today. It is played on Twelfth Night by thirteen men—the Lord, the Fool, and eleven Boggins, presumably some sort of minor spirit. These are the formal participants, but spectators join in the action, which is a disorganized scrummage to get thirteen canvas hoods into particular goals. The last hood—the Haxey Hood itself—is made of leather, representing the head of a sacrificial bull. This has to be shoved and heaved, apparently with the maximum amount of hysterical force and the minimum of efficiency, to an inn. The game is then "won" and the drinking can begin. If it all sounds a bit foolish, that is much the point of it; the rest is in the symbolism—the sacrificial bull, the Lord and Fool, and the hoods, remnants of the masks of Misrule.

Mumming is another survival from the Misrule and hence from Saturnalia. It means masquerading in America, literally "playing in masks" in England, and it is echoed back and forth across Europe in countless variations. The German *Dreikönigssängers*—"Three kings singers"—go from house to house attired and crowned as kings, offering incense and receiving tokens in exchange. English masked plays, dating back to the time of the Crusades, usually featured St. George versus a Turkish knight, the knight being slain by George only to be revived by a mysterious doctor. Cross-gartered ribbons, a magical prop of pagan witches, are still traditional mummers' wear. Every seven years in Germany, the thirteen Wild Men of Oberstdorf, dressed entirely in fir fronds, perform an intricate play-dance of Teutonic origins that is widely believed to be the oldest prehistoric ritual in Europe. It has much in common with Christmas mumming.

America avoided most of these Christmas game traditions because of the Puritan influence of many of the early settlers. It was not until the late nineteenth century that the sternly nonfrivolous attitude toward Christmas was eased. The first states to declare Christmas a legal holiday were in the South. Massachusetts took until 1856 to get around to it, and only in 1890 did Oklahoma become the last state to celebrate Christmas officially.

While Americans were frowning at Christmas frivolities, the English were giggling at them. In 1723 the first pantomime appeared on a London stage, John Thurmond's production of *Harlequin Dr. Faustus* at the Drury Lane Theater. The title alone reveals much about the early pantomime, which was created by grafting classical Italian comedy figures onto a drama. Thus one of the early pantomimes was called *The Dramatick Entertainment Called Harlequin a Sorcerer with the Loves of Pluto and Proserpine.* Another was *Andromeda with the Rape of Columbine; or the Flying Lovers.*

The origins of the pantomime, which has developed into the strongest surviving Christmas entertainment in Great Britain, are found in the Saturnalia and the Italian theater. The Harlequin figure, initially found in every pantomime, was a popular clown figure throughout Europe, dating back to before the twelfth century. An old French *Harlekin* is found in folk

literature as early as 1100, when he had already become pro-verbial as a demoniacal ragamuffin. In 1262 a number of Harlequins appeared in a play by Adam de la Halle. But it was Italy that brought him to life as a dramatic figure as *Arlecchino*, one of the motley four.

The four are sometimes said to represent the seasons: Harlequin, with his nimble dancing and skittishness, spring; Columbine, in her white robes, summer; the Clown, autumn; and the lean Pantalone, winter. This interpretation would link the modern pantomime to early harvest ceremonies as well as to the ancient Roman pantomimists. It would also link it with other traditional Christmas entertainments by way of the clown, clearly a scion of the Lord of Misrule.

In another interpretation of the characters, Harlequin represents Mercury; his wand, a magic sword. Columbine stands for Psyche, the human spirit; Pantaloon for Charon, ferryman of the River Styx; and the clown for Momus, merrymaker with a gaping mouth.

Whatever the origin of the characters, the dramatic themes of pantomimes became swiftly established. There were the spirits of good and evil—usually the fair queen and the demon —engaged in a struggle, with a lot of broad jokes and falling-about thrown in to lighten the plot. It was all a substantial stride away from the original Greek pantomime, which was literally "all mime," or movement without words.

The pantomime, with its basic moral themes and simple good humor, appealed to families that had not been able to go out together to music halls, which were rough-seated, sawdust-strewn, and peppered with coarse humor. Even so, a great deal of the material in early pantomime was culled from the music hall and cleaned up a little; and pantomimes became well known for providing a mosaic of the popular music-hall tunes of the year. In their first few years of existence, English panto-mimes became a mammoth success with the British public. Wrote one contemporary observer:

"The splendour of the scenes, the vastness of the ma-chinery, and the grace of Rich himself [John Rich, one of the first pantomime actor/managers and producer of *The Beggar's Opera*] raised harlequinade above Shakespeare. During the nights of its attraction the prices of admission were raised by one-fourth and the weekly receipts advanced to a thousand pounds."

Prime Minister Robert Walpole remarked, after a visit to a later pantomime in 1782, "How unlike the pantomimes of Rich, which are full of wit and coherent, and carried a story." His comment on the declining quality of the art has been regularly echoed since then, along with unfulfilled prophecies of its imminent demise. It is interesting to note that the pantomime Walpole compared unfavorably with typical Rich fare—such as *Harlequin Executed; a New Italian Mimic scene between a Scaramouch, a Harlequin, a Country Farmer, his wife, and Others*—was *Robinson Crusoe,* said to have been adapted by Richard Sheridan from Daniel Defoe's novel.

About the middle of the eighteenth century, the early pantomime themes gave way to folk and fairy stories, and by 1806 *Harlequin and Mother Goose; or, The Golden Egg* was produced at Covent Garden, with Joseph Grimaldi as the clown. Grimaldi gave clowns their lasting name, Joey, and left an indelible mark on pantomimes and their performance for more than a century. Unfortunately, when he took *Mother Goose* to New York, he was hissed and booed off the stage and gave up after four nights, having failed to sell the pantomime to the American people. The Victorian era saw Dan Leno as the pantomime's chief clown; Leno was able to turn audiences into shaking, shrieking, giggling heaps with songs such as "The Hard Boiled Egg and the Wasp," in which he repeated the chorus, "The hard boiled egg, the hard boiled egg, the hard boiled egg," while audiences agonized by laughter begged him to stop even as they folded up with fresh bouts of mirth.

The oldest and best-known pantomime is *Cinderella,* which is known in slightly different versions in every European country. The "glass slipper" around which the flimsy plot revolves is probably the result of a bit of careless translation from the French version, in which a *pantoufle en vair,* a fur slipper, was rendered as a *pantoufle en verre,* or glass slipper.

The Babes in the Wood is based on a true story of two English children who were abducted and abandoned in Norfolk in the fifteenth century. One of the kidnappers confessed, and the incident was so gruesome that it left an impression even on that tough age and was handed down in song and story.

Dick Whittington, real-life hero of another favorite panto-mime, married the daughter of his master, Alderman Fitz-warren, and became Lord Mayor of London three times before he died in 1423. But he never had a cat, nor did he visit Morocco —both essential details of the pantomime. He did, however, invest his savings in a ketch that traded to Morocco, and there are various explanations of how the cat got into the act, again involving mistranslation from the French.

The Arabian Nights was translated from the French in 1704, and with Sinbad the Sailor and Aladdin had Arab or Persian roots.

All of these pantomimes began their Christmas stage life as harlequinades, the characters being transformed into harle-quin-style heroes and villains halfway through the proceedings, and the whole play culminating in a rough-and-tumble on stage. But gradually the harlequinade was pushed later and later in the evening, until in 1900 it occupied a mere twenty minutes. And today the Harlequin, if he appears at all, speaks only an epilogue and sometimes a prologue. It was largely Grimaldi's personality that downgraded the traditional Harlequin.

Grimaldi's stage debut was by modern standards cruelty to children. In 1782 a pantomime clown appeared at Sadler's Wells with a small monkey on a chain. He swung the creature round his head so violently that the chain broke and the monkey flew off into the orchestra pit. Out of the monkey-skin climbed a tearful three-year-old child, Joseph Grimaldi. And from 1782 to his last performance in 1828, Grimaldi never missed one year of pantomime.

That story can be taken with a grain of salt, but his influ-ence on pantomime, and thus on Christmas entertainment, can scarcely be exaggerated. It was he who introduced the practice of having the audience join in the chorus of his songs, by leaving out the last word of each verse. Thus he would sing:

"The little old woman, she thought it no sin to warm her-self up with a quartern of . . . "

And the audience would scream "gin," while Grimaldi pre-tended to look shocked. It was not subtle, but it was fun.

Pantomime began life as a mongrel and remains one today, with the now-traditional stories being altered and updated, and the leading roles played by popular singers.

The Circumcision, by Rembrandt

The Baptism of Christ, by Nicolas Poussin

Christ Cleansing the Temple, by El Greco

Christ at the Sea of Galilee, by Il Tintoretto

James Glover, for many years musical director of Drury Lane around the turn of the century, wrote of his pantomimes in 1921:

"They have always been made up of a mosaic of the good, bad and indifferent. The good I associated with the greater masters which have always done duty for the larger musical development of the production. If I found the finale of the second act of *Lohengrin* better than my own humble efforts, why should I not give Wagner a chance? It popularises Wagner, and saves me trouble."

William Makepeace Thackeray, a pantomime addict, was faintly—if pleasurably—horrified by the same sort of practice more than a century before.

"At the Fancy," he wrote, "we saw *Harlequin Hamlet, or Daddy's Ghost and Nunkey's Pison*. After the usual business, that Ophelia should be turned into Columbine was to be expected, I confess I was a little shocked when Hamlet's mother became Pantaloon and was instantly knocked down by Clown Claudius."

SANTA CLAUS

IF A FAT jolly old fellow with a long white beard and a sackful of gifts, wearing robes as red as his cheeks, arrived breathlessly down your chimney on December 6, you'd know who he was but not what he was playing at. Could it be that Santa Claus's memory was going, or that his calendar was fast, or just that he was having a practice run to see if he needed to knock a few pounds off before the great day? It is more likely that he had simply decided at last to assert himself and distribute his largesse on his *own* anniversary.

For Santa Claus, although he has been many different people in his time, from Kriss Kringle to the maiden Kolyada, is most at home with his best-known alias, St. Nicholas. And St. Nicholas' day is December 6, which is when many European children hang out their pillowcases and stockings. It would be accurate to say that Santa, or Father Christmas as he is universally known, works in two shifts: a pre-Christmas session of present-giving for Europeans, followed by a Christmas Eve round for Americans, Britons, and most of the remainder of the Christian world.

St. Nicholas was a ubiquitous character, if legend is to be believed (and who dares question it at Christmas?). We know that he was bishop of Myra in Asia Minor in the fourth century. At the time of the Emperor Diocletian, he was persecuted and imprisoned for his faith, but never martyred, although from what we know of him he would cheerfully have borne it. For as a child he fasted on Wednesdays and Fridays, and when his parents died he dedicated the remainder of his life to the service of God. This dedication led him to make a voyage to Palestine, during which he is said to have stilled a storm at sea, which later led to his being recognized as patron saint of sailors in much of East Europe, Italy, and Greece.

His connections with children stem from another legend. Three boys were murdered by an innkeeper, their bodies cut up, and the pieces pickled in a barrel of vinegar. St. Nicholas discovered the pieces, sorted them out like a jigsaw puzzle, and with a prayer joined them up and brought the boys to life again.

The giving part of his nature first manifested itself when he saved the three daughters of an impoverished father from lives of shame by providing them with dowries—three bags of gold that he threw in through their window. This not only qualified him for the role of Christmas philanthropist, but further made him the patron saint of bankers and of pawnbrokers, whose trade sign of three golden balls is said to represent St. Nicholas' wedding gifts.

Not that St. Nicholas is always portrayed as indiscriminately benevolent. He, as well as some of the other traditional Christmas-gift-bearing figures, was in some countries accompanied by a dour servant armed with a rod to beat naughty children instead of giving them presents. In France the judicial one was St. Fouettard, a horrible-looking old man with a long pointed nose who preceded his master on the eve of December 6, politely inquiring of mothers how their children had behaved during the year. Good behavior earned a few bonbons, with promises of more to come from St. Nick himself; bad behavior, the rod. This unforgiving old informer is mistily mirrored in the German Pelznickel, or Fur Nicholas, a fur-clad figure whose once-terrifying nature has mellowed over the years.

Like almost everything else long associated with Christmas celebrations, Santa Claus has his pagan links. His arrival down the chimney is an instance. Early hearth gods and gods of the Yule used the chimney as their door. So did witches; in fact, it was almost certainly their use of the chimney to sneak out to covens, coupled with their addiction to hallucinatory drugs such as belladonna, that gave them the impression they were flying and the reputation of traveling by airborne broomstick.

A jovial figure of some sort has always featured midwinter festivals, whether it was the Saturnalian feast king, the Druid priest-king, or the medieval Lord of Misrule. It is worth noting, however, that none of them was especially concerned with children.

St. Nicholas is the chief figure behind Father Christmas, but there are others who contributed something to today's Santa Claus. There is the white-robed Kolyada of prerevolutionary Russia, a girl who arrived in a sleigh with attendant carol singers on Christmas Eve. There are the gift-bearers descended from the Magi (remember how the "threes" crop up in the St. Nicholas legends): Italy's Befana, Russia's Babouschka, and Spain's *Tres Reyes Magos*.

The name Kriss Kringle is a corruption of Christkindl, the Christ Child, who provides gifts for German children. He was substituted for St. Nicholas during the Reformation. Christkindl is not supposed to be Jesus himself, but an angelic messenger announcing Jesus' coming. Perhaps surprisingly, the original Kriss Kringle was a girl. In a few German homes one of the women of the family still dresses in white, with golden wings and a veil to cover her face, and climbs through a window in the room where the Christmas tree stands. When the children are allowed to enter the room, they feel a mysterious chill in the air and see a pale, unrecognizable figure. Recently, German households have taken to leaving a window open, as if the Christkindl had just departed.

The name Santa Claus comes from Holland's variant of St. Nicholas, Sante Klaas. His popularization is American-inspired; in fact, the modern concept of Santa Claus as a jolly fat man is almost wholly the creation of two men.

One of them was Dr. Clement Clarke Moore, of Columbia University. In 1822 Dr. Moore set out on a sleigh journey on Christmas Eve with his Dutch servant, Pieter. They were delivering presents to Moore's parents in Greenwich Village, and in the cold and snowy night Dr. Moore sang a little spontaneous song as they sleighed back to his wife and nine children. The next morning Dr. Moore surprisingly remembered the gist of his lyrics and put them on paper. Called "A Visit from St. Nicholas," the poem gave Santa Claus a specific description for the first time: a plump jolly little fellow with a white beard, fur clothes, and a sleigh pulled by reindeer. Santa Claus has followed Dr. Moore's pattern ever since, just as generations of children have read his poem with delight:

'Twas the night before Christmas, when all through the house
Not a creature was stirring, not even a mouse. . . .

Half a century later another American, the well-known political cartoonist Thomas Nast, translated Dr. Moore's Santa Claus into cartoon form in *Harper's Weekly*. And his cartoon became the visual prototype of all subsequent Santas. It was Nast, too, who settled on the name Santa Claus as the definitive one, which it has remained in America and Britain. Since Nast's time, red has been introduced into Santa's dress, and in Britain he wears a hood in place of America's tasseled cap. But the changes in the last century are minimal.

Europe still retains some of its older variations on the theme. In the church at Bari, in southeastern Italy, the feast of St. Nicholas is celebrated in great splendor on December 6. For in the church lie the remains of the Saint, reportedly brought there from Myra. In part of Switzerland the red-robed Santa, at first glance looking like an American version, is accompanied by—and some say married to—St. Lucy.

Swedish children receive their gifts from the gnomish figure Jultomten, along with junior gnomes called Julnissar. The gift, called a *Julklapp,* is enclosed in layer upon layer of wrappings like a practical joke and is either delivered by a stranger or, with less ceremony, thrown in through a window. The Swedes have a demanding time of it at Christmas; with every gift they must write a dedicatory verse, the longer the better.

Gifts are not given on Christmas at all in Spain. Christmas Eve is taken up in prayer and, later at night, in feasting; Christmas Day, with sleeping off the previous night's feast, only to feast again. It is the eve of January 6, Epiphany, that is the special time for Spanish children. They put their shoes, filled with straw, out on a windowsill or balcony, and while the camels of the Three Kings are eating the straw the Magi leave gifts in gratitude.

French children have the best of both worlds, with St.

Nicholas bringing gifts in early December in the east of the country, Père Noël officiating on Christmas Eve, and—near the Spanish border—the Three Kings calling in January.

Italy, like Spain, waits for January for the gift-giving, which is done by the wistful witch Befana, whose name comes from Epiphania. Legend has it that, at the birth of Jesus, Befana was told by the shepherds of what was taking place and shown the star of Bethlehem to guide her. But she did not set out immediately and lost sight of the star, and so she was destined for eternity to search for Jesus, leaving presents at every house in case he might be there.

Syria has the camel from the manger scene bringing the presents, whereas in Poland a mother star is the giver. And in Finland Santa Claus is traditionally Old Ukko, a fur-clad man with droopy moustaches but no beard.

Most of these varying traditions are slowly losing out to the cheery, uncomplicated Santa Claus of Dr. Moore. As one city becomes increasingly like another anywhere in the world, so it drops the centuries-old traditions of its own country and adopts more cosmopolitan ways. Santa Claus looks as if he is in for a long run yet, as Francis Church charmingly predicted in the New York *Sun* of 1897 in reply to an eight-year-old girl's query: Is there a Santa Claus? For half a century Church's reply was published each Christmas:

". . . Yes, Virginia, there is a Santa Claus. He exists as certainly as love and generosity and devotion exist, and you know they abound and give to your life its highest beauty and joy. Alas, how dreary would be the world if there were no Santa Claus. It would be as dreary as if there were no Virginias. . . .

"Not believe in Santa Claus! You might as well not believe in fairies! You might get your papa to hire men to watch in all the chimneys on Christmas Eve to catch Santa Claus, but even if they did not see Santa Claus coming down, what would that prove? Nobody sees Santa Claus, but that is no sign that there is no Santa Claus. The most real things in the world are those that no children or men can see. Did you ever see fairies dancing on the lawn? . . .

"No Santa Claus! Thank God! he lives, and he lives for ever. A thousand years from now, Virginia, nay ten times ten thousand years from now, he will continue to make glad the heart of childhood."

Today it is the multiplicity of Santa Clauses to be seen in stores all over the world that might cause children to wonder a little. Which is the real Santa out of all those white-whiskered, red-garbed philanthropists who hand out pre-Christmas gifts or accept lists of Christmas wants from children. And where does he live when he is not on duty in the store? There are almost as many answers to the latter question as there are store Santas.

Thousands of children in all quarters of the globe have received letters from Santa Claus through the mail, in response to letters they have sent him telling him what they'd like to find under the tree on Christmas morning.

Some of these letters are postmarked "Reindeerland." These were sent by Santa's "secretaries" in Stockholm, Sweden,

who answer letters sent to "Reindeerland" or "Toyland" or "the North Pole," for many such letters end up in Lapland, part of Swedish territory. "Santa Claus, Greenland" on the envelope of a letter has found Santa Claus's secretaries in Denmark. In 1959 a Swedish woman founded a letter-answering service on behalf of Santa in Finland. She began with just a handful of letters, but by the mid-1960's thousands were pouring in each Christmas, and replies were being sent off in Finnish, Swedish, French, and English to countries as distant as Kenya and Australia.

Young Americans have corresponded with Santa for many years. The U.S. Air Force weather station in Alaska has served as a convenient dropping-off point to the great man, and the postmark "Santa Claus, North Pole" has gladdened many children's hearts. What will philatelists make of it hundreds of years from now?

There is even a town called Santa Claus in Indiana. How it came to be named that is still disputed, but it has a built-in industry for as long as it cares to operate its post office. Every Christmas it is snowed under with parcels requiring a "Santa Claus" postmark.

A few years ago someone in England thought of the bright idea of registering himself with the Board of Trade under the business name Father Christmas, in the hope that anyone using the name in future would have to pay him for the privilege. Then he discovered that another firm had registered under the name Father Christmas (Presents), and the two of them asked the Board of Trade to rule on which was entitled to use of the name. The happy ending to this modern fable is that the Board of Trade ruled the name to be common property, no doubt allowing the *real* Father Christmas to sigh with relief.

Graduates of the Santa Claus school of Albion, New York, know just what it takes to become a store Santa, and they have B.S.C. (Bachelor of Santa Claus) degrees to prove it. The Santa school was the idea of Charles W. Howard, a toy designer, showman, farmer, and later self-styled chief Santa. He dreamed of perfect Santas fulfilling the children's fantasies, and so he set up his school to clean up the twilight world of tinpot Santas. He further coined the phrase: "Until you've had a Howard-trained Santa, you've never had Christmas at your store."

Howard died in 1966, but his assistant, Mason Doan, took over the fur-trimmed mantle and carried on the school.

Entrance qualifications are stringent. A potential Bachelor of Santa Claus must be middle-aged, well-educated, quick-witted, an easy conversationalist, reliable, physically fit, a thinker, willing to learn and take responsibility, and good-natured without being a buffoon. More specifically, he must be between 5 feet 6 inches and 6 feet tall, weigh between 185 and 250 pounds, and have blue eyes and a full face. Candidates who meet these requirements go through a stiff course of lectures, discussions, and study to prepare them for their responsible roles.

A Silver Chimney, a scaled-down model of his traditional means of entry, is tangible evidence that a graduate has passed the Santa test. For every three successive years of service to children as Santa, he receives three Silver Bricks to pin on his chest like medals. After fifteen years of service he receives a Silver Fireplace. And if he survives twenty-five years at the sack, he is awarded a ruby to be set in the coveted Fireplace. Which makes him as perfect a Santa as you're ever likely to see.

CHRISTMAS CHEER

"CAROLS ARE DITTIES which now exclusively enliven the industrious servant and the humble labourer," wrote William Hone in his *Everyday Book* in 1826. His patronizing tone grates a bit today. "Silent Night" is not exactly a ditty, and senior clergymen conducting carol services in abbeys and cathedrals can scarcely be described as humble laborers. Yet Hone, writing at a time when carols seemed to be dying out, was very close to the spirit of previous centuries in his description.

The early Roman Church had its hymns, but they were theological in content and sung by the priests, and to the great majority of people they were remote and mysterious.

In contrast, the carol—from the old French *carole*, meaning a dance with a song—was a popular song with simple words and simple sentiments: a song of celebration.

Not until the fifteenth century did carols have any connection with Christmas, other than their being sung to celebrate it as they were sung to celebrate any festival or happy occasion. For the next two centuries carols enjoyed enormous popularity, and during that period some of the best were written. During that period, too, they began to be associated directly with Christmas and the Nativity. Subsequently, although carols were still for a time sung at Easter, they came to be reserved for Christmas.

Then came the Puritan wave across Europe, and carols, never warmly embraced by the Christian Church, were largely suppressed. It took them two hundred years to re-emerge, and

Charles Dickens, who played so large a part in the revival of Christmas festivities, did them no harm by naming his most famous novel *A Christmas Carol*.

The French word *carole* is in turn connected with both the Greek and the Latin word for chorus. The word was also later used to describe a ring shape, such as a circle of stones, and in the Middle Ages it was in general use for a ring dance or song.

One of the earliest carols, by an unknown composer, is about a shepherd coming upon Jesus in the manger:

> Jesu, I offer to thee here my pipe,
> My skirt, my tarbox and my scripe;
> Home to my felowes now will I skipe,
> And also look unto my shepe.
> Ut hoy!
> For in his pipe he made such joy . . .

This was the fond, humanized language of carols that had never found its way into hymns. And although it was not entirely typical of medieval carols, it was echoed by Jacopone, a great writer of Christian popular songs.

The Blessed Jacopone of Todi, as he later came to be known, was born at Todi in Umbria about 1230. He married a beautiful girl, but only a year later she was a guest at another wedding when a balcony on which she and other guests were standing collapsed. No one was killed but her. This tragedy changed Jacopone completely. He became a deeply devout Franciscan monk, an ascetic who mortified his flesh to an extent that disturbed even his brethren. He even died meaningfully, on Christmas Day, 1306.

What Jacopone *could* do joyfully was write carols. He has been described as the man who wrote "the first real outburst of Christmas joy in a popular tongue." A verse from his "Il Presepio" ("The Manger") contrasts in its familiar tone with hymns written up to that time:

> Little angels all around
> Danced, and carols flung;
> Making verselets sweet and true,
> Still of love they sung;

Calling saints and sinners too
With love's tender tongue;
Now that heaven's high glory is
On this earth displayed . . .

Such popularization of Christianity and Christmas was echoed in Germany at about the same time, with the Dominican order taking the lead. "In Dulce Jubilo," to this day one of the favorite carols, came from this period. The story goes that a band of angels brought comfort to a mystic, Heinrich Suso, during his sufferings, taking his hand and leading him to sing and dance. One of the songs sung by the angels was a happy one about Jesus; a sixteenth-century Scottish translation captures its spirit:

In dulci Jubilo, Now Lat us sing with myrth and jo
Our hartis consolatioun lyis in praesipio,
And schynis as the Sone, Matris in gremio,
Alpha es et O, Alpha es et O.
O Jesu parvule! I, thrist sore after the
Confort my hart and mynde, O puer optime,
God of all grace sa kynde, et princeps gloriae
Trahe me post te, Trahe me post te.
Ubi sunt gaudia, in ony place bot thair
Quhair that the Angellis sing Nova cantica,
Bot and the bellis ring Nova cantica, in regia cantica curia,
God gif I war thair, God gif I war thair.

This is fairly intelligible even today, and unfamiliar words can easily be guessed. But John Audelay, a Shropshire priest who popularized carols in England shortly after Germany and Italy were producing theirs, wrote in a style that is barely comprehensible to the modern reader. The title under which he produced them, however, is plain enough: "Syng these Caroles in Cristmas."

Although France gave the word carol to the English language, it called its own Christmas songs Noëls. They became popular rather later than their counterparts in the rest of Europe, and they tended to differ from locality to locality, often being adaptations of earthy and definitely nonreligious popular songs.

The Reformation frowned on carols, and they suffered throughout Europe; the French Revolution later helped to snuff out Noëls. By the early nineteenth century, carols had become quaint old hangovers from the past, about as popular at Christmas as boars' heads are today.

A nineteenth-century book entitled *Ancient Mysteries Described*, written by William Hone several years before he described carols as "ditties," remarked:

"The custom of singing carols at Christmas prevails in Ireland to the present time. In Scotland where no church feasts have been kept since the days of John Knox, the custom is unknown. In Wales it is still preserved to a greater extent, perhaps, than in England. . . . After the turn of midnight at Christmas Eve, service is performed in the churches, followed by singing of carols to the harp. Whilst the Christmas holidays continue, they are sung in like manner in the houses. . . ."

Another contemporary writer, William Sandys, also wrote of the existence of carols as if they were a curiosity in the final stages of dying out:

"In the metropolis a solitary itinerant may be occasionally heard in the streets, croaking out 'God rest you merry, gentlemen,' or some other old carol, to an ancient and simple tune. Indeed, many carols are yet printed in London for the chapmen, or dealers in cheap literature; and I have some scores of half-penny and penny carols of this description. . . . Some of these carols, I was informed by the publishers, are in considerable request, and are printed off as the demand requires. The custom also prevails in Ireland and Wales. . . . There was a notice recently of the death of a Welsh poet, David Jones, at Rhuddlan in Flintshire, aged sixty nine, who for the last fifty three years had annually sung a carol, of his own composing, at Christmas day in the church there."

Sandys reprinted many Christmas songs and carols, including several French Noëls. "The First Nowell" and "I Saw Three Ships" were among them, Sandys mentioning that they were "of considerable antiquity."

The revival of interest in carols, initiated by antiquarians concerned largely with their historical worth, was swiftly and apparently spontaneously taken up by composers and by the mass of ordinary people for whom carols were originally intended. During the first half of the nineteenth century several major carols were written. Perhaps the most famous lyrical carol of all was composed in 1818 in Austria, in legendary circumstances worthy of Christmas.

It was Christmas Eve in the tiny Tyrolean village of Oberndorf. Snow lay all about, the villagers were completing their preparations for the festivities, and Father Joseph Mohr, the village priest, was panic-stricken. The bellows of the church organ had broken, and in a few hours the villagers would be filing into the old church for midnight Mass.

Father Joseph had sent to the neighboring town of Fuegen for the organ builder, but he might not be able to repair the instrument in time, and for the first time in centuries the midnight Mass would have to be conducted without musical accompaniment. To the devout and tradition-conscious Austrian villagers, this would be a disaster.

The priest had one idea that might save the situation. He rummaged around in his desk for a poem he had written a few years earlier, inspired by the sight of his parishioners coming to midnight Mass on another Christmas. Finding it, he rushed to the home of Franz Xavier Gruber, the village schoolmaster and organist. Thrusting the yellowing piece of notepaper into Gruber's hand, Father Joseph asked whether he could compose some simple music for it that the choir children could learn in the couple of hours remaining. Gruber sat down with his guitar . . .

The moon was high in the sky as Gruber made his way to the church with his finished score. The choir was already in church, waiting to practice the new song as soon as it appeared, while sighs and wheezes came from the organ loft where the repairman labored to mend the bellows. Even as the choir were looking over the music, he pronounced the bellows irreparable; field mice nesting in the church had eaten clean through them. As he was packing up his tools, about to leave, the choir struck up the new song. They sang it almost perfectly the first time. The organ builder was moved and impressed by its simple beauty, and asked for a copy to take back to Fuegen with him.

The Oberndorf villagers loved it, too, when it was sung during the Christmas Mass; so did the villagers of Fuegen, who heard it the same night.

Somehow the song came to the ears of the Director-General of Music in Saxony, and thence to people all over Austria. Within the next decade it was being sung in many different languages by Christians the world over.

Father Joseph and Gruber were not credited with the composition until many years later, when the King of Prussia ordered inquiries to be made into its origins. By this time the priest was dead and the schoolteacher living in another part of the country. But to this day Gruber's guitar is preserved and exhibited, and a nest of hungry mice can be thanked for the moving carol that begins:

Stille Nacht, Heilige Nacht
Silent Night, Holy Night

About the time that "Silent Night" was first heard around Europe, two English clergymen, John Mason Neale and Thomas Holman Helmore, were collecting songs for their *Carols for Christmastide*. From Sweden they obtained a copy of *Piae Cantiones*, a collection of religious songs compiled by Theodoricus Petrus of Finland in the sixteenth century. One of the ancient tunes they found in the *Cantiones* was a sturdy marching song, for which Neale wrote some lyrics. "Good King Wenceslas" was the result, and in true carol tradition it has weathered criticisms that it is doggerel and corny and has remained popular ever since.

Not only is "Good King Wenceslas" doggerel, with an altered spelling of the king's name, but also it appears to contain a historical blunder. King Wenceslaus was the son of Emperor Charles IV, and he acquired his first kingdom—Bohemia, now central Czechoslovakia—when he was two years old in

1363. He was married by the age of nine and sole ruler of Germany and Bohemia at seventeen. He was, however, anything but the benevolent, compassionate ruler eulogized in the carol.

Apoplectic, idle, and a drunkard, according to historians, Wenceslaus abandoned most of his kingdom to the anarchic clashes between nobles and townsmen and took to his sickbed in Bohemia. In the next few years he was seized by his cousin Jobst of Moravia, freed by his brother Jan, seized once again, this time by his own nobles, and compelled to appoint Jobst "governor" of his kingdoms. In 1400 he was forced by his German princes to abdicate his throne because of his neglect of the kingdom. Thereupon he was seized yet again, this time by another of his brothers, Sigismund, and handed over to the Dukes of Austria, who imprisoned him for a further year. All this before his thirty-third birthday. Broken and ill, Wenceslaus retired to his palace in Prague, where he died, reportedly of apoplexy, aged forty-eight. Not a distinguished reign, even by medieval standards, and certainly not worthy of being recorded for posterity in a cheerful carol.

King Wenceslaus appears to have benefited from confusion with a namesake who lived almost 500 years earlier. He, too, was Bohemian, but he was a duke, not a king. This Wenceslaus was converted to Christianity and founded the cathedral of St. Vitus, the burial place of Bohemian kings. He was murdered by his heathen brother and later canonized, appearing as St. Wenceslaus in the Roman Catholic calendar and remaining the patron saint of Bohemia.

Another stirring carol written around this time was Thomas Haynes Bayly's "The Mistletoe Bough." Children particularly were awed by its tragedy, and rumors of its origin placed it all over England. Bayly in fact adapted it from an Italian legend, adding the English local color. "The Mistletoe Bough" has not survived popularly as have "Silent Night" and "Good King Wenceslas," but, as different from them as they are from each other, it deserves to survive, if only as a fine piece of gothic storytelling:

The Mistletoe hung in the castle hall,
The holly branch shone on the old oak wall;

The Conversion of St. Paul, by Il Tintoretto

The Baptism of Christ, by Alessandro Magnasco

The Holy Family, by Il Giorgione

Holy Family on the Steps, by Nicolas Poussin

And the baron's retainers were bright and gay,
And keeping their Christmas holiday.
The baron he held, with a father's pride,
His beautiful child, young Lovell's bride;
While she, with her bright eyes, seem'd to be
The star of the goodly company.
    Oh! The Mistletoe bough!
    Oh! The Mistletoe bough!

"I'm weary of dancing now," she cried;
"Here tarry a moment—I'll hide—I'll hide.
And Lovell be sure thou'rt first to trace
The clue to my secret hiding place."
Away she ran—and her friends began
Each tower to search and each nook to scan;
And young Lovell cried, "Oh! Where dost thou hide?
I'm lonesome without thee, my own dear bride."
    Oh! The Mistletoe bough! etc.

They sought her that night! And they sought her next day!
And they sought her in vain when a week pass'd away!
In the highest—the lowest—the loneliest spot
Young Lovell sought wildly—but found her not.
And years flew by, and their grief at last
Was told as a sorrowful tale long past;
And when Lovell appear'd the children cried,
"See! the old man weeps for his fairy bride."
    Oh! The Mistletoe bough! etc.

At length an oak chest, that had long lain hid
Was found in the castle—they raised the lid—
And a skeleton form lay mouldering there,
In the bridal wreaths of that lady fair!
Oh! Sad was her fate—in sportive jest
She hid from her lord in the old oak chest,
It closed with a spring!—and, dreadful doom,
The bride lay clasp'd in her living tomb!
    Oh! The Mistletoe bough! etc.

    Not, perhaps, everybody's idea of Christmas, but a moving
song all the same.

With new carols such as these and the rediscovery of many older ones, the revival of carols was well under way by the middle of the nineteenth century. Then in 1871 two scholars of Magdalen College, Oxford, published *Christmas Carols New and Old*, containing forty-two carols. Their selection was not particularly distinguished, but the book sold hugely and in the next two decades was increasingly used in churches; for the first time carols and hymns had formally met.

In France in the same period Father François Perenne's *Dictionnaire des Noëls et des Cantiques* was repopularizing carols there, and the story was similar throughout Europe.

In this century new carols have been brought together by such talented composers as Vaughan Williams and Cecil Sharp, and poets of stature such as Robert Frost, G. K. Chesterton, T. S. Eliot, and Walter de la Mare have written about Christmas. But little modern work has the vigor and simplicity of the early carols or their nineteenth-century descendants.

For sheer Christmas spirit and earthy tenderness, no amount of scholarship or literariness can better "King Arthur's Waes-Hael," written by Robert Hawker, a Cornish parson, in the middle of the last century and never, alas, set to music:

Waes-hael for knight and dame!
O merry be their dole!
Drink-hael! In Jesu's name
We fill the tawny bowl;
But cover down the curving crest,
Mould of the Orient Lady's breast. . . .

Waes-hael! in shadowy scene
Lo! Christmas children we:
Drink-hael! behold we lean
At a far mother's knee;
To dream that thus her bosom smiled,
And learn the lip of Bethlehem's child.

It is hard to imagine Christmas without Christmas cards. Friends we have not seen for years, members of the family living far away, acquaintances we want to keep in touch with —all are brought together briefly in thought at Christmas by the sending of brightly printed cards that require little effort or expense to buy and send. Yet Christmas cards are not much more than a century old; they are only as old, in fact, as an efficient and cheap postal service.

The custom of giving friendship tokens at festivals is ancient. New Year gifts were given in ancient Egypt; small blue-glazed bottles inscribed with New Year greetings have been found in tombs of the Pharaohs. Ancient Romans, too, exchanged gifts, traditionally olive or laurel branches, and visits at New Year. But the Christmas card can probably be traced most accurately back to Japan.

The Japanese had learned block-printing—halfway house between handwriting and press printing—from its Chinese inventors by the eighth century. About 770 the Empress Shayautoku ordered "millions" (probably meaning a large number) of printed texts from Buddhist scriptures. Later the Japanese *surimono* or colored silk print became a popular way of sending greetings or messages. Nineteenth-century European aesthetes were greatly taken by anything Chinese or Japanese, and it was widely thought that *surimono* were exclusively New Year cards. It was only later realized that in Japan they were used to announce a change of address or name, the birth of a son, or any other event of interest to friends. For example, one designed by Niho announced that a man who had been temporarily blind had recovered his sight. For many years after the first European Christmas cards were printed, Japanese designs and influences were apparent in them.

The New Year's greeting card predates the Christmas card by a good four hundred years. In much of Europe, especially in countries with a strong Latin influence, such as France, Italy, and Spain, the first of January was the time to exchange gifts, and thus the appropriate time to exchange remembrances.

Master E. S. designed one of the first recorded New Year's cards in 1466. It is an engraving of Jesus as a little boy, dressed in a mantle and topped by a halo, stepping forward onto an elaborate flower, which also bears a wooden cross. The legend is *Ein guot selig ior*—"a good and happy year," in the language of Lower Germany. The majority of fifteenth-century New Year's cards followed the same sort of pattern, picturing Jesus with a flower or a bird, a custom frowned on, like so much that smacked of pleasure, by the Reformation.

Another card shows Jesus working the sails of a ship on the high seas, and also carrying a figure thought to represent Charity. Most of the cards that survived the Reformation did so because they were placed in Bibles as devotional pictures.

New Year's cards appear to have waned in the two centuries following the Reformation, but wall calendars became popular in the early eighteenth century. These, whether from Latin or Germanic countries, shared the custom of depicting a utopian state of affairs along with New Year's greetings. Whether they depicted bountiful nature or the political scene, all was well with the world (or at least with the world belonging to the designers; their enemies were often shown suffering defeat).

The quodlibet, a contrived picture made up of several smaller pictures arranged as though haphazardly, became popular around the early 1700's. Dealers began using them as advertisements, adding salutations so that they could double as greeting cards, very like much present-day advertising. Craftsmen, news vendors, ballad sellers, messengers, town criers, theater staffs, lamplighters, and persons in all kinds of occupations began using printed greetings, often in the form of doggerel, accompanied by a woodcut picture. These were distributed around Christmas, usually as a reminder for a Christmas bonus. The custom spread to America, where it survived into the nineteenth century after it had faded in Europe.

Quodlibets developed into Christmas broadsheets that featured the accomplishments and services of their senders. Newspaper sellers, for example, would distribute a broadsheet carrying long verses bearing the latest news of wars at home and abroad, court events, and generally, bad news from abroad and good news from home. These verses were usually bordered by woodcut scenes of topical events or illustrations from the scriptures.

During the first half of the nineteenth century it became the custom for schoolchildren to write their own verses or goodwill messages in the center of printed and decorated broadsheets. These were presented to parents at Christmas as evidence of their children's writing proficiency. The less fortunate "charity boys" exhibited them in the streets and solicited small gifts for their hard work and talent.

The first Christmas card proper was designed in 1843 by John Calcott Horsley, later a Royal Academician, for Henry Cole, who was later knighted. It was published in London's Bond Street by Joseph Cundall, who wrote with surprising vagueness, ". . . many copies were sold, but possibly not more than 1,000." It cost one shilling a copy. Thirty-seven years later, Sir Henry Cole proudly pointed out in his memoirs that the Christmas-week post handled by the Post Office was 11,500,000 in excess of the normal weekly mail.

The card showed a family toasting an absent friend in a border of trellised ivy, with the message "A Merry Christmas and A Happy New Year to You"—a message hard to better, and one that is reproduced on many modern cards. Cole, who was a controversial character—a reformer, an educator, and a prominent figure in the foundation of the Victoria and Albert Museum, the penny post, and postcards, among many other things—was strongly criticized for his Christmas card. The most common complaint was that it encouraged drunkenness.

"The idea was Cole's; the execution of the trifle mine," wrote Horsley in the London *Times* in the 1880's. And it was clearly intended as a trifle, for Horsley wrote in the copy he sent to Cole the verse:

> To his good friend Cole
> Who's a merry young soul
> And a merry young soul is he
> and may he be for years to come!
> hoo-ray!

There were other contenders for the honor of having invented the Christmas card, including one of Queen Victoria's favorite painters, W. Dobson; and Thomas Sturrock and Charles Drummond of Leith, Scotland, whose card bore a laughing face and the legend, "A Guid New Year an' Mony o' Them." But they appeared, in fact, a year or so after the Cole-Horsley card.

Christmas cards would almost certainly not have caught on as they did without the advent of the penny post. When postal charges were high and were paid by the recipient of the letter, quantities of mail bearing no message other than seasonal compliments might not have been universally welcome.

William Wordsworth, it is recorded, once paid £7 (a vast sum in those days) for letters from admirers of his work. Cost depended on distance, which would have prejudiced much of the point of Christmas cards—to greet friends and family far away.

In the half century after their invention, Christmas cards became the center of much critical appraisal. As they appeared in the days before Christmas, they were reviewed in the press as if they were paintings or books. They were a great status symbol, although not everybody agreed on the type of status they represented.

"With too much of them thrust upon us," complained *Punch* magazine in 1880, in a lengthy attack on Christmas cards in general,

> "E'en soft sweet things seem hard.
> Must Punch, must England, old and young,
> Henceforth 'live by the card'?"

Three years later, however, the *Times* published a eulogy on Christmas cards, praising them not only for the moral good they did but for the work they provided for printers and other craftsmen all the year round. The article remarked that the cheapest cards came from Germany but claimed that the highest-quality ones were the product of English skill:

"Let us remember the poet, who, as can be imagined, has his inventive faculties well tested on providing Christmas sentiment for the million and more individuals, each with a taste of his own."

Welcome as the *Times*'s support of Christmas cards was, this last bit must have been considered excessive even by the "poets" themselves. For the quality of Christmas-card verse has changed little over the intervening years, and the most generous attitude to take has always been that it is the thought that counts.

Early Christmas cards tended to be smaller than their modern counterparts. They were often highly ornate, decorated with a variety of ribbons and silks and glitter, and their subjects were quite varied. But gradually the traditional

Christmas associations—holly and ivy, Yule logs, robins and wrens, the boar's head, and turkeys, as well as the more obvious religious scenes—became standard Christmas-card subjects.

An early card from Louis Prang—leader of the early American Christmas-card business, which had developed simultaneously with the British card as English families sent greetings to their transatlantic relatives—featured holly and mistletoe, along with children carrying banners proclaiming "Joy" and "Mirth." It bore a good-hearted six-line verse, a form that came to characterize American cards.

> Ho! For the merry, merry Christmas-time,
> With its feast, and fund, and its pantomime,
> When good humour reigns, and a gay content
> Is boon companion in all merriment.
> Such a CHRISTMAS bright, with its frolic joys,
> Belongs to all good little girls and boys.

Christmas trees began appearing on cards by the end of the century, and hot on their trail, the poinsettia first turned up in American cards. Poinsettia, which now rivals holly as the prime Christmas greenery in America, has its legend, too. A poor Mexican boy, Pablo, picked a branch of this forest weed to offer Jesus at the shrine of the Nativity. When it was placed in front of the altar, the top leaves of the branch miraculously turned flame-red, transforming the boy's makeshift gift into a dazzling flower.

Flowers played another, more devious, part in the development of Christmas cards. Victorians were very conscious of the "language of flowers," pointing to the Greeks and Romans as their inspiration. Each flower had a meaning of its own, mostly concerned with love, jealousy, trysts, and the like. So in an age when parents exercised stringent censorship over their children's letters, not to say their behavior with members of the opposite sex, Christmas cards came to be for many a means of communication. By painting small flowers on their cards, or better still, putting pressed flowers inside them, young lovers could smuggle their sentiments to each other. It didn't make for snappy conversation, but it was an annual treat.

Wars and Christmas have little in common; but wars are

fought through Christmases, and people continue to live their normal lives as best they can, so inevitably there are Christmas cards with a wartime flavor. Understandably, it is the humorous aspect of war that appears among the holly, as an American card of 1918 illustrates. The card, satirizing the economy drive of Herbert C. Hoover, at the time Food Administrator of the United States, was printed on cheap gray cardboard and tied with string, described on the card as "camouflaged ribbon." Scant wisps of holly and mistletoe are labeled "This is holly" and "This is mistletoe," and a scrawny creature is captioned "a bluebird." The rhyme inside reads:

> I've Hooverized on Pork and Beans
> And Butter, Cake and Bread,
> I've cut out auto-riding
> And now I walk instead;
> I've Hooverized on Sugar,
> On Coal and Light and Lard,
> And here's my Xmas Greeting
>   On a Hoover Xmas Card.
> I wish you a very M.C. and H.N.Y.

The Hooverized card was certainly not the first to use the economical form of writing Xmas for Christmas, and the spelling has some foundation in Christmas tradition. X, the Greek letter *chi,* is the initial of the Greek name for Christ and is sometimes used as a symbol for His name.

A card also popular among Americans during World War I was the "kissing card," decorated with the Stars and Stripes and with a gummed space that the sender kissed, leaving an imprint of her lips. The verse beneath said:

> For Uncle Sam you're fighting
> And it makes me love you so
> That I send a kiss in the space above
> To take wherever you go!

Another card, showing a soldier standing in France and reaching out to hug a girl in America, asked:

> What's a little Ocean between friends
> When it's Christmas—OVER HERE.

Christmas cards have inevitably been used for political ends. The British statesman Joseph Chamberlain was depicted as a young blood straddling a globe under a benign sun, saying —in a quotation from the Gilbert and Sullivan operetta *The Mikado*—"I mean to rule the earth, as he the sky." And a suffragette's Christmas card bore the message:

> Downtrodden women now arise,
> No more let men thus tyrannize;
> Let's push the tyrant from his throne,
> And have a Christmas of our own.

Poor children were frequently featured on Christmas cards in Victorian times, but more in the spirit of instant compassion for their hard lot at a time when others were rejoicing, than from any reformist sentiments. Receivers of such cards were expected, perhaps, to give more generously to Christmas boxes and the like; they were not expected to ask what could be done

to change the lot of the poor. As an American writer observed in 1926: "Cards are rarely published today that indicate or even intimate the idea that unhappiness exists. They would fall quickly by the wayside, for everyone is intent on scattering sunshine and joy."

Trick cards have always been popular; cards that open out to show three-dimensional scenes, cards that pretend to be one thing on the outside only to turn out entirely different when opened. Cards in the style of banknotes, checks, railroad tickets, wills, and I.O.U.'s were widespread at the end of the last century. In both England and America, some of the cards that represented banknotes or bills were banned because they looked too much like real money. A line had to be drawn, even at Christmas.

CHRISTMAS AROUND THE WORLD

THROUGHOUT THE WORLD Christmases have more in common than they have differences. Over the centuries, various races and cultures have developed their own Christmas customs, but without much strain on the imagination almost all of them can be traced back to the Roman Saturnalia, to pagan solstitial rites, or to early Christian practices. Christmas in one city is much like Christmas in most other cities, and the similarities increase with the years and the growth in international communication. It is in the rural areas, the small towns and villages, that the time-honored national customs survive; and that applies as much to England and the United States as it does to Chile and Greece.

America has more different Christmas customs across its length and breadth than any other country in the world. Dutch, Italian, German, English, Swedish—all carried the traditions of the old countries to their new home, and Christmas customs seem to outlive most others. The United States has itself contributed substantially to modern Christmas lore.

The turkey and the poinsettia are American innovations that have spread around the world. But the communal Christmas tree is America's special Christmas trademark. All over the country can be seen giant evergreens, decorated with fairy lights—a generous, sharing gesture that underlines the traditional goodwill of the season.

In America's neighbor to the south, Mexico, Christmas is a festival in the fullest sense. It incorporates pageantry, joy, feasting, and all the traditional ingredients of the season.

Las posadas (processions) begin nine days before Christmas, when Mary and Joseph are thought to have begun their journey to Bethlehem, and continue unabated until Christmas. Sometimes nine families take turns in making the *posada,* one on each night; a few families make it on each of the nine nights. The *posada* comprises two groups, the travelers and the hosts, or innkeepers. The head of the household leads prayers; then the entire family, and as many friends as wish to attend, set out as travelers and march through the house carrying candles, with children in the lead bearing tiny replicas of Joseph and Mary. An innkeeper guards each room, and as the travelers pass asking for admittance, the innkeeper refuses. All the while the participants are chanting the Litany of Loretto:

"Who knocks at my door, so late in the night?"

"We are pilgrims, without shelter, and we want only a place to rest."

"Go somewhere else and disturb me not again."

"But the night is very cold. We have come from afar and we are very tired."

"But who are you? I know you not."

"I am Joseph of Nazareth, a carpenter, and with me is Mary, my wife, who will be mother of the Son of God."

"Then come into my humble home and welcome! And may the Lord give shelter to my soul when I leave this world."

When the travelers reach the room where the altar has been prepared—a Nativity scene complete with Mary and Joseph but, until Christmas Eve, lacking Christ—they enter and say a prayer. Then the party begins, complete with the *piñata.*

The *piñata* is an earthenware jar molded in the form of an animal or bird or even a human being, and filled with sweets and toys that can be obtained only by breaking the jar. It is hung from the ceiling, and each child is blindfolded and given a stick. The children take turns in trying to smash the *piñata,* and when one succeeds—which can take time, since it is often fairly sturdy and their swings are wild—the rest join him in a scramble for the spoils.

America's neighbor to the north, Canada, preserves the traditions of the two countries that contributed most heavily to its population. In French-speaking Quebec Province, the Christmas customs of France are enjoyed in the rural areas, although the major cities of Quebec and Montreal have acquired much of the sophistication of metropolises the world over. The other, English-speaking, provinces tend to maintain many of the colorful traditions of an English Christmas.

In the frozen north, many Eskimos still gather, as in pre-Christian times, for a solstitial feast. For the occasion they build a communal igloo that may stand fifteen feet high and is made elaborately from the foundations of six other igloos. Caribou meat and fish are laid in, and for the whole of the festival there are story-telling and drum dances and games of skill.

Although naturally influenced by North American traditions, Puerto Ricans maintain many of their own, and Christmas is a Latin American fiesta rather than a more staid American festival. Groups of *trullas,* or carol singers, still travel the countryside—in some parts on horseback—singing traditional songs, for which they receive sometimes money, more often food and drink. Families may spend right up to the hilt to load their tables for the *trullas* over Christmastime.

Children flock each year to the church of San José to watch the animated *nacimiento*. The church has a crucifix and an altar dating to the sixteenth century, but it is the *nacimiento* that draws the youngsters. It is an almost complete community, with villagers engaged at their work or riding on miniature trains that move back and forth through the village—and all centered around the two-thousand-year-old manger scene.

In Latin American countries, the period from the end of November until the first of February has five special fiestas: the Feast of Purissima (the Immaculate Conception) on December 8, Nochebuena (Christmas Eve), Christmas Day, Holy Innocents' Day on December 28, and the Feast of the Three Kings on January 6. Purissima is a day for prayer. Christmas Eve is dominated by the manger scene built by every family; the day culminates in a midnight Mass de Gallo, or Mass of the Rooster, to commemorate the tradition that a cock crowed in Bethlehem at midnight. Christmas Day is of less importance than Christmas Eve; and gifts are usually given at Epiphany.

Holy Innocents' Day is reminiscent of April Fool's Day or Hallowe'en, a time for the playing of practical jokes. Most countries celebrate the feasts in much the same way, although with minor variations.

In Brazil, children put out their shoes for Papa Noel to fill. Before going to midnight Mass, families set their tables with food for the Holy Family to eat if they stop by and are hungry. Christ is placed in his crib, and the last Advent candle is lit. After Mass, families celebrate until dawn. On Christmas Day the children search for their gifts, which Papa Noel has hidden, and serve their parents breakfast in bed.

Chilean Christmas centers around the small community of Andacollo, which is visited annually by thousands of pilgrims to carry out ancient rituals, including dancing in honor of the Virgin. The Virgin in this case is a three-foot-tall statue, discovered in a miraculous manner. Many years ago, a villager had a dream in which an angel told him, "Go to the hills, for wealth and happiness await you." The man, whose name was Collo, did as the angel bade, and on the way, while he was hacking his way through the undergrowth, his machete struck a half-buried object. He dug it out and found it was a statue of the Virgin, for which he made a shrine in his home. The villagers started to venerate the figure, and Collo was established as its guardian. Today, at Christmas the statue is decked out in the robes of royalty—a white robe edged with gold and a crown inlaid with precious stones.

Globos, paper balloons up to five feet or more in diameter, are a Christmas tradition peculiar to Colombia. To make a *globo,* a special type of thin, brightly colored paper is cut into sixteen triangles and glued together into a globe shape. When the balloon is inflated, father takes over the operation, which now becomes hazardous. Rags soaked in gasoline are suspended from the base of the balloon. Father sets the rags afire and, turning round three times, releases the balloon, which drifts off blazing. The launching of *globos* is illegal throughout Colombia, but so ingrained is the tradition that the law turns a blind eye at Christmas.

In Costa Rica at Christmas, orchids are everywhere, a custom growing out of a whim of nature, for the exotic flowers are abundant at the season. Collecting orchids and arranging them in hollowed logs set with candles is a Christmas tradition. The manger scene, in Costa Rica called *portal,* is often heavily decorated with their blooms. The *portal* is the focus of Christmas in Costa Rica. Towns set up kiosks to sell figurines, candy, flowers, and colored sawdust for use in making them, and families vie with one another to achieve the grandest. Although Christmas trees are fairly common, the *portal* dominates the Christmas scene.

Guatemala has a special holiday of its own just before Christmas. Called *el Dia de Guadalupe,* the Day of Guadalupe, it falls on December 12 and celebrates the appearance of the much-loved Virgin of Guadalupe, who first appeared in a vision to a little Indian boy called Santiago on that date. She is now the patron saint of all South American Indians. Children dress in traditional costume for this festival. Carrying miniature baskets of food and jugs of water, they parade to the accompaniment of firecrackers—and camera shutters, for the children proudly take photographs of themselves back to their families.

On the ninth day before Christmas another unusual ceremony is performed. Statues of Joseph and Mary are placed on a platform and carried through the night streets on the shoulders of two men, accompanied by family and friends. As they march, the men of the procession play tortoiseshell drums in a rare off-beat rhythm never heard except at Christmas. The paraders carry *farolitos,* brightly painted lanterns, and they proceed to a friend's house and sing a traditional carol asking for shelter. The would-be hosts, who expect their visitors, refuse to admit them, and a drama of questions and answers is enacted before the paraders announce that they are Joseph and Mary, upon which they are invited in. Their statues are placed by a prepared crib, and prayers are said. Then there is music and dancing for the rest of the night.

The city of Mérida, in Venezuela, has its own centuries-old Christmas tradition, *La Paradura del Niño,* or the Standing Up of Jesus. Every family, whatever its status, builds a *pesebre,* a complete village scene with Jesus' crib at the center. On the first day of the New Year the figure of Jesus must be taken from the crib and placed standing up until February 2, the Feast of Candelaria. If any family fails to stand the Christ figure up and his neighbors spot the lapse, they steal the figure and hide it.

Facsimile of possibly the first Christmas card published, *circa* 1843, designed by J. C. Horsley for Henry Cole

American card, *circa* 1881, published by L. Prang & Co., Boston

English Christmas card, *circa* 1865

American Christmas card, *circa* 1877, published by L. Prang & Co., Boston

Snowed Up on Christmas Eve—Appeals for Help, lithograph from the picture by Frank Dadd

The offender then is obliged to give a party for his neighbors, a *Paradura* party. Two men and two women are chosen as "godparents," to hold the four corners of the silk stretcher on which the figure will be returned to the crib. The godparents lead the march to the house where the figure is believed to be hidden, singing a long traditional carol that includes the lines:

> Godparents and shepherds,
> We come to kiss the Child,
> This sacred kiss
> We give with affection.
> And as we give this kiss
> To the blessed Child Jesus
> The godparents will stand him up
> And he will remain standing.

When the figure has been replaced in its original crib, children bring gifts to the infant Jesus and then respectfully cover Him with a cloth so that the dancing and merrymaking can begin.

Charles Dickens' picture of a Victorian Christmas still breathes over English Christmases today—the carol singers and the puddings, the stage coaches on Christmas cards, and the snow—again mostly on Christmas cards, since it rarely snows at Christmas.

Outside of the cities, England is a country heavy with tradition, and many ancient Christmas ceremonies are still celebrated. Queen's College at the University of Oxford, for instance, still celebrates the boar's head ritual. Bedecked with bay, rosemary, and holly, and with an orange in its mouth, the boar's head is borne in to the assembled fellows and dons and their guests to the fanfare of trumpets and the singing of the college choir. The head, on a silver platter, is finally placed in front of the Provost, who denudes it of its trappings and distributes them among the choir, the orange going to the soloist of the year.

Christmas bell-ringing is an ancient English custom that has waned, but not died. One specific custom that has survived for seven hundred years in Yorkshire is "Tolling the Devil's

Knell." On Christmas Eve a team of ringers toll the Dewsbury church bell once for every year since Christ's birth, timing the last stroke to fall precisely at midnight. Legend has it that the custom began in the thirteenth century, when a local nobleman presented the bell to the church, instructing that it should be rung each Christmas Eve to remind him of his murder of a servant.

In Somerset they burn the faggot (a bundle of ash sticks bound together) on Christmas Eve. The practice was begun in the ninth century by Saxon soldiers building fires to keep themselves warm before going into battle; ash was the only wood that burned when still green.

In England's fellow Commonwealth country, Australia, Christmas is bikini time on the beaches. Inland, it is the season to watch out for bush fires or their converse, the Big Wet. Whereas bush fires can range across country faster than a man can run, the Big Wet can bring such torrential rain that districts are cut off for days by floods. With such extremes of weather, it is not surprising that Australia celebrates Christmas differently from most of the rest of the world.

The great Australian tradition is open-air caroling. The custom began in 1907, when the city of Melbourne organized large-scale community singing, and it spread to other cities. Six years later Norman Banks wrote the "Melbourne Carol," perhaps not the greatest carol in the world, but certainly the first Australian one:

> Yuletide in Melbourne means mass jubilation
> And carols by candlelight on Christmas Eve.
> Thousands assemble in glad dedication
> To hail Him with joy, and the vow "I believe."

Special candles are sold for the Melbourne caroling, with the profits going to charity, and some two hundred thousand people assemble to sing by candlelight. The origins of the mass caroling lie with Cornish miners in South Australia in the nineteenth century, who on Christmas Eve sang Wesleyan carols by the light of their miners' lamps.

Talk about winter festivals to a Scotsman and he will think of Hogmanay, or New Year's Eve. No one is certain what the word originally meant, but to Scotsmen today it signifies a public holiday and a surfeit of drinking and rejoicing in the streets. On the hour of midnight, church bells ring throughout the country, and people everywhere link hands and sing "Auld Lang Syne," a song of remembrance of friends past and present.

First footing is another age-old tradition still kept very much alive in Scotland. The first footer is the first person to cross the threshold of a home in the New Year. He or she should bring a piece of coal, a piece of bread, a little money, and some salt; in return he will be given food and, more important, drink. There is great competition to be a first footer, because of the luck he brings to a household. On the other hand, a woman first footer is believed to bring bad luck. Dark men are said to be luckier than fair men, and a man known to have been born feet first is ideal. A bachelor is often considered better than a married man, as long as he is not flat-footed; he must have feet that "water runs under." The first footer should enter the house without speaking and poke the fire before he or anyone else in the house says a word.

In Wales, carol singing is not only festive but also competitive. Annual carol-singing contests are held between the highly trained choirs for which Wales is famous, and there is much competition to discover a new carol, which will be sung all over the country the following year.

The tradition of Mari Llwyd, a very old and strange cousin of Saturnalia, is on the wane but still to be seen in some country districts. Traditionally, one of the villagers plays the role of Mari Llwyd, wandering in white robes and mask and carrying a horse's skull on the end of a pole. Everyone he meets, his horse "bites"—it has movable jaws—and the only way to be free of the beast is to give him money.

Ireland, a country not noted for Christmas traditions, celebrates St. Stephen's Day, on December 26, with vigor. Village boys go from home to home bearing a straw "wren" on the end of a branch and singing a brief song in return for a few coins:

> The Wren, the Wren, the King of all Birds,
> St. Stephen's Day was caught in a furze,
> Although he is small, his family is great.
> Open up, lady, and give us a trate.

In a few parts of Ireland the village church bell is tolled from eleven o'clock to midnight on Christmas Eve, a custom referred to as "the Devil's Funeral," from the belief that the Devil died before Christ was born.

Denmark gave the world Hans Christian Andersen, the children's Charles Dickens of modern Christmas. Andersen wrote several fairy tales about Christmas, but "The Fir-tree" is the all-time favorite. Andersen wrote, "Life itself is the most wonderful fairy tale of all," and he passed this feeling on to children. Denmark also gave the world the blue-and-white porcelain Christmas plates on which at one time the wealthy presented sweetmeats to the poor, and which are now cherished by collectors.

For themselves the Danish have kept the Nisse, a small elf who is the survivor of the many fairy creatures who figured in ancient Danish Christmases. The Nisser—as they are called in the plural—get into all sorts of mischief, but they are essentially kindly and they guard household pets, which is why on

Christmas cards they often appear in company with a cat. Nisser have families and they are easily distinguished; the old head of the household wears a red cap like the rest of his family, but he also has a long white beard. On Christmas Eve a plate of rice pudding is put outside the kitchen door as a treat for the household Nisser, and if the cat eats it—well, it just shows that the Nisser know how to look after their friends.

Danes look after all animals carefully at Christmas. Sheaves of grain are put out everywhere for birds; if they eat well and in large numbers, it foretells a good year. Hunting and fishing are banned over the Christmas season, and farm animals get double rations of food, with the toast: "Eat well, keep well; this is Christmas Eve."

The Danes themselves eat well at Christmas, too, and they usually place a lighted candle in the window as an invitation to strangers to join them. At Christmas Eve dinner the *Julebaal*—Yule log—is lit in the hearth.

Norway has rediscovered its Julesvenn in recent years. Julesvenn was an ancient Norse figure in the mold of Santa Claus, except that he brought a bunch of lucky barley into the home to be found on Christmas morning. Today he brings more contemporary gifts. Straw dolls are still sold in Norwegian shops around Christmas, reflecting the old custom of strewing the floors of a house with straw at the time. On Christmas Eve the entire household, including servants, slept on the floor, and after Christmas the straw was spread about the fields to ensure a good harvest.

In the Norwegian countryside, people still put out a bowl of porridge for the barn elf in the hayloft at Christmas. The offering guarantees that the elf will not play any irritating tricks in the year to come.

In modern Sweden, St. Lucia vies for popularity with St. Nicholas. St. Lucia is celebrated as the Queen of Light, a fourth-century Sicilian martyr who traditionally helped Sweden in a time of famine. Every year on December 13, the eldest daughter wakes the rest of the family with Christmas cakes, singing an old Sicilian song, "Santa Lucia." During the day each city elects its own Lucia to preside over festivities.

Julafton, or Christmas Eve, is the high spot of the Swedish season and a time for family feasting. St. Stephen's Day, December 26, is the day for the animals, when they are given an especially generous meal.

St. Knut's Day falls on January 13 and officially ends Christmas—thirty days of it, which explains the old saying that "Christmas lasts a month in Sweden."

Belgium retains a particularly religious aura in its Christmas customs. On Christmas Day the children march in procession to church, carrying shrines and crucifixes decorated with bright ribbons. One boy, dressed as St. John the Baptist, leads a small white lamb.

St. Nicholas calls twice in Belgium. His first visit, at the beginning of December, is to learn how children have behaved during the year. Two days later, on December 6—his feast day —he returns with gifts or, for the worst children, switches. Children let him know where they live by leaving food and water for his horses outside their front doors, and St. Nicholas in return leaves evidence of his visit, other than his gifts, by turning the contents of children's rooms upside down. This topsy-turvy remnant of Saturnalia used to be reflected in the Feast of St. Thomas, too. On December 21 the children hobbled a hen and a rooster with a piece of string and let them loose. Then they chased the pair of one-legged animals. The girl who caught the hen was "Queen"; the boy who caught the rooster was "King." Schoolchildren either locked their teacher out of the schoolhouse until he promised to treat them, or bound him to a chair and carried him to a nearby inn, where he had to buy them refreshments in order to be set free.

Holland specializes in St. Nicholas Eve parties on December 5. St. Nicholas is most important to the Dutch Christmas. Celebration of his day is steeped in tradition, and it influences the whole of the month's festivities. At the St. Nicholas Eve party, guests gather around a dining table and give one another "surprise" gifts, each accompanied by a verse commenting on the recipient, usually in good-natured raillery. The point of the gifts is that they should be disguised to look like something else. A small present might be hidden in a cabbage or in a cake, or in a cavity cut in the pages of a book. A large gift might be disguised as a rubbish bin or a coal scuttle. The more ingenious the camouflage, the more successful the gift. Holland has a saying that the country "goes mysterious" on St. Nick's day;

even businessmen and politicians publicly join in the Saturnalia-flavored madness.

Austria has a strong heritage of Christmas music. Most parishes in the past had their own poet who added to the vast collection of *Hirtenlieder,* or shepherd songs, which sought to capture the emotions of the shepherds of Bethlehem. Many of these songs are still kept alive in rural areas.

Christmas lasts for a month for Austrian children, from the arrival of St. Nicholas with his companion, Krampus, right up to Epiphany, January 6, when the Three Wise Men arrive. On Christmas Eve the *Christkind* brings presents and sometimes helps to decorate the tree.

A roughshod version of kissing under the mistletoe survives on New Year's Eve in Austria. A large wreath is hung from the ceiling of the living room, and an ancient figure with a snowy beard and a crown of mistletoe lurks in a corner. He is Sylvester, representing the Old Year, and he leaps out to hug and kiss anyone who passes under the wreath. At midnight Sylvester is driven out of the room, to make way for the New Year.

When a French family returns from midnight Mass on Christmas Eve, they eat *le reveillon,* or late supper, which may range from turkey for a Burgundian to oysters for a Parisian. Before going to bed, French children leave their shoes in front of the fireplace for Père Noël to fill with gifts. At one time it was the custom to put out sabots, or peasants' wooden shoes rather like Dutch clogs; nowadays, however, sabots are seen only in pastry-shop windows—made of chocolate and decorated with candles.

The *crêche,* or crib, is popular throughout France, but in no region so much as in Provence, where the making of small figures called *santons* provides a year-round hobby for many villagers. The custom began about 1800, when Italian peddlers began selling *santa belli*—bright plaster figurines of saints and holy people—in the streets of Marseilles. Local craftsmen started to copy these figures in clay. At about this time Antoine Maurel wrote a fantasy play about the Nativity; called *Pastorale,* it dramatized the feelings of an entire village led to the stable in Bethlehem by the shepherds. The story seized Provençal imaginations, and the *santons* began to take the shapes of the characters in *Pastorale*—the mayor, the village gossip, the

village idiot, and so on. At that time they wore, as in the play, the costumes of their day; over the years, however, the *santon* makers have evolved characters based on contemporary figures in their own village. The *santons* are an essential part of the modern *crèche* in Provence, helping to make it the envy of Europe.

The German Christmas begins with the first Sunday of Advent, when a wreath bearing four red candles is hung in a window or stood against a wall. On the first Sunday after November 26 the first candle is lit, and the second and third candles on successive Sundays. The last is lit on *Heiligabend*, Christmas Eve. Advent calendars are also used during this period, often with little hinged windows for each day, behind which lie messages or rhymes.

During Advent, young girls have opportunities to foretell their marriage prospects in many outlandish ways. On St. Andrew's Night, November 30, for instance, standing barefoot under a plum tree and listening for a dog to bark will tell a girl from which direction her future husband will arrive. After Christmas, if a girl drops molten lead into cold water—or, more practically, egg white into hot water—she may discover what trade her future husband will follow, for the lead or egg white will set into the approximate shape of the tools of his trade. On St. Thomas' Day, December 21, some young girls still sleep head to the foot of the bed, to encourage dreams about their future spouse.

On a Thursday before Christmas is held *Klopfelnacht*, or Knocking Night. Mummers in hideous masks go from house to house, making as much noise as they can with bells, whips, tin cans, pebbles thrown at windows, and, of course, much hammering on front doors. The Knockers traditionally were asked to leap around in fields to ward off evil spirits and ensure fertility.

Carols and hymns are sung by choir boys called *Kurrende*, or sometimes the Starlings. They often sing from church towers, and the favorite carol is "Silent Night."

Since Germany introduced the Christmas tree to the world, there are naturally many legends attached to it. One of them tells how St. Boniface, the missionary who took Christianity to Germany, learned that the eldest son of the pagan chief Gundhar was to be sacrificed to the gods on Christmas Eve, under a giant oak that was sacred to the god Thor. Boniface, hoping to end the pagan myths by destroying their symbols, set about felling the tree; but as he began, a huge wind blew the oak down. Seeing that he had an awe-stricken audience, Boniface used the opportunity to point out a nearby fir tree, telling the villagers that it was the tree of peace and love because their homes were made of it, that it was a symbol of eternal life because its branches were evergreen, and that it pointed to heaven.

The Greeks have goblins called *Kallikantzaroi*, which they believe are the souls of the dead, and they still burn Yule logs to frighten these spirits away. At one time it was believed that a child born on Christmas Day became a *Kallikantzaroi* unless its toenails were singed; no one, ran the superstition, could become a goblin without toenails. *Kallikantzaroi* spend most of the year trying to chop down the tree that supports the world, only to have it reborn at Christmas just as they are completing their Herculean task. According to a variety of legends, the goblins are dark and swarthy creatures, lame and stupid, with red eyes, cloven hooves, thin hairy arms, and squinting eyes. They feed on worms, frogs, and anything else slithery, and they pester people continuously.

To the Greeks, Easter is a more important feast day than Christmas, but December 6, St. Nicholas Day, is observed with great devotion because St. Nicholas is the patron saint of sailors. The sea is inextricably bound up with everyday Greek life, and no Greek ship or boat sails without an icon of the saint and some boiled wheat on board. The wheat is to be thrown on the water in a storm, with the words: "Dear St. Nicholas, cease your rush."

During Advent every Greek household cooks its *Christopsomo*, or Christ bread, decorated with appropriate frosted figures—perhaps a plough and oxen on a farmer's loaf, sheep and a sheepfold on a shepherd's. Various areas have special traditions associated with the bread. In Kozánē the loaves are made harness-shaped, dedicated to the land and crops, and are nailed on a wall, where they remain through the year. In Messenia the first slice of the loaf is given to the first beggar who passes; the crumbs, considered sacred, are scattered around fruit trees to make them fecund in the coming year.

Spaniards begin Christmas celebrations at the Feast of the Immaculate Conception, which starts on December 8 and lasts a week. In many areas, balconies and porches are decorated with flowers and flags, and candles burn in windows throughout the night.

Christmas Day is reserved for feasting and exchanging presents. The Urn of Fate is also consulted on Christmas Day. Slips bearing the names of unmarried men and women are put in a large urn and jumbled around, then drawn out in pairs—a primitive kind of matchmaking ceremony.

Meeting the Magi is the Spanish Epiphany tradition, one shared with Portugal. All the villagers gather up cakes and fruit and straw and, to the clatter of handbells, horns, and rattles, walk to the edge of the village to meet the Three Kings. But the Kings always seem to have taken another road, leaving the children to eat the goodies. When the people return to the village, they find the Kings gathered in the church around the *nacimiento,* or manger. This companionable custom is unfortunately giving way to more modern Christmas celebrations in much of Spain.

The *presepio,* or crib, is the great Christmas love of Italy. Even grocery stores find ways of combining a manger scene with their window dressing at Christmas, whether carved out of butter or molded of almond paste and baked as a cake. St. Francis of Assisi is credited with popularizing the crib, and he succeeded admirably, the concept of the small child and the poor mother appealing particularly to the Latin temperament.

In Rome, Christmas was long heralded by the arrival of the *pifferari,* or Calabrian minstrels. Their *zampogne*—not unlike bagpipes—wailed and droned as the minstrels moved from street to street playing before statues of the Madonna and before carpenters' shops "in politeness to St. Joseph." Naples had similar pipers, who for a pittance would play a whole novena (nine days' prayers) before the Madonna of any house. Sicily had a like custom, except that the instruments used were violins. Unhappily, the custom has almost completely died out.

Among the countryfolk of Switzerland, it is traditional on Christmas Eve to forecast the weather of the coming year. An onion is cut into twelve segments, one for each month, and the segments are filled with salt. Examined the next morning, the

segments in which the salt is dry represent dry months, the wet segments, wet months.

To the rest of the world, a Swiss Christmas is made unique by the sound of bells. Echoing across the valleys, the church bells merge with Alpine horns and sleigh bells to make a really joyful Christmas sound.

In Poland, St. Sylvester Eve, December 31, is traditionally a time when every man can do what he wishes, regardless of his station in life. Although Poland is now a Communist-governed country, doubtless the old traditions are still remembered by many, if no longer practiced. Poles, like other Slavs, looked to the sky at Christmas, for the Star of Bethlehem was their most significant Christmas symbol. The first star to appear in the sky on Christmas Eve heralded the end of the Advent fast, and at the evening breakfast, *oplatki*—small Host-like wafers distributed by the clergy—were eaten. The priest also blessed the meal and the candles that lit it, and the table was often set with one extra place for the absent Jesus.

Following the meal, the Star-man, a more religious version of Santa Claus (usually the village priest in disguise), appeared to give gifts to good children and scold bad ones. The test of gift-worthiness was recitation of the Catechism. The stars brought the gifts, according to legend; and the Star-boys, three village boys dressed as the Wise Men, accompanied the Star-man as his porters, singing carols as they went.

Russia, like Poland, no longer officially recognizes Christmas as a religious festival, but the country is so steeped in traditions that Christmas customs are virtually ineradicable. Father Christmas is now generally called Grandfather Frost, and the Christmas tree has become the New Year tree, but Communism finds it as hard to stamp out Christian traditions as early Christians did to eradicate pagan ones; the names may change, but the characters remain much the same.

Among traditional Russian customs were the singing of carols, known as *Kolyadki;* and the Advent fast and the Christmas Eve supper, with straw placed beneath the tablecloth to represent the straw in the manger. Russia also had the old woman Babouschka and the young maiden Kolyada, both delivering gifts to good children.

In country areas girls played a game called "burying the

gold," which is thought to have symbolized the disappearance of the sun during the winter season. The game involved a circle of girls handing round a gold ring, with much feinting and sleight of hand, chanting "Gold I bury, gold I bury." One girl in the center of the circle tried to find out who had the ring; as soon as she spotted it, another girl took her place.

The celebration of Christmas in Japan dates back only about a century. This is not surprising, since the Christian population is less than 1 percent; yet in the past twenty-five years Christmas festivities have grown to enormous proportions. The observance is mainly commercial and closely tied to American urban Christmas. Western carols are sung in Japanese, Christmas trees are laden with lights, turkeys are fattened, and mistletoe and holly are hung. Hoteiosho, an old Japanese god, stands in for Santa Claus, and he checks children's behavior without the aid of a helper—he has eyes in the back of his head.

Oshogatsu, New Year's Day, is Japan's real holiday. Houses are thoroughly cleaned and decorated with straw, bamboo, and pine to represent family ties and long life. Children fly kites, and adults visit friends and pay respects to their ancestors.

FAMILY
ACTIVITIES

T HE THANKSGIVING TURKEY has been carved and served on its traditional Thursday in November. By Sunday the remnants have been totally consumed as sandwiches, croquettes, à la king, and turkey salad. As the noble bones are dropped into the kettle as the basis for a hearty soup, up go the merchants' Christmas decorations, in comes the extra sales help, and off we all go on our annual Christmas shopping safaris.

Few of us give a thought to Christmas until after Thanksgiving. The season is somehow not officially upon us until the shops unveil their special Christmas windows and gift boxes are piled high behind counters. Eleven months of leisure shopping time—lost. Eleven months of seasonal sales—lost. Eleven months of relatively sane, unhurried, unharried salespeople who know their stock and their business—lost. Eleven months of thoughtful list-making, sweater-knitting, fruitcake baking—all lost.

So let's begin with a New Year's resolution or two.

1. I will do my Christmas shopping early. (January 2 is as early as you can make it, so why not begin then?)

2. As a gift-giver, I will not purchase or otherwise contrive to give a single necktie, pair of hose, bottle of cologne, scarf, pair of gloves, or bottle of liquor, even for the most remote business obligation. (Those are the types of gifts that tell the recipient that you felt obliged to give him something and did so with as little thought as possible.)

3. If the man in the family breaks his electric razor in

September, I will not wait to replace it as a "gift for Christmas." (Ideally, Christmas gifts for adults are those special somethings—not necessarily luxuries—that people yearn for but would not dream of buying for themselves.)

SHOPPING FOR CHRISTMAS

Assuming that you are not busy on January 2 returning unwanted ties, perfume, and scarves, what are the specific advantages of keeping a Christmas eye out so early? January white sales, for one thing. Clearance sales, for another.

In the broad category of white sales (and there are traditional white sales in August besides in January), there are electric blankets, luxurious towels, magnificently patterned sheets and pillowslips, and splendid beach towels for use on patio, lawn, and sand.

Although clearance sales are often planned to dispose of merchants' miscalculations and mistakes, there are excellent buys to be had of most desirable postseason items: Handbags and pocket accessories, sumptuous sweaters, high-fashion "at home" clothes for men and women, furniture and accessories, small appliances. Golf, tennis, baseball, and camping equipment is sale priced in September and October; ski, skating, and football equipment in March and April. The list is endless, and so are the sales.

One of the most efficient ways to put these seasonal sales to best use—and to ensure total success in Christmas shopping whenever you do it—is to keep an "I've always wanted a . . ." dossier for everyone on your list. How often have you heard someone remark during the course of a year about a particular something he'd love to have—some day. By early December, when most of us normally begin to shop, you've either forgotten what that something is, or there is no longer a wide selection to choose from. It can't happen if you've written it down.

Such a list could helpfully include someone's special enthusiasms that don't fall into the usual gift-shopping category. For example, Aunt Jean's favorite performer has a hit show on Broadway, and Aunt Jean plans an Easter trip to New York. Aunt Jean's Christmas gift is a pair of tickets for the show, presented to her on December 25 but dated for an evening during Easter week. There is always the chilling possibility that the star will leave the cast in the interim, but the idea and execution of the gift are worth the risk. As another example, a nine-year-old on your list is an ardent fan of a particular baseball team. Is there someone you know, however remotely, who could get a ball autographed by the entire team, or a personally dedicated and signed photograph of the players? Could there be a more exciting, treasured gift for that nine-year-old? If you yourself are not tuned in to sports, jot down a note the next time you hear that boy waxing ecstatic about his heroes. If you have no way of getting through with a personal contact, get in touch with the team's publicity office early in the season, to allow plenty of time for the arrangements to be made.

There are many other gift possibilities along these lines. For a 19-year-old interested in aviation, consider a gift certificate for a flying lesson or two—if, of course, there is an airfield near his home or college. For a 16-year-old (or someone of any age) who is concerned about our vanishing wildlife, make a contribution in his name to a national organization devoted to the preservation of wildlife and give him a subscription to one of the handsome magazines on the subject. Among such organizations are National Wildlife Federation and the Sierra Club, to name only two.

Instead of the obvious gifts of golf balls for the links devotee or a fancy apron for the chief cook, let your imagination stretch to the limit of your purchasing power.

For the golfer, perhaps a major tournament is scheduled near enough to your home to make a day there practicable. The resident professional at your golfer's regular course or club or the sports editor of the local newspaper can give you this information. Most professional tournaments are held at private club courses, so simply write to the management of the club, explaining your Christmas gift purpose and asking how you can insure tickets to one or more days of tournament play. On Christmas Day, the gift may be either the actual ticket, or, more probably, your own reasonable facsimile until the real thing arrives. It might be appropriately attached to a new golf umbrella, a telescopic ball retriever, or a set of covers for the woods.

Detail of Christmas crib and tree decorated with a collection of
18th-century Neapolitan figures at The Metropolitan Museum of Art

Christmas tree at Rockefeller Plaza, New York City

For the chief cook? Even the most experienced cooks sometimes run out of ideas on what to serve next. Cookbooks are a good possibility, especially since any well-stocked bookshop features twenty or thirty or more, with ladles-full published every year. To make such a gift a bit more out of the ordinary, find out if there are any cooking classes in the vicinity. Not just ordinary meat-and-potatoes lessons, but classes in the cuisines of China, Mexico, Russia, Germany, France, Italy; classes in exquisite pastry making, appetizer techniques, and so on.

The idea of lessons can be extended to a broad range of interests: Lessons in horseback riding, tennis, golf, dancing, swimming. Lessons in language, handicrafts, music, voice, acting. Lessons in karate, judo, driving, sewing, painting, sculpture. Individual courses of all types at local colleges and universities. For all the above gifts, that invaluable list you kept is your fountain of ideas.

One of the most successful gifts of recent years, and one that is rapidly growing in popularity, is as available in small towns as in big cities, although it requires a bit of effort in either case. But what could be more pleasing to a dedicated movie fan than enabling him to see his favorite old movie in his own home, without commercial breaks. The idea is especially apt for those who live where art theaters are nonexistent or revival festivals are rare. Rental fees for 16-mm sound projectors are not beyond reach, and there are companies all over the country that rent prints of hundreds of feature films. The gift of a day, a week, or even a month of viewings of a favorite movie is a sure-fire smash. If your local yellow-pages directory does not have a listing for motion-picture film libraries, the camera shop where you arrange for the rental of the projector and screen can probably offer some suggestions on where to write. Your choice need not be restricted to feature films, for these libraries stock thousands of short subjects in a staggering variety, in both 8-mm and 16-mm. A sharp ear for casually dropped remarks and a sharp pencil for jotting them down leave no margin for error. And if you make inquiries early enough in the year, you still will have plenty of time to dream up a substitute gift if that favorite film is simply unavailable for private rental.

For the person whose interest in astronomy has been

piqued by the space probes of recent years, quite inexpensive and quite adequate telescopes and books, including paperbacks, are available for the aspiring stargazer. For the nature lover, there are equally inexpensive binoculars and books (again in paperback) for learning to know birds as well as other regional fauna and flora.

The "how to" books and equipment with which *to* do range as widely in price as they do in projects, from the resurgent interest in macramé (knot-tying) to rug-hooking, leather-working, or raising tropical fish for fun and profit. A leisurely browse through the "how to" section of your library or bookshop can spark the idea for the "perfect" Christmas gift, just as well as a browse through a department-store or mail-order catalogue.

Another source for off-the-beaten-track gifts that can be mined all year long is the antique shop, if you're lucky enough to live where such shops exist or even abound. In the general category of antique shops are those that specialize in genuine antiques, from bric-a-brac to furniture. Others are plain and simple junk shops, but what is sold by a dealer as "junk" may be grist for the Christmas shopper's mill. You need not be expert or even experienced as an antique hunter to shop successfully in these stores. What to look for? Old brass, glassware, utensils, fireplace tools, andirons, picture frames, light fixtures, carvings, decorative wood panels for doorways and walls, lamp bases, old signs for kinds of stores that no longer exist, spool boxes, coat racks, wall racks, brass and wood shelf brackets and bed headboards, jewelry, tiles, artifacts.

In the brass category are antique mortars and pestles to be used as decorative pieces and planters as well as by the gourmet cook who likes to grind her own herbs and spices. There are decorative doorknobs that might even boast the carved initial of the intended recipient. There are lovely old brass door knockers, candlesticks, lamp bases, mailboxes.

If you believe, as many do, that glass stemware need not come in matching sets, there are single treasures to be unearthed. An attractive way to give a single glass to the one who will appreciate it is to fill it with a homemade specialty of your own: jam, paté, candy, chutney. Seal the top, gift-wrap it, and you're either giving the glass filled with goodies, or giving your very special plum jam in a beautiful container. There are wine and liquor decanters of cut glass or leaded crystal, as well as bowls, stemware, ink stands, and vases. Collector's glass may be had in a variety of shapes; colors include the lovely cranberry red glass as well as a spectrum of other colors popular in America's past and suitable for the most modern color scheme.

In junk and antique shops you can dig for very old and very usable kitchen utensils and crockery. There are the enormous wooden bowls once used for mixing homemade bread dough; some are as much as 20 inches across and 6 to 8 inches deep at the center of the base. Stained a deep, glowing walnut, they can toss off a magnificent salad for an army of guests. Serving pieces large enough to honor these gargantuan bowls may be hard to find, but they are available in houseware shops or in the new breed of gourmet shops that are springing up around the country.

In the good old days, tools were made to be ornamental as well as useful. Frequently, utilitarian carpenter's levels were made of beautiful wood and edged and otherwise decorated in brass. Today they are as welcome for display as they are for the workshop.

The idea in junk-shop shopping, a pleasure to nurture, is to browse with your mind as wide open as your eyes, looking at each object for possible applications other than its original purpose. Merchants once displayed stocks of thread in spool cases, usually made of fine wood and in a variety of heights.

For today's home they are attractive as ottomans, if low enough, or as unusual end or lamp tables, if high enough. All are eminently giftworthy.

It should be admitted now that one *can* leave the Christmas shopping to December, shop only in department and specialty shops, and come up with stacks of gifts that are creative, imaginative, and sure to be received with pleasure. But going off the beaten track "out of season" gives an added dimension to what can often prove to be a wearying task.

Thoughtful shoppers are sometimes reluctant to buy a practical item as a gift because it doesn't seem festive enough. When practicality is dressed up, however, the gift becomes the ugly duckling turned swan. This type of gift works best as an inexpensive "extra" to the major gift. Following are several examples, which hopefully will inspire an avalanche of ideas.

If someone on your list is a gardener and is always misplacing his tools, buy him a new trowel and fill it with goodies —hard candy, cookies, nuts, personalized or decorative matches, a pouch or two of his favorite pipe tobacco, cigars, small desk gadgets. If you'd like to give a work-shop organizer (plastic boxes for holding nails, nuts and bolts, and the like), fill the containers with surprises—fishing lures, sinkers, golf tees, penny candy, or more expensive items such as jewelry, cigarette lighter, collector's coins, stamps. Do the same for gifts of drawer dividers, personalized drinking mugs, desk letter trays, sieves, colanders. If it can contain something, fill it. The other side of this coin involves making edibles the gift and the container the "extra." If you like to give homemade jams, candies, cookies, or cakes at holiday time, find a useful and unusual receptacle for them that will last long after the edibles have been enjoyed— preserves packed in a mug or glass, cookies in a child's toy truck, a fruitcake in a new lunch box. Extending the idea, you might enclose a roll of hair ribbon in a cellophane tape dispenser, or arrange paintbrushes bouquet-like in a pencil cup or a vase.

No matter when you do your shopping, keep in mind the attractive possibilities of gift containers that are not the usual box. If, for instance, you have decided on the color scheme for your tree decorations, one of your gifts may fit perfectly into a colored-straw tissue dispenser, which makes its own good-looking wrapping, beribboned and gift-tagged. A small waste-basket of straw or plastic will accommodate any number of types of gifts. Other gift containers that are their own best wrappings are teapots, perhaps filled with a selection of exotic teas; bread or flower baskets; a wine rack, filled or dotted with a variety selection of wines. In short, gifts that are two in one and save the need for wrapping.

An important factor in gift shopping and giving is the psychological impact of the gift; and frequently too little attention is paid to this aspect of Christmas, especially where children are concerned. Subconsciously if not consciously, the child evaluates his status in the family by the gifts he receives. We can each probably recall a specific gift, or the absence of it, that remains a painful memory carried into adulthood. Conversely, we can each recall one special Christmas that years later still brings a smile. How does this happen? How can disappointment be avoided?

Each child nurtures certain fantasies that are quite unrealistic—the city child who dreams of having his own pony, for example; but these disappointments are not in the category we are discussing here. There have been jokes and cartoons by the hundreds about the father who buys his three-year-old son or eight-year-old daughter an elaborate set of electric trains. The child senses that the gift was not really for him, but for his father, who perhaps was fulfilling his own childhood dream. It is no joke to the youngster.

In too many instances, a blue-jeaned little tomboy receives a frilly dress or a fragile doll because "all little girls love frills and dolls"; or the boy who spends his spare time reading is given a football and helmet because Dad wants him to be an athlete and "all little boys love football." The message is clear. The tomboy daughter and the bookworm son are unacceptable to the adults in their lives. The dress is never voluntarily worn, the football never thrown. The children have experienced a subtle type of rejection in the guise of a gift at Christmas time. One can be rejected, admonished, and pressured by a gift as well as by the absence of a gift.

There are other examples of gifts designed on the surface to please but bound to disappoint. For instance, the child who mows lawns, washes cars, and delivers papers to earn the money to buy the very special bicycle his heart is set on, and finds on Christmas morning that his parents have bought the bike for him. He will accept it, admire it, and ride it, but it will never have the same meaning for him as it would had he bought it himself with the money he earned. Despite the best intentions in the world, the joy of owning a coveted possession is diminished.

When planning the "I really must" gifts to the postman, the mechanic, the regular delivery men, remember that letting these gifts be obvious afterthoughts is as thoughtless as not giving a gift at all. The postman won't be any more pleased than you were by the dreary Christmas tie someone gave you last year. Your beautician will get the message when you give her the off-brand bottle of gardenia cologne you bought at the last minute or had stowed away in a closet. Christmas is no time for expressions of resentment or indifference. As a solution to the "really must" dilemma, the residents of one street might pool their gift resources for their postman and buy him an electric foot massager; the milkman might enjoy a pair of electric mittens as a joint gift from several of his customers; the newspaper delivery boy, tickets to a forthcoming sports event or a book of tickets to the local movie house.

Gifts *from* children establish early in their lives their own sense of values as well as yours. Children who are not yet old enough to have a regular allowance but are old enough to understand the spirit of Christmas giving can give to their parents, brothers, and sisters without hypocrisy. The saying, "It's not the gift, but the thought behind it" is as true for the five-year-old as for the adult. It also establishes a valid sense of proportion at a very early age.

The small child should be encouraged to make his own Christmas offerings at nursery school or kindergarten, or from materials at home. He may even choose to part with a treasure that someone has admired—baseball cards, a special shell found at the shore, marbles, an object he modeled from clay. If adults buy a relatively sophisticated present and give it in the child's name, he cannot experience true participation and he senses that something is wrong even if he cannot consciously define it. When a child is old enough to receive a regular allowance or to learn the value of money by earning it at assigned

chores, he can purchase the gifts he wishes to give. Just as an adult does not buy a child a gift that only the adult can enjoy, the small child can be gently guided away from buying an adult a gift the child really wants for himself. You can and should help a small child set a financial limit on each gift, and, if necessary, feed him ideas in such a way that he'll believe he made the decision alone. There are hundreds of items under a dollar that a child can give—a "special" coffee mug, a dialing gadget for the inveterate telephoner in the family, decorative candles, a name plate for a bicycle, a roll of camera film, ball-point pens, bags of marbles, modeling clay, a catnip mouse for the family cat, a rawhide "bone" for the dog.

So, even for the youngest member of the family, Christmas gift shopping can be an all-year-round pleasure, but decorating the home for this very special holiday is confined to the few short weeks before Christmas.

DECORATING THE HOME

Since Christmas is wholly a festive holiday, the outside as well as the interior of your home can reflect the season's spirit, and the decorations can range from the elaborate to the simple.

Although decorating is a matter of personal taste, over-decoration diminishes the effect of your efforts. Santas on the roof, reindeer on the lawn, strings of lights outlining the entire frame of the house, wreaths lighting every window, an itchy trigger finger on the spray-can of snow—the spirit is willing but the impact is weak. The art of decoration is the art of balance, focus. If one errs, it should be on the side of under-statement. The not-so-secret secret is to decide on and carry through one major focal point. Since this is usually the Christmas tree itself, all else should complement and lead to it.

If you are fortunate enough to have a live evergreen tree on your front lawn, a string of lights, either multicolored or all white (which gives the effect of tracings of delicate ice or snow), and/or simple weatherproof decorations is a welcome and welcoming sight. One well-placed floodlight trained on the tree gives it all the added nighttime emphasis it needs.

The old-fashioned front gate is a rare sight these days, but if you have one fronting your property it should be given a touch of seasonal decoration. A small wreath or basket is enough for openers. If you choose a basket, make it at least 4 inches deep, line it with a container that will hold water, and fill it with evergreen branches accented with berries or other small fruits such as grapes (real or artificial), crabapples, lady apples, sickle pears, and the like. Or arrange the basket with combinations of wheat stalks, cattails, pepper berries, acorns, pine cones, or whatever other fruits and vegetables you wish.

If you use Indian corn and gourds for your Thanksgiving decorations, they can be spray-painted, or left *au naturel*, and used again at Christmas time. Fasten the basket to the fence gate, and your holiday welcome is established.

Lampposts, too, are natural outdoor frameworks for seasonal welcomes. They lend themselves best to festooning with evergreen ropes accented with splashes of colorful berries.

Roping is one of those rare words that mean exactly what they say. The basis for an evergreen rope is a length of rope—clothesline being the best for thickness, strength, and proper flexibility.

First, cut the rope to the length wanted. Use pieces of evergreen no more than 4 or 5 inches each for best results. Wrap them together with fine wire (30 gauge is universally considered the most desirable), leaving enough wire to fasten the sprays securely to the rope, overlapping as you go, so that a full effect of foliage, not stems, is achieved. You'll find that you get the most attractive results most easily if you tie the ends of the rope to stationary objects while you work, so that it is held straight, with no slackness. Besides trimming lampposts, ropes of evergreen do well on bannisters and newel posts.

Garlands of evergreen, which are effective over doorways, mantels, and windows, are made in the same way as ropes. They look best if made so that the greens face in opposite directions.

If you wish, you can relieve the total greenness of the sprays by securing pine cones, berries, or fruits to the ropes and garlands.

Through the front gate, up the garden path, and to the front door, where we'll linger a while, for it is one of the important areas to receive holiday decorating attention.

The wreath is the most popular of all door decorations, and the number of types that can be bought or handmade is boundless. The first consideration is size—in relation to the dimensions of the door, the house itself, and the distance of the house from the street. Proper scale once more is an important factor in design in addition to color and texture. There is no "right" or "wrong" in these combinations if the elements please you, but remember that dark colors seem to recede, light colors to advance, and that the lighting, artificial or natural, that will fall on the colors will also diminish or accentuate them.

To begin with the frame, it can be handmade either of smooth, firm wire or of crinkle-textured wire, both purchasable at florists. Another type of frame for do-it-yourself wreathing is of styrofoam; it resembles a life preserver and is available at variety stores in a large selection of sizes, thicknesses, and colors. You can also fashion a wreath frame from the ubiquitous wire coat hanger, or you can use slender lengths of shrub branches that will bend to your will.

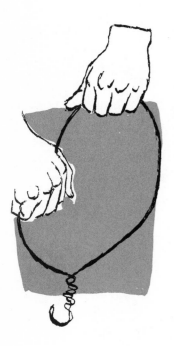

A time-honored technique for attaching the sprays of greens to the frame is to wind narrow strips of scrap cloth around the frame, overlapping firmly so that the sprays can be tucked into the resulting "slots." The ideal length for the sprays is the same as that recommended for roping—no more than 5 inches. Next comes interweaving colorful or textural additions to the wreath. If you use a frame of styrofoam, the technique of attaching its finery is different but the possibilities are wider, including berries, pine cones, etc. Lay the styrofoam circle out flat, and arrange your decorative pieces lightly until you achieve the design you like. Next, press each piece hard into the foam to make a permanent indentation, remove it and apply a bit of glue to the groove, and replace the piece firmly. When all the decorative pieces are back in place, allow time for drying before the wreath is hung.

Simple sprays of ribbon-tied greens, or the more elaborate swags dotted with fruits, colorful baubles, or any of the previously mentioned decorative touches can be used to accent the wreath if there is suitable wall space beside the door. Swags also look well on gates or window shutters. You might also consider Christmasing your winter-empty window boxes with sprigs of holly, evergreen sprays, or whatever else strikes your fancy.

If your attic doesn't yield lengths of old-fashioned sleigh bells, the treasure houses known as junk or antique shops might. They are well worth searching for—not only as attractive and nostalgic decorative additions to your outdoor areas, but also as prime symbols of winter and the Christmas season.

One more suggestion for outdoor home decorating, and then we'll move inside and warm up to the subject of interiors.

In Scandinavia it has long been a Christmas tradition to prepare a bird-feeding tree for happiness and luck. Obviously, this includes happiness and luck for the birds as well. In this country in recent years, we have all become aware of the plight of our wildlife—species after species becoming extinct or in danger of extinction from chemicals, forests shrinking as population centers spread, threatening food supply and breeding places. Christmas is as appropriate a time as any to decorate an outdoor bird-feeding station, a gift to your Christmas celebration and a gift of life to the bird population in your area.

A small potted evergreen set in the garden or on the lawn serves as this tree of life, and it can be planted later as a permanent addition to your landscaping. Any tree presently growing will do as well, of course. It remains for you to stock it with food. The branches can be hung with garlands of popcorn and cranberries, containers of peanut butter (birds are wild for it, and it is marvelous nourishment for them, keeping their natural body oils replenished for protection against the winter cold), bags of suet rolled in wild-bird seed and tied with colorful ribbon—baubles with a purpose. Pans or plastic containers filled with seed also make fine cafeterias when decorated and hung from tree branches. Planning and setting up these bird feeders and keeping the food and water supply replenished is an instructive and exciting responsibility for children. No professional artist or designer could create the colorful and random arrangements made by the reds, blues, buffs, browns, and iridescent blacks and purples of the flocks of birds that will take advantage of your largesse.

The major stumbling block to making your own Christmas decorations is a mental one. A preconviction that the job is just too difficult and time-consuming prompts many people to give up before they try. There is nothing wrong with buying your decorations ready-made. However, if you do wish to experience the fun and enormous satisfaction of producing your own originals, then shift your mental gears, unlock your imagination, and go! If you begin early enough before Christmas week, you can experiment, rip apart and start over, invent your own

methods and shortcuts, and still have time, should all efforts fail
to satisfy you, to buy the ready-mades.

It is important, especially for neophytes, to assemble all
the materials in a spot set aside for the project, and to lay out
what you'll require for easy access and continued momentum.
The basic equipment useful to have at the ready includes:
lengths of clothesline, not necessarily new; spools of fine-gauge
wire (#30); spools of heavier wire (#24); wreath frames; aqua
picks; florist's clay; pin holders for supporting heavier branches;
glue; heavy toothpicks; wire cutters, awl, and scissors; chicken
wire; and styrofoam, in precut frames or blocks, or precut into
spheres or whatever shapes you fancy. Florists, garden centers,
variety stores, and lumberyards will yield just about everything you'll need. Keep on hand a supply of ribbon in several
widths and textures; and surround yourself with the greenery,
fruits, nuts, baubles, berries, wheat stalks, dried or artificial
flowers, shells (both seashells and halves of walnut shells, which
take paint well and can cradle miniature objects); buttons, bells,
cones, hard candies, beads, and costume jewelry. There are undoubtedly other decorations not included in this list that you
might like to try. The next time you're in a hardware or variety
store, look at the wares displayed as though they were featured
for Christmas decorations, then pick and choose. This will
break you out of the holly-and-tinsel rut, and something that
catches your eye may inspire your entire decoration theme.

The bird feeders are full and appropriately decorated for
Christmas, the path to your front door is glowing with a display
of garlands and wreaths. Over the threshold and into the house,
where most of us focus our major efforts.

We'll begin with the first area that strikes the eye—the
foyer. The wisest and safest course here is understatement. The
major decorative focal point will be the tree itself, normally in
the traditional place of honor in the living room, so the decoration of the entrance hall should be the overture to the magnifi-
cence to come.

A smaller version of the front-door wreath and hung back
to back with it, so to speak, keeps the season's spirit coming and
going. Since the indoor decorations are protected from the
weather, wood carvings and ceramic pieces can be included.
A small grouping of greens for the foyer shelf or table, a poin-

settia plant or two attractively placed may be all the touch of Christmas you'll want there. Indoors, the decorations must share the viewer's attention with your furnishings, and although modern and traditional mix well, do not let your choice overpower the furniture.

Simple drops of pine cones, perhaps spray-painted silver, gold, or a color and combined with any of the wreath-making materials, do well under foyer wall sconces or between bands of wall molding.

A topiary tree is a popular solution to foyer decoration. Genuine topiary trees are small living trees trained and cut to grow in fanciful shapes. For purposes of Christmas decoration, a topiary tree can be created with a pot of plastic or papier mâché, a trunk of wood molding, and foliage of evergreens attached to a sphere of chicken wire or styrofoam. Because such trees are not usually more than 2 or 3 feet high, they can accent a foyer corner or, in pairs, frame the door either inside or out. Another treatment of the topiary tree is to "cut it in half," attach it to a panel, and mount it on the wall. Cut the pot vertically, make the trunk of half-round molding, and attach the foliage to a half sphere of chicken wire or styrofoam. This type of topiary tree thus becomes part of the architecture and offers no competition to the important tree in the living room.

The dining room deserves your serious decorating attention, even if you do not plan elaborate entertaining during the twelve days of Christmas. Of course, the kind of small sprays and wreaths that have been described can be placed around the room, on the sideboard, and centering the dining table. In keeping with the purpose of the room, edibles—both real and artificial—come beautifully into play here. You can use pineapples, for example, with the spiky green leaves traced with cranberries, sprigs of edible greens such as mint leaves, or topped with wisps of evergreen. You can use a large compote or bowl filled with the traditional colors of the season in bright red apples mixed with green apples, limes, or greengage plums. As your decorating scheme is eaten, you merely replenish it from the refrigerator. Pomegranates, red onions, red and green cabbages, even tiny Brussels sprouts piled into a small tree-like pyramid make handsome groupings. If you decide to decorate with food, consider a wreath of dark evergreens combined with the long thin variety of red and green peppers; bowls of radishes mixed with pimiento-stuffed olives, pimiento slices over stalks of asparagus, radishes, and Brussels sprouts. The wreath or garland you hang on the dining room wall could not survive the season if it were constructed with edibles. You *can* use bright red tomatoes and strawberries, however, if they are the kind originally intended for use as pincushions. This type of whimsy costs a bit initially if you use a mixture of fifteen or twenty of each on a wreath, topiary tree, or whatever, but they will serve beautifully and tastefully for years.

Groupings of plump candles set in beds of evergreen sprays —the greens sprayed with fireproofing material, and the candles never left lit when the room is empty—symbolize the glow of the season. Make use of your best silver serving pieces, polished to a fare-thee-well, as receptacles for evergreens on table and sideboard. If you wish to confine your important seasonal decorating to the living room, the warmth of silver by candlelight is sufficiently suggestive of the holidays to stand alone.

As for the rest of the home, aside from the living room focal point, it is a question of choice whether or not you "do" the bedrooms, den, bathrooms, and kitchen. A simple spray, swag, or wreath on the doors may be all you'll expend of your time, money, and energy.

The Mistletoe, old print

Some people maintain that to decorate every room in the house is equivalent to a woman's wearing all her jewelry at one time. Others are equally convinced that Christmas *is* in every room in the house, so why not acknowledge the fact.

If you subscribe to the latter view, you can frame the medicine cabinet or mirror with a rope or garland of evergreens, use Christmas-motif disposable guest towels on the rack, and a dish of red and green soap balls at the sink. For the children's rooms, consider a stocking topped with evergreen sprays hung on the door, a small artificial tree in the room, and perhaps a seasonally appropriate mobile hung from the ceiling fixture. For the adults' bedrooms, you might limit the decorations to door wreaths but make them meaningfully appropriate to the occupants. For the car-struck young man, a wreath or spray can be constructed entirely of miniature model automobiles; for the teen-age girl, one made of painted hair rollers and clips; for the sewing room, one of pincushions, tape measures, tailor's chalk, thimbles, spools of thread, buttons, and bows. For Dad's workshop or den, plan a wreath of miniature or toy tools, or of colorful fishing lures, painted lead sinkers, or anything appropriate to his hobby. For a small child—*her* wreath dotted with beads, jacks, and dominoes; *his* door identified by a wreath of marbles, checkers, trading cards. For all of these wreaths, glue the objects to styrofoam or wire and circle them with seasonal foliage.

A major center of Christmas interest is the kitchen. At Christmas time we sometimes sigh for the huge old country kitchen, with its sit-down table for the whole family and its enormous stove from which emerged fragrant pies and cakes and roasts and pans of cookies. Millions of Americans make do with small efficiency kitchens in their homes or apartments, but if elaborate Christmas decorating is no longer practical, at least a touch or two is possible.

Tradition tells us that the mistletoe should hang in the hall, but surely tradition can be broken where these romantic berries are concerned; a sprig could be hung from the kitchen light fixture, where the cook can often be rewarded for her efforts with kisses as well as clean plates. For minimal decoration, tape some of the Christmas cards to the refrigerator door as a constant and happy reminder of the good wishes of friends

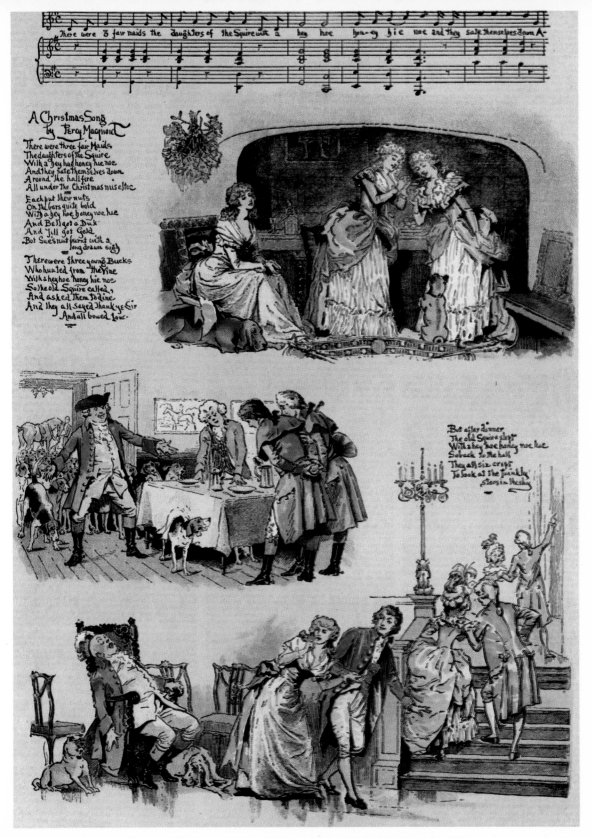

Love at Christmas Time, lithograph by Percy Macquoid, 1889

Love at Christmas Time, lithograph by Percy Macquoid, 1889

and family. Enwreath the kitchen wall clock. Use decals on the
window panes. Fill the breadbasket or fruit bowl with signs of
the season. Fashion a countertop lollipop tree from a styrofoam
cone—the lollipop sticks are their own attaching devices.
Break up a wall with an espalier tree, a frame of heavy wire
wrapped with your choice of evergreens, flowers, small artificial
fruits, nuts, or colorful plastic cutlery. Such a tree can be made
as tall or short as you like. Since it goes flat against the wall, it
can be held upright with colored or see-through tape if the
decorations are not too heavy. Just check the wall first to be
sure that bits of paint or wallpaper won't be removed with the
tape when the tree comes down.

The best is now to come—the living room, where the tree
will be nobly ensconced and the family and guests will spend
the most time. This is the room where most of your creative
efforts—and of your decorating budget—will be expended.

It is the rare homeowner who has the money and the
storage space to indulge in separate Christmas-theme china,
glassware, linens, and other accessories. Displays in department
stores and illustrations in the December issues of magazines
spare no expense, and the layouts are designed by professionals.

In the face of all this splendor, it is easy to become discouraged from trying your hand in your own home. But if you cannot duplicate something you like, you can at least adapt it to your own budget and skills.

Because the tree and the fireplace, if any, are the centers of interest in the living room, they should get most of the emphasis. Always plan one center of interest per room for maximum effect.

You might do well to choose a theme other than the usual red and green, candy canes and Santas. The theme might be religious, it might be concerned with the sea, with flowers, with animals, with light, with shapes, bells, or colors. Any theme can be expanded to whatever extent your time and imagination take you, and it can be applied to the windows (transparencies, decals, wreaths, lights, hand-painted designs of your own invention) and to touches on the wall sconces, chandeliers, lamps, and occasional tables.

To execute the religious theme, you can choose among reproductions of the works of hundreds of artists and sculptors who have celebrated the story of the first Christmas. You may already own, or wish to create, a crèche to grace the mantelpiece or place beneath the tree. For the Christmas season you can cover the pictures hanging in the room with reproductions of religious scenes, suitably matted, if necessary. A framed hanging mirror might be covered temporarily by the thematic picture. Almost any depiction of a mother and child takes on the significance of the holiday when surrounded by other evidence of the religious theme. The tree will similarly receive its treatment of the theme with your versions of the star of Bethlehem, angels, manger animals, and the three Magi with their gifts of gold, frankincense, and myrrh.

The Zodiac, popular down the ages, has seen a recent resurgence of interest, and it might make a light-hearted theme for your holiday season. The twelve signs of the Zodiac lend themselves well to fanciful decorating: Capricorn, the goat; Aries, the ram; Sagittarius, the archer; Libra, the scales; Gemini, the twins; Pisces, the fish; Cancer, the crab; Taurus, the bull; Virgo, the Virgin; Scorpio, the scorpion; Leo, the lion; and Aquarius, the water bearer. You can use them all, or only the birth signs of family members, and you can be as representational or as stylized as you please throughout the house.

The decorations inside and outside the house might be called the supporting cast in the annual revival of the Christmas pageant. The star, the leading player, is the tree. You and the family, as the playwrights, directors, and producers of this holiday presentation, are the ones to make the star shine to standing ovations and glowing reviews. The theme for the tree should dictate the theme for the other decorations, for that which lends itself best for hanging on a tree can be expanded in areas less constrained in terms of space and shape.

DECORATING THE TREE

Before discussing some of the infinite suggestions for decorating the Christmas tree, let's take a moment to consider the selection of the tree itself.

From the 60-foot tree, carefully chosen in northern forests, that is a tradition at Rockefeller Plaza in New York City, to the littlest pines brought into homes all over the country, the ceremony of decorating and lighting is undertaken with equal seriousness and anticipation. The mammoth tree in the Plaza symbolizes the Christmas greetings of a city. In your home, the tree is your own personal statement of your approach to Christmas and the holiday season.

The most popular and desirable tree for indoor use is the balsam fir, for several good reasons. The foliage is shiny, the shape is an ideal pyramid, and the branches are strong enough to support heavy and elaborate decorations, yet the needles are soft, so that no one is painfully pierced during the decorating process. In addition to all these virtues, the balsam firs are the poodles of the tree world—they don't shed.

The Douglas fir has all of the attractive balsam qualities, with one exception. Because its branches are less firm and solid, the decorations must be less densely hung and lighter in weight. If this presents no drawback, then consider the Douglas fir, as it does extremely well indoors.

Other popular evergreens are the Norway pine and the spruce, but their needles are quite sharp, as are those of the red cedar and the arbor vitae.

Nurserymen will tell you that the tree will look its best for a long stay indoors if it is properly prepared. You may store the cut tree outdoors well before you are ready to decorate it, but it must be protected from hard winter winds and sun. The more rain or snow sprinkling it gets, the better. Bring it indoors in two stages, rather than risk shock by a sudden switch to a heated room. A short stopover in a basement or garage is recommended. Make certain that the base of the tree is cut on a longish diagonal or a V, so that as much surface as possible is exposed to the water or moist sand you set it in.

Many ecology-conscious Americans are turning to the purchase of living trees, rather than killing a tree to use and then dispose of a week later. The variety that does best for this purpose is the Norwegian spruce. It is placed, root ball and all, into a proper container, about which your indispensable nurseryman can advise you. It enjoys its days of glory as the setting for your decorations and gifts, and then lives on, replanted outdoors—a gift to the earth.

Proper scale is the next consideration when buying a tree. An 8-footer dwarfed by the skyscrapers of Rockefeller Plaza would look as ill-chosen as it would in a small, low-ceilinged living room. Naturally, you'll measure the tree you like, so that it won't require top-lopping once you bring it home. If you err by buying a tree too slender or too short for the spot you had in mind, it is a simple matter to find a location in the room that will keep it in eye-pleasing scale.

Now that the perfect tree is in the ideal spot, the real challenge presents itself—how to decorate. If the theme is traditional, then red and green is the predominant color scheme, and the ornaments are colorful balls, tinsel, strings of lights, and cotton or spray-on "snow," all symbols of the old-fashioned Christmas.

If you're ready to break away from the traditional, there is a world of ideas to explore. For the tree whose theme is simply color, key it to the predominant color scheme of your living room. If the scheme is blue, all the decorations, ornaments, trimmings, and gift wrappings can run the gamut from palest ice blue to deepest navy. Carry the blue all through the room— blue candles, blue flowers, blue wreaths, and evergreens either naturally bluish in cast, or artificial, or spray-painted. An occa-

The Christmas Tree, from HARPER'S WEEKLY, 1858

sional touch of silver or gold can break up this sea of blue if it seems overwhelming.

Golds and browns combined radiate warmth, and materials for decorating are plentiful in these colors: nuts, pine cones, wheat, dried plants such as dock and pepper weed, teasel heads, bleached barley, real or artificial chrysanthemums, and so on, right through dried autumn foliage.

You might use flowers for your theme, decorating the tree with artificial (fabric or paper) posies, bouquets, and single blossoms in a riot of color. It is possible to decorate the tree with real flowers, if you place the stems in slender glass containers that resemble laboratory test tubes, fasten them to the branches, and keep them supplied with water. The gift wrapping paper can be flower patterned, the wreaths can bloom with flowers, and bouquets of real or artificial flowers can dot the room.

You can design a tree and a room on a theme of birds— paper birds, plastic birds, feather birds, birds of whatever substance you can imagine and fashion them of, realistic birds, fanciful birds, birds seeming to nest among the greenery, creating a small bird sanctuary within the walls of your home.

The theme might be national, representing your family's place of origin. Reminiscent of a Scottish heritage, for example, would be plaid ribbons for plaid-patterned gift wrappings, thistle, heather, tiny bagpipes, toy Scottish terriers, Shetland ponies, a sporran, and for the mantelpiece stockings, Argyle socks!

You could salute the modern miracle of miniaturization: tiny transistor radios, playing cards no larger than match covers, miniature models of ships and cars, bite-size cameras and their tiny rolls of real film, unbelievably small books, whatever wonders you can turn up in Lilliputian dimensions.

Other themes: Geometric shapes; the sea (shells, driftwood, tiny model ships, coral, fishes, sponges); the sky (stars, planets, model spacecraft); music (notes, small instruments, 45-rpm records); fairy-tale characters cut from illustrated books and fastened to hangable backings.

The area under the tree should share in the decorative attention, and the theme of the tree be carried through in the pattern or color of the gift wrappings. A magnificent tree with an unfinished base is akin to a beautifully gowned and groomed woman who forgets her shoes. The tree is just not complete without those finishing touches at its base.

HOLIDAY ACTIVITIES

In most homes, the outdoor and indoor decorations begin to go up during the week preceding Christmas, climaxed by the trimming of the tree on Christmas Eve. The fundamental religious aspect of Christmas—celebration of the birth of the Savior—draws the whole family to special church activities. The youngsters, perhaps, participate in Nativity pageants or plays. Parents and children as well may take part in carol services at the church, or tour the neighborhood or community singing carols under the stars. And on Christmas Day, many families make a tradition of going together to church to mark the most joyous festival of Christianity. And there is plenty more to keep everyone busy on Christmas Day, exchanging and opening gifts, preparing the festive dinner, receiving guests, or visiting family or friends.

But Christmas is not only a day, it's a season, traditionally spanning twelve days and ending with Epiphany, or Twelfth Night, heralded on January 6 with "twelve drummers drumming."

The excitement of Christmas Day is often followed by a letdown on December 26. The working members of the family head back to their jobs, even though they can anticipate the festivities of New Year's Eve, only six days away, and perhaps a round of evening parties to give or go to in between. The children have their gifts and their freedom from school schedules, but their unbounded energy must be harnessed somehow for the remainder of their holiday. Much still remains to be planned and done to help keep adult spirits at a festive level and children's energy well channeled.

One of the pleasantest undertakings for the holidays is a progressive dinner. It may be planned for Christmas Day itself, and by its nature it allows large groups of people to share each other's Christmas at home and offer and receive each other's gifts.

A progressive dinner works like this. At least four, and preferably more, women decide on an all-out, spare-no-expense, spare-no-effort dinner. The courses may be chosen by lot, and whichever course each participant draws she is responsible for. On the other hand, the hostesses may decide among themselves who takes which course, especially if one is an expert at magnificent pastries, another a whiz with salads, and so on. Drinks and appetizers begin at one home, enjoyed at leisure by all the families involved. A little while before time for the next course, the hostess responsible for it leaves the group and prepares for her guests. By the time the group has polished off the last canapé and driven to the second-course home, an unflustered and thoroughly prepared hostess is ready and waiting. When her gifts have been exchanged and her family's decorating efforts admired, she serves the soup, the fish, or whatever her course may be. Thus the dinner progresses from house to house.

When dessert and coffee are finished, so is the dinner—unless later in the evening, when the children are asleep, it is given a final topping off with demitasse and nightcaps. If wine is to accompany only the main course, an equitable arrangement can be reached so that, say, the salad expert can contribute most

or all of the wine. Breads, relishes, and anything else wanted to round out the meal can be similarly arranged for.

The advantages of such an arrangement are self-evident. No one hostess has the responsibility for shopping, cooking, and serving an entire meal for a large number of guests. She isn't locked into the kitchen—and no matter how many hands are willing to help, a hostess is pretty much confined to the kitchen. When her turn at serving a course is over, she can relax and enjoy being a guest for the rest of the day.

Since she is responsible for only one course (the main meat or poultry course and accompanying side dishes may be shared by two women in the same kitchen), she has the time and can afford to undertake a complicated dish and prepare it with exquisite care and the finest ingredients. Another advantage to all is that, in the face of such an elaborate menu, all the guests have time between courses to do a little digesting and keep their appetites and enthusiasm sharp. A progressive dinner is somewhat like an old-fashioned barn raising, done in the true spirit of the season and of neighborliness.

A stationary version of this type of entertaining can be encouraged among the children with one home as the focal point, unless the weather and the proximity of the houses involved allows for traveling. Each child contributes a lunch or dinner dish he or she has prepared. The menu could include sandwiches, hot dogs, hamburgers, punch, cookies, and enough hot cocoa for all.

If you are lucky enough to have a working fireplace, a Yule log hunt is a marvelous outdoor game for everyone. For a traditional Yule log ceremony as practiced in New England and other colder regions, a suitably large and impressive log is chosen, decked out with ribbons and greens or mistletoe, and hidden in a woodsy area before Christmas Day. The Yule log hunters, and this can include even the smallest toddlers, gather at a central meeting place, sing carols, and then begin the search. At one time the successful hunting party hauled the log to its destination, with the smallest member of the party riding it in triumph. The modern substitute is the trunk of a large car or a station wagon. Then the log is lit, traditionally with a piece saved from last year's log, and heartily toasted by the assemblage. The Yule log symbolizes good fortune, as well as the

warmth, good food, hospitality, and peaceful hopes of the season.

Among activities in which the whole community can share and benefit is a group undertaking to decorate the town's (or neighborhood's) public buildings and churches. Other activities produce a gift to the town and the environment, and what better time than Christmas for such a gift! Several years ago, an entire town literally waded in and cleaned up their once pretty little river and its banks, which had become the town junk heap. The fire department lent wading boots, local merchants and the sanitation department provided trucks for hauling away the debris, and a Girl Scout troop contributed coffee, doughnuts, and sandwiches to the workers. In one Sunday afternoon, the river was bubbling along between litter-free banks, cleared of truckloads of mess that had made it an eyesore.

In most parts of the country December is too cold a month for garbage-fishing, even if the river or stream isn't frozen over, but it is all too easy today to find a once-beautiful park, field, or other public spot that would benefit from a clean-up detail. Representatives of such an undertaking can turn to city officials to coordinate use of municipal facilities, equipment, and personnel. The local newspaper, service organizations, Scout troops, and church groups can be enlisted to make such a gift to the community a shining reality.

Turning indoors, where typical December weather may force everyone to stay, many activities can fill the leisure hours. In the 19th century and even into the 20th, reading aloud was a gracious activity that has, sadly, fallen into disuse. What better time to revive this gentle and entertaining art than when all the family, including vacationing college students, is together. The trick is to use material that lends itself to the voice and to choose a first reader who is extrovert enough to give a rousing, dramatic beginning.

Many of the children's classics, read aloud to one or two little sleepyheads by Mom and Dad during the year, lend themselves perfectly to reading aloud to a roomful of adults. These are the stories written on two levels, the narrative line for children, the deeper humor or philosophy to be savored by the grown-ups. Among prime examples are *A Christmas Carol*, *Alice in Wonderland*, *Through the Looking Glass*, *Charlotte's*

Web, *Stuart Little,* *The Wind in the Willows,* and the *Pooh* stories.

The works of Jane Austen are even more delightful read aloud than to oneself, as are those of Louisa May Alcott, Edgar Allan Poe, and Mark Twain, the Tarzan series, collections of ghost stories, and the ingenuous adventures of Frank Merriwell, the Rover Boys, and Dink Stover. Reading poetry aloud is a bit trickier, but taking turns reading the collected verse of Rudyard Kipling, James Thurber, or Ogden Nash requires no classical training.

Reading plays aloud, with as many participants as there are roles, is sure-fire entertainment. You need not confine the subject matter to traditional Christmas plays and pageants. You can aspire as high as Shakespeare or as low as an early melodrama, played as seriously or as campily as you please. You can even try recent Broadway productions. Most plays are available in book form (many in the indispensable paperbacks), and no royalty payment is required for home readings. The drama sections of the bookstores and libraries should yield anthologies of "Best American Plays" and single editions of recent hits, as well as classics. Chekhov, Strindberg, Albee, and Williams might prove too heavy for holiday consumption, but the choice, of course, is yours.

On Twelfth Night, January 6, the Christmas season officially ends. You may choose to end your Christmas season a
bit earlier, but rather than just letting it fade away and discarding the stripped tree, you might try one of several traditional activities that end the season with ceremony and style.
A particularly attractive tradition that originated in Scandinavia is called "Plundering the Tree," which is far less sinister
than it sounds. A group of families arrange the number of
households to be involved, unless the community is small
enough to include all. Each family removes the tree decorations and ceremoniously puts them on display, along with refreshments. Enter the plunderers, each family of which selects
one ornament to keep for use on its own tree next year. All
then move on to "plunder" the decorations of the next home.
When all the participants have plundered all the homes, the
trees are gathered and burned—providing, of course, that a
safe spot is available and the fire department gives its blessing.
A final carol is sung, and if the ceremony is held on New Year's
Eve or New Year's Day, a lusty chorus of "Auld Lang Syne"
winds up the festivities.

And now it's January 2 again. Isn't it time you began thinking about next Christmas?

CAROLS

THE SELECTION OF carols given here attempts to indicate the broad range of songs that fall into the category. They come from many lands—including our own. They range in mood from reverence to jollity. Some are chosen especially with children in mind; others lend themselves well to group performance, with soloists and chorus, as, for instance, "Kings of Orient" and "The Twelve Days of Christmas."

All the carols have been specially arranged for this book with a view toward simplicity. The very feature of carol singing that endears it to families at Christmas is its ability to bring people together in a mutual expression of the joyousness of the season and the spirit of "peace on earth, goodwill toward men" that is its special meaning in our century of turmoil and strife.

Anyone with a basic ability to play the piano and read simple music at sight will have no difficulty with the arrangements. The hope of the editors is that families will be motivated to group themselves around the piano and enjoy a spontaneous celebration of Christmas according to their own interpretation of its meaning.

NOTES ON THE CAROLS

"Angels We Have Heard on High" is a French carol believed to date from the eighteenth century. The melody is often used for the hymn "Angels from the Realms of Glory" by

James Montgomery (1771–1854), author of a number of popular Protestant hymns.

"Away in a Manger" is anonymous in both music and verse. Although both have been widely credited to the Protestant reformer Martin Luther, modern researchers find no evidence to support the attribution. The verse is frequently sung to the familiar tune "Flow Gently, Sweet Afton."

"Deck the Hall" is a traditional Welsh tune for a secular carol entitled *"Nos Galan,"* marking the New Year.

"God Rest You Merry, Gentlemen" is traditional English in both words and music. A version of the carol appeared in a collection of ballads published about 1770. The phrase "God rest you merry" means "God keep you merry"; the occasional placement of a comma after ". . . rest you" is an error that alters the sense of the line. The carol has another, entirely different, tune, but the one given here is the more widely known.

The tune of "Good King Wenceslas" was originally a spring carol, the verse beginning "Spring has now unwrapped the flowers." Its transformation was accomplished by the Reverend John Mason Neale (1818–1866), English writer and translator of hymns. He had come into possession of a rare volume of songs entitled *Piae Cantiones,* compiled in 1582 by Theodoricus Petrus of Nyland, Finland. Neale wrote new verses for a number of the lovely tunes in the *Piae Cantiones,* among them "Good King Wenceslas." Critics have been less than kind regarding the merits of his verses. Be that as it may, however, he was certainly guilty of historical error in the person of his hero; the story of the error in identity is told in the chapter CHRISTMAS CHEER. Literary and historical quibbles aside, "Good King Wenceslas" has achieved a secure place in the roster of favorite Christmas carols.

"Go Tell It on the Mountain" is a modern American addition to Christmas carol lore. It is a Negro spiritual born in the Southern states, different in mood and style from the "typical" carol, but deeply reverent and moving nonetheless.

"Hark! The Herald Angels Sing" is perhaps the most famous of the thousands of hymns written by Charles Wesley (1707–1788), brother of John Wesley and with him a founder of Methodism. The melody to which it is sung today was written by the German composer Felix Mendelssohn (1809–1847),

but not as a setting for Wesley's hymn; it was originally a movement of a secular choral work. The joining of verse and music did not occur until years after both men were dead.

"I Saw Three Ships" is a traditional carol tune that has been found in many parts of England.

"It Came Upon a Midnight Clear" is American in both music and verse. The words were written by Edmund Hamilton Sears (1810–1876), a Unitarian clergyman. The music was composed as a Christmas carol by Richard Storrs Willis (1819–1900), but it was not until some time later that the felicitous combination was made.

"Jingle Bells" is not a Christmas carol in any sense of the term. Nevertheless, its simplicity, gaiety, and celebration of the pleasures of the snowy world that is traditionally associated with the Nativity have made it an inevitable part of the roster of Christmas songs. Both words and music are the work of the American Unitarian clergyman and poet John Pierpont (1785–1866).

The verse of "Joy to the World" was written by Isaac Watts (1674–1748), an English clergyman who published some 750 hymns and paraphrases of the Psalms. Our carol falls into the latter category, having appeared in Watts's *The Psalms of David Imitated in the Language of the New Testament*. The composer of the melody is unknown, although George Frederick Handel is often incorrectly credited with it.

"Kings of Orient" is one of the more widely accepted modern carols. It was written and composed about 1857 by Dr. J. H. Hopkins (1820–1891), rector of Christ's Church, Williamsport, Pa. The carol is especially effective when performed in dramatic fashion, with soloists representing the three kings and the entire chorus joining in the refrain.

"O Come, All Ye Faithful," a Roman Catholic hymn, is highly uncertain in attribution. In its Latin version, *"Adeste, Fideles,"* it was probably first sung in England at the Portuguese Embassy in London. The first known manuscript of the hymn was signed by John Francis Wade (1711–1786), a music copyist, and many scholars credit the music to him. The current, almost universal, English version has evolved over the years from many less successful translations.

"O Holy Night" is another carol written by a composer

of classical stature—the Frenchman Adolphe Charles Adam (1803–1856)—although he is best remembered for his ballet music, notably *Giselle*. The verse, by Cappeau de Roquemaure, was translated by John Sullivan Dwight (1813–1893), American music critic and Unitarian minister who was also instrumental in founding the Boston Philharmonic Society.

"O Little Town of Bethlehem" is one of the best loved of all Christmas hymns. The verse is by the American Episcopal bishop Phillips Brooks (1835–1893), who wrote it while he was a pastor in Philadelphia, Pa., in the 1860's; and the music was composed for it by the church organist, Lewis H. Redner (1831–1908).

"O Tannenbaum" is a favorite German carol, the words of which are sung in the original language by many English-speaking people. The translation given here is by the editors, for those who find the German text difficult to encompass.

"Silent Night, Holy Night" is a lovely lyrical carol that has a charming true story attached to its creation. The tale of the emergency collaboration between an Austrian clergyman and the village schoolmaster and organist is told in full in the chapter CHRISTMAS CHEER.

"The First Nowell" is an English carol believed to date from the seventeenth century. Although widely sung at Christmas, its verses are actually more appropriate to the Epiphany season, or Twelfth Night.

"The Twelve Days of Christmas" is an old English cumulative song that celebrates the winter solstice and the New Year rather than the Nativity. Nevertheless, it has become exceedingly popular as a carol and lends itself to many forms of presentation.

"The Wassail Song" is a carol for the New Year. It and others like it were widely sung by the "waits," troups of men and boys who strolled among English villages during the holiday season, performing carols and expecting gifts of refreshments or money.

The melody of "What Child Is This?" is the centuries-old English folk tune "Greensleeves," which has been put to many and diverse lyrics from as far back as the sixteenth century. The current hymn verses are by William Chatterton Dix (1837–1898), a British hymn writer and businessman.

Angels We Have Heard on High

Swiftly, joyously

An-gels we have heard on high, Sweet-ly sing-ing o'er the plains,

And the— moun-tains— in re-ply, Ech-o - ing their— joy - ous strains.

2. Shepherds, why this jubilee?
   Why your joyous strains prolong?
   What the gladsome tidings be
   Which inspire your heav'nly song?
   Gloria in excelsis Deo,
   Gloria in excelsis Deo.

3. Come to Bethlehem and see
   Him whose birth the angels sing;
   Come, adore on bended knee,
   Christ the Lord, the newborn King.
   Gloria in excelsis Deo,
   Gloria in excelsis Deo.

Away in a Manger

Slowly, with gentle movement

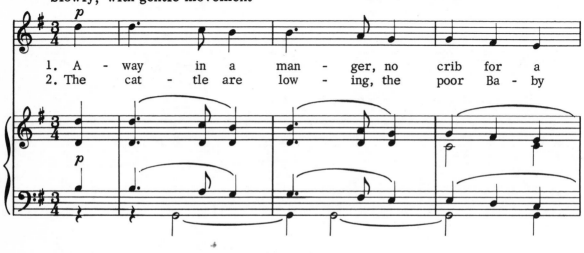

1. A - way   in a   man - ger, no   crib   for a
2. The   cat - tle are   low - ing, the   poor Ba - by

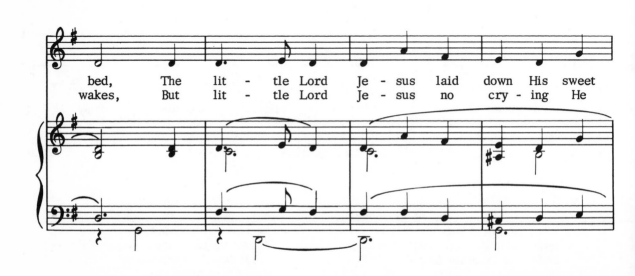

bed,   The   lit - tle Lord   Je - sus   laid   down His   sweet
wakes,   But   lit - tle Lord   Je - sus   no   cry - ing   He

head; The stars in the sky   looked down where He
makes; I love Thee, Lord Je - sus! look down from the

poco rit.

lay, The lit - tle Lord Je - sus, a - sleep on the hay.
sky, And stay by my cra - dle till morn-ing is nigh.

3. Be near me, Lord Jesus, I ask Thee to stay
    Close by me forever, and love me, I pray;
    Bless all the dear children in Thy tender care,
    And take us to heaven, to live with Thee, there.

Deck the Hall

Gaily

1. Deck the hall with boughs of hol-ly,
2. See the blaz-ing Yule be-fore us,   Fa, la, la, la, la,   la, la, la, la.
3. Fast a-way the old year pass-es,

L.H.

'Tis the sea-son to be jol-ly,
Strike the harp and join the cho-rus,   Fa, la, la, la, la,   la, la, la, la.
Hail the new, ye lads and lass-es,

Don we now our gay ap-par-el,
Fol-low me in mer-ry mea-sure, Fa, la, la, la, la, la, la, la, la.
Sing we joy-ous all to-geth-er,

Troll the an-cient Yule-tide car-ol,
While I tell of Yule-tide trea-sure, Fa, la, la, la, la, la, la, la, la.
Heed-less of the wind and weath-er,

The First Nowell

Moderately

1. The __ first __ Now - ell the __ an - gel did say, Was to
2. They __ look - èd __ up and __ saw __ a star, Shin-ing

cer-tain poor shep-herds in fields as they lay; In __ fields __ where __
in __ the East, __ be - yond __ them far; And __ to __ the __

they lay __ Keep-ing their sheep In a cold win-ter's night __ that
earth it __ gave __ great light, And __ so it con - tin - ued both

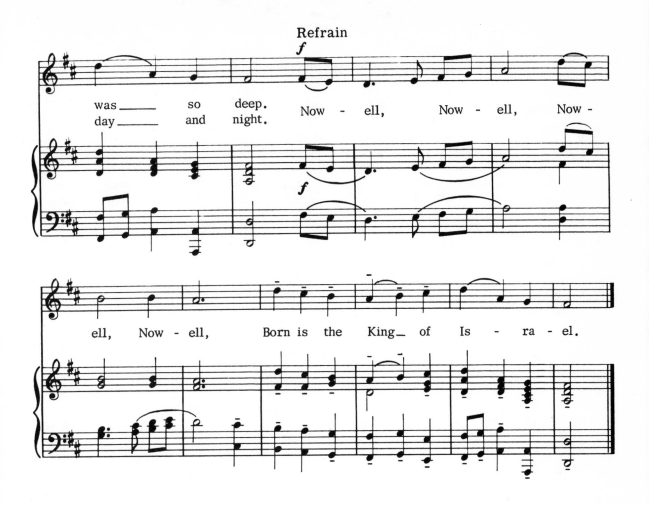

Refrain

was____ so deep. Now-ell, Now-ell, Now-ell, Now-ell, Born is the King_ of Is - ra - el.

3. And by the light of that same star,
   Three wise men came from country far;
   To seek for a king was their intent,
   And to follow the star wheresoever it went.

   Refrain

4. This star drew nigh to the northwest,
   O'er Bethlehem it took its rest,
   And there it did both stop and stay,
   Right over the place where Jesus lay.

   Refrain

5. Then entered in those wise men three,
   Fell reverently upon their knee,
   And offered there, in His Presence,
   Both gold, and myrrh, and frankincense.

   Refrain

6. Then let us all with one accord,
   Sing praises to our Heavenly Lord,
   That hath made heaven and earth of nought,
   And with His Blood mankind hath bought.

   Refrain

God Rest You Merry, Gentlemen

With spirit

1. God rest you merry, Gen-tle-men, Let noth-ing you dis-may, For
2. In Beth-le-hem, in Jew-ry, This bless-ed Babe was born, And

Je-sus Christ our Sav-iour Was born up-on this day, To
laid with-in a man-ger Up-on this bless-ed morn; The

save us all from Sa-tan's pow'r When we were gone a-stray.
which His moth-er Ma-ry, Did noth-ing take in scorn.

Refrain

O ___ ti - dings of com - fort and joy, com - fort and

joy, O ___ ti - dings of com - fort and joy.

3. From God our heav'nly Father,
   A blessèd angel came,
   And unto certain shepherds
   Brought tidings of the same;
   How that in Bethlehem was born
   The Son of God by name.

   Refrain

4. "Fear not," then said the angel,
   "Let nothing you affright,
   This day is born a Saviour
   Of virtue, power, and might;
   So frequently to vanquish all
   The friends of Satan quite."

   Refrain

5. The shepherds at those tidings
   Rejoicèd much in mind,
   And left their flocks a-feeding,
   In tempest, storm, and wind:
   And went to Bethlehem straightway,
   This blessed Babe to find.

   Refrain

6. But when to Bethlehem they came,
   Whereat this Infant lay,
   They found Him in a manger,
   Where oxen feed on hay;
   His mother Mary kneeling,
   Unto the Lord did pray.

   Refrain

7. Now to the Lord sing praises,
   All you within this place,
   And with true love and brotherhood
   Each other now embrace;
   This holy tide of Christmas
   All others doth deface.   Refrain

Good King Wenceslas

Quickly

1. Good king Wen-ces - las look'd out   On the Feast of Ste - phen,
2. "Hith- er, page, and stand by me,   If thou know'st it, tell - ing,

When the snow lay   round a - bout,   Deep and crisp and   e - ven:
Yon-der peas- ant,   who is he?   Where and what his   dwell - ing?"

Brightly shone the moon that night, Though the frost was cruel,
"Sire, he lives a good league hence, Underneath the mountain;

When a poor man came in sight, Gath-'ring winter fuel.
Right against the forest fence, By Saint Agnes' fountain."

3. "Bring me flesh, and bring me wine,
    Bring me pine logs hither,
Thou and I will see him dine,
    When we bear them thither."
Page and monarch, forth they went,
    Forth they went together;
Through the rude wind's wild lament,
    And the bitter weather.

4. "Sire, the night is darker now,
    And the wind blows stronger;
Fails my heart, I know not how,
    I can go no longer."
"Mark my footsteps, my good page,
    Tread thou in them boldly:
Thou shalt find the winter's rage
    Freeze thy blood less coldly."

5. In his master's steps he trod,
    Where the snow lay dinted;
Heat was in the very sod
    Which the saint had printed.
Therefore, Christian men, be sure,
    Wealth or rank possessing,
Ye who now will bless the poor,
    Shall yourselves find blessing.

Go Tell It on the Mountain

Lively

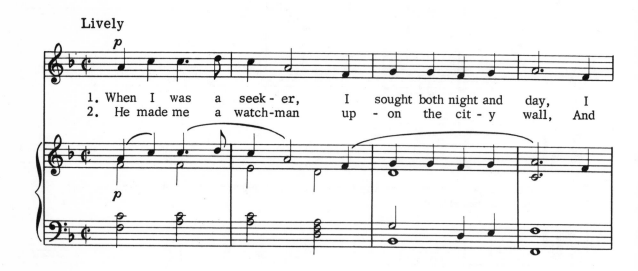

1. When I was a seek - er, I sought both night and day, I
2. He made me a watch-man up - on the cit - y wall, And

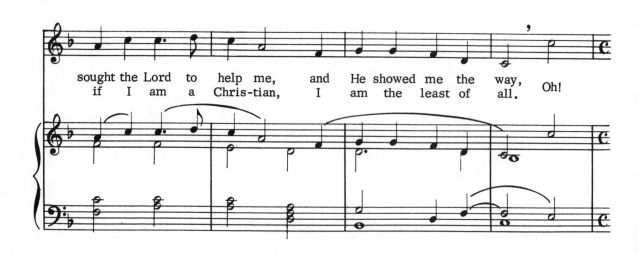

sought the Lord to help me, and He showed me the way, Oh!
if I am a Chris-tian, I am the least of all.

Hark! The Herald Angels Sing

In stately fashion

1. Hark! the her - ald an - gels sing,__ Glo - ry to the
2. Christ, by high - est heav'n a - dored,__ Christ, the ev - er-

new - born King; Peace on earth and mer - cy mild,__
last - ing Lord; Late in time be - hold Him come,__

God and sin - ners re - con - ciled! Joy - ful, all ye na - tions, rise,__
Off - spring of the Vir - gin's womb. Veil'd in flesh the God-head see,__

Join the tri - umph of the skies;_ With th'an - gel - ic
Hail th'In - car - nate De - i - ty,_ Pleased as Man with

host pro - claim, Christ is__ born in Beth - le - hem.
man to dwell, Je - sus__ our Em - man - u - el!

Refrain

Hark! the her - ald an - gels sing, Glo - ry_ to the new-born King.

Mild He lays His glory by,
Born that man no more may die;
Born to raise the sons of earth,
Born to give them second birth.
Ris'n with healing in His wings,
Light and life to all He brings,
Hail, the Son of Righteousness!
Hail, the heav'nborn Prince of Peace!

Refrain.

I Saw Three Ships

Briskly and merrily

1. I saw three ships come sail - ing in,
2. And what was in those ships all three? On

Christ - mas Day, on Christ - mas Day, And what was in those

sail - ing in, On Christ - mas Day in the morn - ing.
ships all three?

3. Our Saviour Christ and His lady,
4. Pray, whither sailed those ships all three?
5. O they sailed into Bethlehem,
6. And all the bells on earth shall ring,
7. And all the angels in heaven shall sing,
8. And all the souls on earth shall sing,
9. Then let us all rejoice amain,

It Came Upon a Midnight Clear

Moderately

1. It came up-on__ a mid-night clear, That glo - rious song__ of
2. Still through the clo - ven skies they come, With peace - ful wings__ un-

old, _____ From an - gels bend - ing near the earth, To
furl'd; _____ And still their heav'n - ly mu - sic floats O'er

touch their harps__ of gold: _____ "Peace on the earth,__ good-
all the wea - ry world; _____ A - bove its sad__ and

will to men, From heav'n's all gra - cious king"; _____ The

low - ly plains They bend_ on hov - 'ring wing._____ And

world in sol - emn still - ness lay To hear the an - gels sing._

ev - er o'er_ its Ba - bel sounds The bless- ed an - gels sing._

3. O ye, beneath life's crushing load,
    Whose forms are bending low,
Who toil along the climbing way
    With painful steps and slow,
Look now, for glad and golden hours
    Come swiftly on the wing:
O rest beside the weary road,
    And hear the angels sing.

4. For lo! the days are hastening on,
    By prophets seen of old,
When with the ever-circling years,
    Shall come the time foretold,
When the new heaven and earth shall own
    The Prince of Peace their King,
And the whole world send back the song
    Which now the angels sing.

Jingle Bells

Oh, what fun it is to ride In a one-horse o - pen sleigh!__

Jin - gle bells, jin - gle bells, Jin - gle all the way!

Oh, what fun it is to ride In a one-horse o - pen sleigh!

Joy to the World

Maestoso

1. Joy to the world! the Lord is come; Let
2. Joy to the world! the Sav - iour reigns; Let

earth re - ceive her King; Let ev - 'ry ___
men their songs em - ploy; While fields ___ and ___

3. He rules the world with truth and grace,
   And makes the nations prove
   The glories of His righteousness
   And wonders of His love,
   And wonders of His love,
   And wonders, and wonders of His love.

Kings of Orient

Slowly

All: 1. We three kings of O - ri-ent are; Bear - ing gifts we

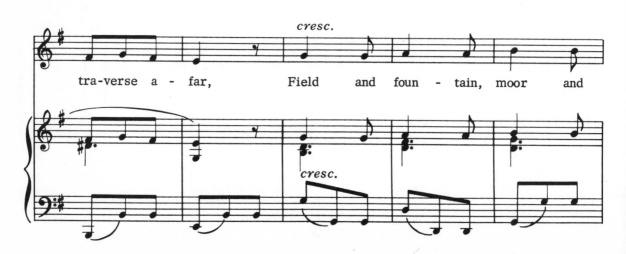

tra-verse a - far, Field and foun - tain, moor and

still pro - ceed - ing, Guide us to thy per - fect light.

Melchior

> Born a King on Bethlehem plain,
> Gold I bring, to crown Him again
> King forever, ceasing never,
> Over us all to reign.
>
> Refrain

Caspar

> Frankincense to offer have I,
> Incense owns a Deity nigh,
> Prayer and praising all men raising,
> Worship Him, God most high.
>
> Refrain

Balthazar

> Myrrh is mine; its bitter perfume
> Breathes a life of gathering gloom,
> Sorrowing, sighing, bleeding, dying,
> Sealed in a stone-cold tomb.
>
> Refrain

All

> Glorious now behold Him arise,
> King and God and Sacrifice,
> Alleluia, alleluia,
> Earth to the heav'ns replies.
>
> Refrain

O Come, All Ye Faithful

(Adeste, Fideles)

With spirit, but not too fast

1. O come, all ye faith-ful, joy-ful and tri - um - phant, O
1. Ad - es - te, fi - del - es, lae - ti tri - um - phan - tes, Ve -

come ye, O come ye to Beth - le - hem:
ni - te, Ve - ni - te in Beth - le - hem:

Come and be - hold Him, born the King of an - gels: O
Na - tum vi - de - te, Re - gem an - ge - lo - rum: Ve -

2. Sing, choirs of angels, sing in exultation,
   Sing, all ye citizens of heav'n above!
   Glory to God, all glory in the highest;
   O come, let us adore Him, O come, let us adore Him,
   O come, let us adore Him, Christ, the Lord.

3. Yea, Lord, we greet Thee, born this happy morning;
   Jesus, to Thee be glory giv'n;
   Word of the Father, now in flesh appearing;
   O come, let us adore Him, O come, let us adore Him,
   O come, let us adore Him, Christ, the Lord.

2. *Cantet nunc Io chorus angelorum,*
   Cantet nunc aula caelestium;
   Gloria, gloria in excelsis Deo;
   Venite adoremus, venite adoremus,
   Venite adoremus Dominum.

3. *Ergo qui natus die hodierna,*
   Jesu, tibi sit gloria;
   Patris aeterni verbum caro factum;
   Venite adoremus, venite adoremus,
   Venite adoremus Dominum.

O Holy Night

1. O ho - ly night!___ the stars are bright - ly shin - ing, It is the night of the dear Sav-iour's birth! Long lay the

2. Led by the light___ of faith se - rene - ly beam - ing, With glow - ing hearts' by His cra - dle we stand. So, led by

world,___ in sin and er - ror pin - ing, 'Till He ap-
light of a star___ sweet - ly gleam - ing, Here came the

peared, and the soul felt its worth. A
wise men ___ from the Or - ient land. The

thrill of hope the wea-ry world re-joic - es, For yon - der breaks a
King of kings lay thus in low-ly man-ger, In all our tri - als

mf

new and glor-ious morn! Fall on your knees! O
born to be our friend; He knows our need, to our

hear_____ the an-gel voi - ces! O night_____ di-
weak - ness no stran - ger; Be-hold_____ your

vine! _____ O night_____ when Christ was born! _____ O
King! _____ Be-fore _____ the Low-ly bend! _____ Be-

175

O Little Town of Bethlehem

Not too fast

1. O lit-tle town of Beth-le-hem, How still we__ see thee lie, A-
2. For Christ is born of Ma - ry And gath-ered__ all a-bove, While

bove thy deep and dream-less sleep The si - lent__ stars go by; Yet
mor-tals sleep, the an - gels keep Their watch of__ won-d'ring love. O

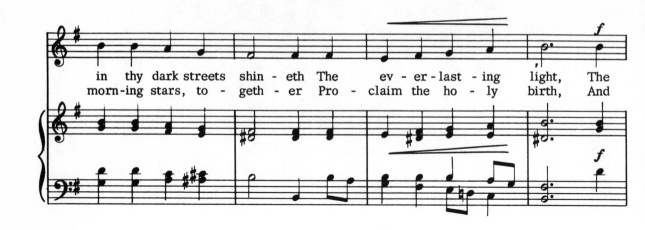

in thy dark streets shin - eth The ev - er - last - ing light, The
morn-ing stars, to - geth - er Pro - claim the ho - ly birth, And

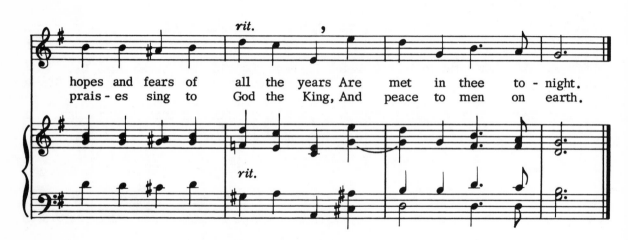

hopes and fears of all the years Are met in thee to - night.
prais - es sing to God the King, And peace to men on earth.

3. How silently, how silently
   The wond'rous gift is given!
   So God imparts to human hearts
   The blessings of His heaven.
   No ear may hear His coming,
   But in this world of sin,
   Where meek souls will receive Him still,
   The dear Christ enters in.

4. O holy Child of Bethlehem,
   Descend to us, we pray;
   Cast out our sin, and enter in,
   Be born in us today.
   We hear the Christmas angels,
   The great glad tidings tell;
   O come to us, abide with us,
   Our Lord Emmanuel.

O Tannenbaum

Sturdily

1. O Christ-mas tree, O Christ-mas tree, how faith-ful is thy fo-liage;
1. O *Tan - nen-baum,* O *Tan - nen-baum Wie treu sind dei - ne Blät-ter!*

You keep your green and love - ly glow in sum-mer and in win-ter snow.
Du grünst nicht nur zur Som-mers-zeit, Nein, auch im Win-ter, wenn es schneit.

O   Christ-mas tree, O   Christ-mas tree, how faith-ful is thy   fo - liage.
O   Tan - nen-baum, O   Tan - nen-baum,Wie treu sind dei - ne   Blät - ter!

2. O Christmas tree, O Christmas tree,
   You give us so much pleasure.
   At Christmas time we gaze on you
   And feel great joy that thou art true.
   O Christmas tree, O Christmas tree,
   You give us so much pleasure.

2. *O Tannenbaum, O Tannenbaum,*
   Du kannst mir sehr gefallen.
   Wie oft hat nicht zur Weihnachtszeit
   Ein Baum von dir mich hoch erfreut!
   O Tannenbaum, O Tannenbaum,
   Du Kannst mir sehr gefallen.

Silent Night, Holy Night

Slowly, with expression

1. Si - lent night, Ho - ly night! All is calm, all is bright,

'Round yon Vir-gin Moth-er and Child, Ho-ly In-fant so ten-der and mild,

Sleep in heav-en-ly peace,___ Sleep_ in heav-en-ly peace!_

2. Silent night, holy night!
Shepherds quake at the sight,
Glories stream from heaven afar,
Heav'nly hosts sing Alleluia;
Christ, the Saviour, is born,
Christ, the Saviour, is born.

3. Silent night, holy night!
Son of God, love's pure light,
Radiant beams from Thy holy face,
With the dawn of redeeming grace,
Jesus, Lord, at Thy birth,
Jesus, Lord, at Thy birth.

The Twelve Days of Christmas

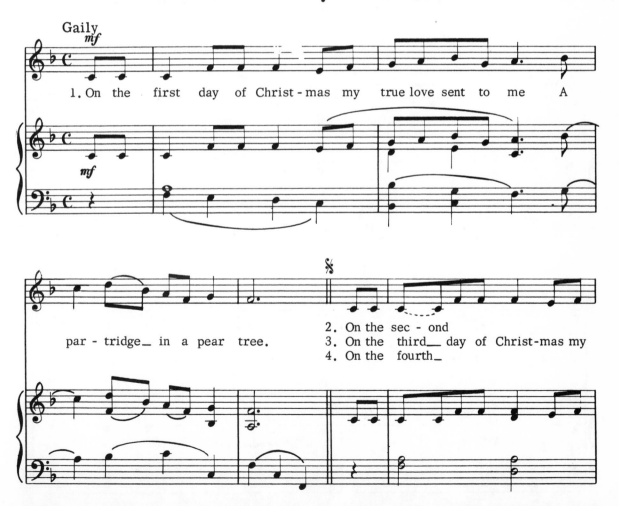

1. On the first day of Christ-mas my true love sent to me A par-tridge in a pear tree.

2. On the sec-ond
3. On the third day of Christ-mas my
4. On the fourth

Two tur - tle doves .... and a par-tridge_ in a pear

true love sent to me   Three French_hens, (Two, etc.)

Four call - ing birds, (Three, etc.)

repeat as necessary

D. S. 𝄋

tree. .... On the fifth day of Christ-mas my true love sent to me

D. S. 𝄋

f $\oplus$ *mf*

Five gold___ rings!   5-12. Four_ call-ing birds, three French hens,

f

L. H.
mf

Fine

two__ tur-tle doves, And a par - tridge__ in a pear tree.

Fine

6. On the sixth __
7. On the sev - enth
8. On the eighth__
9. On the ninth__ day of Christ- mas my true love sent to me
10. On the tenth __
11. On the elev - enth
12. On the twelfth__

(Last time) to ⊕

Six__ geese a - lay - ing, Five gold__ rings!
Sev - en swans a - swim - ming (six, etc.)
Eight__ maids a - milk - ing (seven, etc.)
Nine__ la - dies danc - ing (eight, etc.)
Ten__ lords a - leap - ing (nine, etc.)
Elev-en pi - pers pi - ping (ten, etc.)
Twelve__ drum- mers drum- ming (eleven, etc.)

to ⊕

repeat as necessary

Wassail Song

Gaily

1. Here we come a-was-sail-ing A-mong the leaves so
2. We are not dai-ly beg-gars That beg from door to

green,⸺ Here we come a wand'-ring so fair to be
door, But we are neigh-bors' chil-dren Whom you have seen be-

Refrain
(♩. = ♩) **f**

seen: Love and joy come to you, And to you your was-sail
fore:

too, And God bless you, and send you A hap - py New

Year, And God send you a hap - py New Year.

3. Our wassail cup is made
   Of the rosemary tree,
   And so is your beer
   Of the best barley.

   Refrain

4. Bring us out a table,
   And spread it with a cloth;
   Bring us out a mouldy cheese,
   And some of your Christmas loaf.

   Refrain

5. God bless the master of this house,
   Likewise the mistress too;
   And all the little children
   That round the table go.

   Refrain

What Child Is This?

Not too fast

1. What Child is this__ Who, laid to rest,__ On Ma - ry's lap__ is
2. Why lies He in__ such mean es - tate,__ Where ox and ass__ are

sleep - ing? Whom an - gels greet__ with an - thems sweet,__ While
feed - ing? Good Chris - tians, fear:__ for sin - ners here__ The

shep - herds watch__ are keep - ing? This, this__ is Christ the King,__ Whom
si - lent Word__ is plead - ing. Nails, spear__ shall pierce Him through, The

shep-herds guard_ and an - gels sing: Haste, haste_ to
Cross be borne_ for me, for you: Hail, hail,_ the

bring Him laud,_ The Babe,_ the Son_ of Ma — ry!
Word made flesh,_ The Babe,_ the Son_ of Ma — ry!

3. So bring Him incense, gold, and myrrh,
   Come, peasant, king, to own Him;
   The King of kings salvation brings:
   Let loving hearts enthrone Him.
   Raise, raise the song on high,
   The Virgin sings her lullaby:
   Joy, joy, for Christ is born,
   The Babe, the Son of Mary!

A CHRISTMAS CAROL

Charles Dickens

As condensed by Charles Dickens
for his own readings

MARLEY'S GHOST

MARLEY WAS DEAD, to begin with. There is no doubt whatever about that. The register of his burial was signed by the clergyman, the clerk, the undertaker, and the chief mourner. Scrooge signed it. And Scrooge's name was good upon 'Change for anything he chose to put his hand to.

Old Marley was as dead as a door-nail.

Scrooge knew he was dead? Of course he did. How could it be otherwise? Scrooge and he were partners for I don't know how many years. Scrooge was his sole executor, his sole administrator, his sole assign, his sole residuary legatee, his sole friend, his sole mourner.

Scrooge never painted out old Marley's name, however. There it yet stood, years afterwards, above the warehouse door, —Scrooge and Marley. The firm was known as Scrooge and Marley. Sometimes people new to the business called Scrooge Scrooge, and sometimes Marley. He answered to both names. It was all the same to him.

Oh! But he was a tight-fisted hand at the grindstone, was Scrooge! a squeezing, wrenching, grasping, scraping, clutching, covetous old sinner! External heat and cold had little influence on him. No warmth could warm, no cold could chill him. No wind that blew was bitterer than he, no falling snow was more intent upon its purpose, no pelting rain less open to entreaty. Foul weather didn't know where to have him. The heaviest rain and snow and hail and sleet could boast of the advantage over him in only one respect,—they often "came down" handsomely, and Scrooge never did.

Nobody ever stopped him in the street to say, with glad-some looks, "My dear Scrooge, how are you? When will you come to see me?" No beggars implored him to bestow a trifle, no children asked him what it was o'clock, no man or woman ever once in all his life inquired the way to such and such a place, of Scrooge. Even the blindmen's dogs appeared to know him; and when they saw him coming on, would tug their owners into doorways and up courts; and then would wag their tails as though they said, "No eye at all is better than an evil eye, dark master!"

But what did Scrooge care! It was the very thing he liked. To edge his way along the crowded paths of life, warning all human sympathy to keep its distance, was what the knowing ones call "nuts" to Scrooge.

Once upon a time—of all the good days in the year, upon a Christmas eve—old Scrooge sat busy in his counting-house. It was cold, bleak, biting, foggy weather; and the city clocks had only just gone three, but it was quite dark already.

The door of Scrooge's counting-house was open, that he might keep his eye upon his clerk, who, in a dismal little cell beyond, a sort of tank, was copying letters. Scrooge had a very small fire, but the clerk's fire was so very much smaller that it looked like one coal. But he couldn't replenish it, for Scrooge kept the coal-box in his own room; and so surely as the clerk came in with the shovel, the master predicted that it would be necessary for them to part. Wherefore the clerk put on his white comforter, and tried to warm himself at the candle; in which effort, not being a man of a strong imagination, he failed.

"A merry Christmas, uncle! God save you!" cried a cheerful voice. It was the voice of Scrooge's nephew, who came upon him so quickly that this was the first intimation Scrooge had of his approach.

"Bah!" said Scrooge; "humbug!"

"Christmas a humbug, uncle! You don't mean that, I am sure?"

"I do. Out upon merry Christmas! What's Christmas time to you but a time for paying bills without money; a time for finding yourself a year older, and not an hour richer; a time for balancing your books and having every item in 'em through

a round dozen of months presented dead against you? If I had my will, every idiot who goes about with 'Merry Christmas' on his lips should be boiled with his own pudding, and buried with a stake of holly through his heart. He should!"

"Uncle!"

"Nephew, keep Christmas in your own way, and let me keep it in mine."

"Keep it! But you don't keep it."

"Let me leave it alone, then. Much good may it do you! Much good it has ever done you!"

"There are many things from which I might have derived good, by which I have not profited, I dare say, Christmas among the rest. But I am sure I have always thought of Christmas time, when it has come round,—apart from the veneration due to its sacred origin, if anything belonging to it *can* be apart from that,—as a good time; a kind, forgiving, charitable, pleasant time; the only time I know of, in the long calendar of the year, when men and women seem by one consent to open their shut-up hearts freely, and to think of people below them as if they really were fellow-travellers to the grave, and not another race of creatures bound on other journeys. And therefore, uncle, though it has never put a scrap of gold or silver in my pocket, I believe that it *has* done me good, and *will* do me good; and I say, God bless it!"

The clerk in the tank involuntarily applauded.

"Let me hear another sound from *you*," said Scrooge, "and you'll keep your Christmas by losing your situation! You're quite a powerful speaker, sir," he added, turning to his nephew. "I wonder you don't go into Parliament."

"Don't be angry, uncle. Come! Dine with us to-morrow."

Scrooge said that he would see him—yes, indeed he did. He went the whole length of the expression, and said that he would see him in that extremity first.

"But why?" cried Scrooge's nephew. "Why?'"

"Why did you get married?"

"Because I fell in love."

"Because you fell in love!" growled Scrooge, as if that were the only one thing in the world more ridiculous than a merry Christmas. "Good afternoon!"

"Nay, uncle, but you never came to see me before that

Merry Christmas, lithograph by Thomas Nast, 1879

The Christmas Dream, lithograph by Jules Taverner, 1871

happened. Why give it as a reason for not coming now?"

"Good afternoon."

"I want nothing from you; I ask nothing of you; why cannot we be friends?"

"Good afternoon."

"I am sorry, with all my heart, to find you so resolute. We have never had any quarrel, to which I have been a party. But I have made the trial in homage to Christmas, and I'll keep my Christmas humor to the last. So A Merry Christmas, uncle!"

"Good afternoon!"

"And A Happy New Year!"

"Good afternoon!"

His nephew left the room without an angry word, notwithstanding. The clerk, in letting Scrooge's nephew out, had let two other people in. They were portly gentlemen, pleasant to behold, and now stood, with their hats off, in Scrooge's office. They had books and papers in their hands, and bowed to him.

"Scrooge and Marley's, I believe," said one of the gentlemen, referring to his list. "Have I the pleasure of addressing Mr. Scrooge, or Mr. Marley?"

"Mr. Marley has been dead these seven years. He died seven years ago, this very night."

"At this festive season of the year, Mr. Scrooge," said the gentleman, taking up a pen, "it is more than usually desirable that we should make some slight provisions for the poor and destitute, who suffer greatly at the present time. Many thousands are in want of common necessaries; hundreds of thousands are in want of common comforts, sir."

"Are there no prisons?"

"Plenty of prisons. But under the impression that they scarcely furnish Christmas cheer of mind or body to the unoffending multitude, a few of us are endeavoring to raise a fund to buy the poor some meat and drink, and means of warmth. We choose this time, because it is a time, of all others, when Want is keenly felt, and Abundance rejoices. What shall I put you down for?"

"Nothing!"

"You wish to be anonymous?"

"I wish to be left alone. Since you ask me what I wish, gentlemen, that is my answer. I don't make merry myself at

Christmas, and I can't afford to make idle people merry. I help to support the prisons and the workhouses,—they cost enough,—and those who are badly off must go there."

"Many can't go there; and many would rather die."

"If they would rather die, they had better do it, and decrease the surplus population."

At length the hour of shutting up the counting-house arrived. With an ill-will Scrooge, dismounting from his stool, tacitly admitted the fact to the expectant clerk in the tank, who instantly snuffed his candle out, and put on his hat.

"You'll want all day to-morrow, I suppose?"

"If quite convenient, sir."

"It's not convenient, and it's not fair. If I was to stop half a crown for it, you'd think yourself mightily ill-used, I'll be bound?"

"Yes, sir."

"And yet you don't think *me* ill-used, when I pay a day's wages for no work."

"It's only once a year, sir."

"A poor excuse for picking a man's pocket every twenty-fifth of December! But I suppose you must have the whole day. Be here all the earlier *next* morning."

The clerk promised that he would; and Scrooge walked out with a growl. The office was closed in a twinkling, and the clerk, with the long ends of his white comforter dangling below his waist (for he boasted no great-coat), went down a slide, at the end of a lane of boys, twenty times, in honor of its being Christmas eve, and then ran home as hard as he could pelt, to play at blindman's-buff.

Scrooge took his melancholy dinner in his usual melancholy tavern; and having read all the newspapers, and beguiled the rest of the evening with his banker's book, went home to bed. He lived in chambers which had once belonged to his deceased partner. They were a gloomy suite of rooms, in a lowering pile of building up a yard. The building was old enough now, and dreary enough; for nobody lived in it but Scrooge, the other rooms being all let out as offices.

Now it is a fact, that there was nothing at all particular about the knocker on the door of this house, except that it was very large; also, that Scrooge had seen it, night and morning, during his whole residence in that place; also, that Scrooge had as little of what is called fancy about him as any man in the city of London. And yet Scrooge, having his key in the lock of the door, saw in the knocker, without its undergoing any intermediate process of change, not a knocker, but Marley's face.

Marley's face had a dismal light about it, like a bad lobster in a dark cellar. It was not angry or ferocious, but it looked at Scrooge as Marley used to look,—with ghostly spectacles turned up upon its ghostly forehead.

As Scrooge looked fixedly at this phenomenon, it was a knocker again. He said, "Pooh, pooh!" and closed the door with a bang.

The sound resounded through the house like thunder. Every room above, and every cask in the wine-merchant's cellars below, appeared to have a separate peal of echoes of its own. Scrooge was not a man to be frightened by echoes. He fastened the door, and walked across the hall, and up the stairs. Slowly too, trimming his candle as he went.

Up Scrooge went, not caring a button for its being very dark. Darkness is cheap, and Scrooge liked it. But before he shut his heavy door, he walked through his rooms to see that all was right. He had just enough recollection of the face to desire to do that.

Sitting-room, bedroom, lumber-room, all as they should be. Nobody under the table, nobody under the sofa; a small fire in the grate; spoon and basin ready; and the little saucepan of gruel (Scrooge had a cold in his head) upon the hob. Nobody under the bed; nobody in the closet; nobody in his dressing-gown, which was hanging up in a suspicious attitude against the wall. Lumber-room as usual. Old fire-guard, old shoes, two fish-baskets, washing-stand on three legs, and a poker.

Quite satisfied, he closed his door, and locked himself in; double-locked himself in, which was not his custom. Thus secured against surprise, he took off his cravat, put on his dressing-gown and slippers and his nightcap, and sat down before the very low fire to take his gruel.

As he threw his head back in the chair, his glance happened to rest upon a bell, a disused bell, that hung in the room, and communicated, for some purpose now forgotten, with a chamber in the highest story of the building. It was with great astonishment, and with a strange, inexplicable dread, that, as he looked, he saw this bell begin to swing. Soon it rang out loudly, and so did every bell in the house.

This was succeeded by a clanking noise, deep down below, as if some person were dragging a heavy chain over the casks in the wine-merchant's cellar.

Then he heard the noise much louder, on the floors below; then coming up the stairs; then coming straight towards his door.

It came on through the heavy door, and a spectre passed into the room before his eyes. And upon its coming in, the dying flame leaped up, as though it cried, "I know him! Marley's ghost!"

The same face, the very same. Marley in his pigtail, usual waistcoat, tights, and boots. His body was transparent; so that Scrooge, observing him, and looking through his waistcoat, could see the two buttons on his coat behind.

Scrooge had often heard it said that Marley had no bowels, but he had never believed it until now.

No, nor did he believe it even now. Though he looked the phantom through and through, and saw it standing before him, —though he felt the chilling influence of its death-cold eyes, and noticed the very texture of the folded kerchief bound about its head and chin,—he was still incredulous.

"How now!" said Scrooge, caustic and cold as ever. "What do you want with me?"

"Much!"—Marley's voice, no doubt about it.

"Who are you?"

"Ask me who I *was*."

"Who *were* you then?"

"In life I was your partner, Jacob Marley."

"Can you—can you sit down?"

"I can."

"Do it, then."

Scrooge asked the question, because he didn't know whether a ghost so transparent might find himself in a condition to take a chair; and felt that, in the event of its being impossible, it might involve the necessity of an embarrassing explanation. But the ghost sat down on the opposite side of

the fireplace, as if he were quite used to it.

"You don't believe in me."

"I don't."

"What evidence would you have of my reality beyond that of your senses?"

"I don't know."

"Why do you doubt your senses?"

"Because a little thing affects them. A slight disorder of the stomach makes them cheats. You may be an undigested bit of beef, a blot of mustard, a crumb of cheese, a fragment of an underdone potato. There's more of gravy than of grave about you, whatever you are!"

Scrooge was not much in the habit of cracking jokes, nor did he feel in his heart by any means waggish then. The truth is, that he tried to be smart, as a means of distracting his own attention, and keeping down his horror.

But how much greater was his horror when, the phantom taking off the bandage round its head, as if it were too warm to wear in-doors, its lower jaw dropped down upon its breast!

"Mercy! Dreadful apparition, why do you trouble me? Why do spirits walk the earth, and why do they come to me?"

"It is required of every man, that the spirit within him should walk abroad among his fellowmen, and travel far and wide; and if that spirit goes not forth in life, it is condemned to do so after death. I cannot tell you all I would. A very little more is permitted to me. I cannot rest, I cannot stay, I cannot linger anywhere. My spirit never walked beyond our counting-house—mark me!—in life my spirit never roved beyond the narrow limits of our money-changing hole; and weary journeys lie before me!"

"Seven years dead. And travelling all the time? You travel fast?"

"On the wings of the wind."

"You might have got over a great quantity of ground in seven years."

"O blind man, blind man! not to know that ages of incessant labor by immortal creatures for this earth must pass into eternity before the good of which it is susceptible is all developed. Not to know that any Christian spirit working kindly in its little sphere, whatever it may be, will find its mortal life too short for its vast means of usefulness. Not to know that no space of regret can make amends for one life's opportunities misused! Yet I was like this man; I once was like this man!"

"But you were always a good man of business, Jacob," faltered Scrooge, who now began to apply this to himself.

"Business!" cried the Ghost, wringing its hands again. "Mankind was my business. The common welfare was my business; charity, mercy, forbearance, benevolence, were all my business. The dealings of my trade were but a drop of water in the comprehensive ocean of my business!"

Scrooge was very much dismayed to hear the spectre going on at this rate, and began to quake exceedingly.

"Hear me! My time is nearly gone."

"I will. But don't be hard upon me! Don't be flowery, Jacob! Pray!"

"I am here to-night to warn you that you have yet a chance and hope of escaping my fate. A chance and hope of my procuring, Ebenezer."

"You were always a good friend to me. Thank'ee!"

"You will be haunted by Three Spirits."

"Is that the chance and hope you mentioned, Jacob? I— I think I'd rather not."

"Without their visits, you cannot hope to shun the path I tread. Expect the first to-morrow night, when the bell tolls One. Expect the second on the next night at the same hour. The third, upon the next night, when the last stroke of Twelve has ceased to vibrate. Look to see me no more; and look that, for your own sake, you remember what has passed between us!"

It walked backward from him; and at every step it took, the window raised itself a little, so that, when the apparition reached it, it was wide open.

Scrooge closed the window, and examined the door by which the Ghost had entered. It was double-locked, as he had locked it with his own hands, and the bolts were undisturbed. Scrooge tried to say, "Humbug!" but stopped at the first syllable. And being, from the emotion he had undergone, or the fatigues of the day, or his glimpse of the invisible world, or the dull conversation of the Ghost, or the lateness of the hour, much in need of repose, he went straight to bed, without undressing, and fell asleep on the instant.

THE FIRST OF THE THREE SPIRITS

When Scrooge awoke, it was so dark, that, looking out of bed, he could scarcely distinguish the transparent window from the opaque walls of his chamber, until suddenly the church clock tolled a deep, dull, hollow, melancholy ONE.

Light flashed up in the room upon the instant, and the curtains of his bed were drawn aside by a strange figure,— like a child: yet not so like a child as like an old man, viewed through some supernatural medium, which gave him the appearance of having receded from the view, and being diminished to a child's proportions. Its hair, which hung about its neck and down its back, was white as if with age; and yet the face had not a wrinkle in it, and the tenderest bloom was on the skin. It held a branch of fresh green holly in its hand; and, in singular contradiction of that wintry emblem, had its dress trimmed with summer flowers. But the strangest thing about it was, that from the crown of its head there sprung a bright clear jet of light, by which all this was visible; and which was doubtless the occasion of its using, in its duller moments, a great extinguisher for a cap, which it now held under its arm.

"Are you the Spirit, sir, whose coming was foretold to me?"
"I am!"

"Who and what are you?"

"I am the Ghost of Christmas Past."

"Long past?"

"No. Your past. The things that you will see with me are shadows of the things that have been; they will have no consciousness of us."

Scrooge then made bold to inquire what business brought him there.

"Your welfare. Rise, and walk with me!"

It would have been in vain for Scrooge to plead that the weather and the hour were not adapted to pedestrian purposes; that bed was warm, and the thermometer a long way below freezing; that he was clad lightly in his slippers, dressing-gown, and nightcap; and that he had a cold upon him at that time. The grasp, though gentle as a woman's hand, was not to be resisted. He rose; but finding that the Spirit made towards the window, clasped its robe in supplication.

"I am a mortal, and liable to fall."

"Bear but a touch of my hand *there*," said the Spirit, laying it upon his heart, "and you shall be upheld in more than this!"

As the words were spoken, they passed through the wall, and stood in the busy thoroughfares of a city. It was made plain enough by the dressing of the shops that here, too, it was Christmas time.

The Ghost stopped at a certain warehouse door, and asked Scrooge if he knew it.

"Know it! I was apprenticed here!"

They went in. At sight of an old gentleman in a Welsh wig, sitting behind such a high desk that, if he had been two inches taller, he must have knocked his head against the ceiling, Scrooge cried in great excitement: "Why, it's old Fezziwig! Bless his heart, it's Fezziwig, alive again!"

Old Fezziwig laid down his pen, and looked up at the clock, which pointed to the hour of seven. He rubbed his hands; adjusted his capacious waistcoat; laughed all over himself, from his shoes to his organ of benevolence; and called out in a comfortable, oily, rich, fat, jovial voice: "Yo ho, there! Ebenezer! Dick!"

A living and moving picture of Scrooge's former self, a young man, came briskly in, accompanied by his fellow-prentice.

"Dick Wilkins, to be sure!" said Scrooge to the Ghost. "My old fellow-prentice, bless me, yes. There he is. He was very much attached to me, was Dick. Poor Dick! Dear, dear!"

"Yo ho, my boys!" said Fezziwig. "No more work to-night. Christmas eve, Dick. Christmas, Ebenezer! Let's have the shutters up, before a man can say Jack Robinson! Clear away, my lads, and let's have lots of room here!"

Clear away! There was nothing they wouldn't have cleared away, or couldn't have cleared away, with old Fezziwig looking on. It was done in a minute. Every movable was packed off, as if it were dismissed from public life forevermore; the floor was swept and watered, the lamps were trimmed, fuel was heaped upon the fire; and the warehouse was as snug and warm and dry and bright a ball-room as you would desire to see upon a winter's night.

In came a fiddler with a music-book, and went up to the lofty desk, and made an orchestra of it, and tuned like fifty stomach-aches. In came Mrs. Fezziwig, one vast substantial smile. In came the three Miss Fezziwigs, beaming and lovable. In came the six young followers whose hearts they broke. In came all the young men and women employed in the business. In came the housemaid, with her cousin the baker. In came the cook, with her brother's particular friend the milkman. In they all came one after another; some shyly, some boldly, some gracefully, some awkwardly, some pushing, some pulling; in they all came, anyhow and everyhow. Away they all went, twenty couples at once; hands half round and back again the other way; down the middle and up again; round and round in various stages of affectionate grouping; old top couple always turning up in the wrong place; new top couple starting off again, as soon as they got there; all top couples at last, and not a bottom one to help them. When this result was brought about, old Fezziwig, clapping his hands to stop the dance, cried out, "Well done!" and the fiddler plunged his hot face into a pot of porter especially provided for that purpose.

There were more dances, and there were forfeits, and more dances, and there was cake, and there was negus, and there was a great piece of Cold Roast, and there was a great piece of Cold Boiled, and there were mince-pies, and plenty of beer.

But the great effect of the evening came after the Roast and Boiled, when the fiddler struck up "Sir Roger de Coverley." Then old Fezziwig stood out to dance with Mrs. Fezziwig. Top couple, too; with a good stiff piece of work cut out for them; three or four and twenty pair of partners; people who were not to be trifled with; people who *would* dance, and had no notion of walking.

But if they had been twice as many,—four times,—old Fezziwig would have been a match for them, and so would Mrs. Fezziwig. As to *her*, she was worthy to be his partner in every sense of the term. A positive light appeared to issue from Fezziwig's calves. They shone in every part of the dance. You couldn't have predicted, at any given time, what would become of 'em next. And when old Fezziwig and Mrs. Fezziwig had gone all through the dance,—advance and retire, turn your partner, bow and courtesy, corkscrew, thread the needle, and back again to your place,—Fezziwig "cut,"—cut so deftly, that he appeared to wink with his legs.

When the clock struck eleven this domestic hall broke up. Mr. and Mrs. Fezziwig took their stations, one on either side the door, and, shaking hands with every person individually as he or she went out, wished him or her a Merry Christmas. When everybody had retired but the two 'prentices, they did the same to them; and thus the cheerful voices died away, and the lads were left to their beds, which were under a counter in the back shop.

"A small matter," said the Ghost, "to make these silly folks so full of gratitude. He has spent but a few pounds of your mortal money,—three or four perhaps. Is that so much that he deserves this praise?"

"It isn't that," said Scrooge, heated by the remark, and speaking unconsciously like his former, not his latter self,— "it isn't that, Spirit. He has the power to render us happy or unhappy; to make our service light or burdensome; a pleasure or a toil. Say that his power lies in words and looks; in things so slight and insignificant that it is impossible to add and count 'em up: what then? The happiness he gives is quite as great as if it cost a fortune."

He felt the Spirit's glance, and stopped.

"What is the matter?"

"Nothing particular."

"Something, I think?"

"No, no. I should like to be able to say a word or two to my clerk just now. That's all."

"My time grows short," observed the Spirit. "Quick!"

This was not addressed to Scrooge, or to any one whom he could see, but it produced an immediate effect. For again he saw himself. He was older now; a man in the prime of life.

He was not alone, but sat by the side of a fair young girl in a black dress, in whose eyes there were tears.

"It matters little," she said softly to Scrooge's former self. "To you, very little. Another idol has displaced me; and if it can comfort you in time to come, as I would have tried to do, I have no just cause to grieve."

"What idol has displaced you?"

"A golden one. You fear the world too much. I have seen your nobler aspirations fall off one by one, until the master-passion, Gain, engrosses you. Have I not?"

"What then? Even if I have grown so much wiser, what then? I am not changed towards you. Have I ever sought release from our engagement?"

"In words, no. Never."

"In what, then?"

"In a changed nature; in an altered spirit; in another atmosphere of life; another Hope as its great end. If you were free to-day, to-morrow, yesterday, can even I believe that you would choose a dowerless girl; or, choosing her, do I not know that your repentance and regret would surely follow? I do; and I release you. With a full heart, for the love of him you once were."

"Spirit! remove me from this place."

"I told you these were shadows of the things that have been," said the Ghost. "That they are what they are, do not blame me!"

"Remove me!" Scrooge exclaimed. "I cannot bear it! Leave me! Take me back. Haunt me no longer!"

As he struggled with the Spirit he was conscious of being exhausted, and overcome by an irresistible drowsiness; and, further, of being in his own bedroom. He had barely time to reel to bed before he sank into a heavy sleep.

THE SECOND OF THE THREE SPIRITS

Scrooge awoke in his own bedroom. There was no doubt about that. But it and his own adjoining sitting-room, into which he shuffled in his slippers, attracted by a great light there, had undergone a surprising transformation. The walls and ceiling were so hung with living green, that it looked a perfect grove. The leaves of holly, mistletoe, and ivy reflected back the light, as if so many little mirrors had been scattered there; and such a mighty blaze went roaring up the chimney, as that petrifaction of a hearth had never known in Scrooge's time, or Marley's, or for many and many a winter season gone. Heaped upon the floor, to form a kind of throne, were turkeys, geese, game, brawn, great joints of meat, suckling pigs, long wreaths of sausages, mince-pies, plum-puddings, barrels of oysters, red-hot chestnuts, cherry-cheeked apples, juicy oranges, luscious pears, immense twelfth-cakes, and great bowls of punch. In easy state upon this couch there sat a Giant glorious to see; who bore a glowing torch, in shape not unlike Plenty's horn, and who raised it high to shed its light on Scrooge, as he came peeping round the door.

"Come in,—come in! and know me better, man! I am the Ghost of Christmas Present. Look upon me! You have never seen the like of me before?"

"Never."

"Have never walked forth with the younger members of my family; meaning (for I am very young) my elder brothers born in these later years?" pursued the Phantom.

"I don't think I have, I am afraid I have not. Have you had many brothers, Spirit?"

"More than eighteen hundred."

"A tremendous family to provide for! Spirit, conduct me where you will. I went forth last night on compulsion, and I learnt a lesson which is working now. To-night, if you have aught to teach me, let me profit by it."

"Touch my robe!"

Scrooge did as he was told, and held it fast.

The room and its contents all vanished instantly, and they stood in the city streets upon a snowy Christmas morning.

Scrooge and the Ghost passed on, invisible, straight to Scrooge's clerk's; and on the threshold of the door the Spirit smiled, and stopped to bless Bob Cratchit's dwelling with the sprinklings of his torch. Think of that! Bob had but fifteen "bob" a week himself; he pocketed on Saturdays but fifteen copies of his Christian name; and yet the Ghost of Christmas Present blessed his four-roomed house!

Then up rose Mrs. Cratchit, Cratchit's wife, dressed out but poorly in a twice-turned gown, but brave in ribbons, which are cheap and make a goodly show for sixpence; and she laid the cloth, assisted by Belinda Cratchit, second of her daughters, also brave in ribbons; while Master Peter Cratchit plunged a fork into the saucepan of potatoes, and, getting the corners of his monstrous shirt-collar (Bob's private property, conferred upon his son and heir in honor of the day) into his mouth, rejoiced to find himself so gallantly attired, and yearned to show his linen in the fashionable Parks. And now two smaller Cratchits, boy and girl, came tearing in, screaming that outside the baker's they had smelt the goose, and known it for their own; and, basking in luxurious thoughts of sage and onion, these young Cratchits danced about the table, and exalted Master Peter Cratchit to the skies, while he (not proud, al-

though his collars nearly choked him) blew the fire, until the slow potatoes, bubbling up, knocked loudly at the saucepan-lid to be let out and peeled.

"What has ever got your precious father then?" said Mrs. Cratchit. "And your brother Tiny Tim! And Martha warn't as late last Christmas day by half an hour!"

"Here's Martha, mother!" said a girl, appearing as she spoke.

"Here's Martha, mother!" cried the two young Cratchits. "Hurrah! There's *such* a goose, Martha!"

"Why, bless your heart alive, my dear, how late you are!" said Mrs. Cratchit, kissing her a dozen times, and taking off her shawl and bonnet for her.

"We'd a deal of work to finish up last night," replied the girl, "and had to clear away this morning, mother!"

"Well! Never mind so long as you are come," said Mrs. Crachit. "Sit ye down before the fire, my dear, and have a warm, Lord bless ye!"

"No, no! There's father coming," cried the two young Cratchits, who were everywhere at once. "Hide, Martha, hide!"

So Martha hid herself, and in came little Bob, the father, with at least three feet of comforter, exclusive of the fringe, hanging down before him; and his threadbare clothes darned up and brushed, to look seasonable; and Tiny Tim upon his shoulder. Alas for Tiny Tim, he bore a little crutch, and had his limbs supported by an iron frame!

"Why, where's our Martha?" cried Bob Cratchit, looking round.

"Not coming," said Mrs. Cratchit.

"Not coming!" said Bob, with a sudden declension in his high spirits; for he had been Tim's blood-horse all the way from church, and had come home rampant,—"not coming upon Christmas day!"

Martha didn't like to see him disappointed, if it were only in joke; so she came out prematurely from behind the closet door, and ran into his arms, while the two young Cratchits hustled Tiny Tim, and bore him off into the wash-house, that he might hear the pudding singing in the copper.

"And how did little Tim behave?" asked Mrs. Cratchit, when she had rallied Bob on his credulity, and Bob had hugged

A MERRY CHRISTMAS AND HAPPY NEW YEAR.

American lithograph, 1869

A Merry Christmas & A Happy New Year in London,
19th-century English lithograph

his daughter to his heart's content.

"As good as gold," said Bob, "and better. Somehow he gets thoughtful, sitting by himself so much, and thinks the strangest things you ever heard. He told me, coming home, that he hoped the people saw him in the church, because he was a cripple, and it might be pleasant to them to remember, upon Christmas day, who made lame beggars walk and blind men see."

Bob's voice was tremulous when he told them this, and trembled more when he said that Tiny Tim was growing strong and hearty.

His active little crutch was heard upon the floor, and back came Tiny Tim before another word was spoken, escorted by his brother and sister to his stool beside the fire; and while Bob, turning up his cuffs,—as if, poor fellow, they were capable of being made more shabby,—compounded some hot mixture in a jug with gin and lemons, and stirred it round and round and put it on the hob to simmer, Master Peter and the two ubiquitous young Cratchits went to fetch the goose, with which they soon returned in high procession.

Mrs. Cratchit made the gravy (ready beforehand in a little saucepan) hissing hot; Master Peter mashed the potatoes with incredible vigor; Miss Belinda sweetened up the apple-sauce; Martha dusted the hot plates; Bob took Tiny Tim beside him in a tiny corner at the table; the two young Cratchits set chairs for everybody, not forgetting themselves, and mounting guard upon their posts, crammed spoons into their mouths, lest they should shriek for goose before their turn came to be helped. At last the dishes were set on, and grace was said. It was succeeded by a breathless pause, as Mrs. Cratchit, looking slowly all along the carving-knife, prepared to plunge it in the breast; but when she did, and when the long-expected gush of stuffing issued forth, one murmur of delight arose all round the board, and even Tiny Tim, excited by the two young Cratchits, beat on the table with the handle of his knife, and feebly cried, Hurrah!

There never was such a goose. Bob said he didn't believe there ever was such a goose cooked. Its tenderness and flavor, size and cheapness, were the themes of universal admiration. Eked out by apple-sauce and mashed potatoes, it was a suffi-

cient dinner for the whole family; indeed, as Mrs. Cratchit said with great delight (surveying one small atom of a bone upon the dish), they hadn't ate it all at last! Yet every one had had enough, and the youngest Cratchits in particular were steeped in sage and onion to the eyebrows! But now, the plates being changed by Miss Belinda, Mrs. Cratchit left the room alone,— too nervous to bear witnesses,—to take the pudding up, and bring it in.

Suppose it should not be done enough! Suppose it should break in turning out! Suppose somebody should have got over the wall of the back yard, and stolen it, while they were merry with the goose,—a supposition at which the two young Cratchits became livid! All sorts of horrors were supposed.

Hallo! A great deal of steam! The pudding was out of the copper. A smell like a washing-day! That was the cloth. A smell like an eating-house and a pastry-cook's next door to each other, with a laundress's next door to that! That was the pudding! In half a minute Mrs. Cratchit entered,—flushed but smiling proudly,—with the pudding, like a speckled cannonball, so hard and firm, blazing in half of half a quartern of ignited brandy, and bedight with Christmas holly stuck into the top.

O, a wonderful pudding! Bob Cratchit said, and calmly too, that he regarded it as the greatest success achieved by Mrs. Cratchit since their marriage. Mrs. Cratchit said that now the weight was off her mind, she would confess she had had her doubts about the quantity of flour. Everybody had something to say about it, but nobody said or thought it was at all a small pudding for a large family. Any Cratchit would have blushed to hint at such a thing.

At last the dinner was all done, the cloth was cleared, the hearth swept, and the fire made up. The compound in the jug being tasted, and considered perfect, apples and oranges were put upon the table, and a shovelful of chestnuts on the fire.

Then all the Cratchit family drew round the hearth, in what Bob Cratchit called a circle, and at Bob Cratchit's elbow stood the family display of glass,—two tumblers, and a custard-cup without a handle.

These held the hot stuff from the jug, however, as well as golden goblets would have done; and Bob served it out with beaming looks, while the chestnuts on the fire sputtered and crackled noisily. Then Bob proposed:—

"A Merry Christmas to us all, my dears. God bless us!"

Which all the family re-echoed.

"God bless us every one!" said Tiny Tim, the last of all.

He sat very close to his father's side, upon his little stool. Bob held his withered little hand in his, as if he loved the child, and wished to keep him by his side, and dreaded that he might be taken from him.

Scrooge raised his head speedily, on hearing his own name.

"Mr. Scrooge!" said Bob; "I'll give you Mr. Scrooge, the Founder of the Feast!"

"The Founder of the Feast indeed!" cried Mrs. Cratchit, reddening. "I wish I had him here. I'd give him a piece of my mind to feast upon, and I hope he'd have a good appetite for it."

"My dear," said Bob, "the children! Christmas day."

"It should be Christmas day, I am sure," said she, "on which one drinks the health of such an odious, stingy, hard, unfeeling man as Mr. Scrooge. You know he is, Robert! Nobody knows it better than you do, poor fellow!"

"My dear," was Bob's mild answer, "Christmas day."

"I'll drink his health for your sake and the day's," said Mrs. Cratchit, "not for his. Long life to him! A merry Christmas and a happy New Year! He'll be very merry and very happy, I have no doubt!"

The children drank the toast after her. It was the first of their proceedings which had no heartiness in it. Tiny Tim drank it last of all, but he didn't care twopence for it. Scrooge was the Ogre of the family. The mention of his name cast a dark shadow on the party, which was not dispelled for full five minutes.

After it had passed away, they were ten times merrier than before, from the mere relief of Scrooge the Baleful being done with. Bob Cratchit told them how he had a situation in his eye for Master Peter, which would bring in, if obtained, full five and sixpence weekly. The two young Cratchits laughed tremendously at the idea of Peter's being a man of business; and Peter himself looked thoughtfully at the fire from between his collars, as if he were deliberating what particular investments he should favor when he came into the receipt of that bewildering income. Martha, who was a poor apprentice at a milliner's, then told them what kind of work she had to do, and how many hours she worked at a stretch, and how she meant to lie abed to-morrow morning for a good long rest; to-morrow being a holiday she passed at home. Also how she had seen a countess and a lord some days before, and how the lord "was much about as tall as Peter"; at which Peter pulled up his collars so high that you couldn't have seen his head if you had been there. All this time the chestnuts and the jug went round and round; and by and by they had a song, about a lost child travelling in the snow, from Tiny Tim, who had a plaintive little voice, and sang it very well indeed.

There was nothing of high mark in this. They were not a handsome family; they were not well dressed; their shoes were far from being water-proof; their clothes were scanty; and Peter might have known, and very likely did, the inside of a pawn-broker's. But they were happy, grateful, pleased with one another, and contented with the time; and when they faded, and looked happier yet in the bright sprinklings of the Spirit's torch at parting, Scrooge had his eye upon them, and especially on Tiny Tim, until the last.

It was a great surprise to Scrooge, as this scene vanished, to hear a hearty laugh. It was a much greater surprise to Scrooge to recognize it as his own nephew's, and to find himself in a bright, dry, gleaming room, with the Spirit standing smiling by his side, and looking at that same nephew.

It is a fair, even-handed, noble adjustment of things, that while there is infection in disease and sorrow, there is nothing in the world so irresistibly contagious as laughter and good-humor. When Scrooge's nephew laughed, Scrooge's niece by marriage laughed as heartily as he. And their assembled friends, being not a bit behindhand, laughed out lustily.

"He said that Christmas was a humbug, as I live!" cried Scrooge's nephew. "He believed it too!"

"More shame for him, Fred!" said Scrooge's niece, indignantly. Bless those women! they never do anything by halves. They are always in earnest.

She was very pretty; exceedingly pretty. With a dimpled, surprised-looking, capital face; a ripe little mouth that seemed made to be kissed,—as no doubt it was; all kinds of good little dots about her chin, that melted into one another when she laughed; and the sunniest pair of eyes you ever saw in any little creature's head. Altogether she was what you would have called provoking, but satisfactory, too. O, perfectly satisfactory.

"He's a comical old fellow," said Scrooge's nephew, "that's the truth; and not so pleasant as he might be. However, his offenses carry their own punishment, and I have nothing to say against him. Who suffers by his ill whims? Himself, always. Here he takes it into his head to dislike us, and he won't come and dine with us. What's the consequence? He don't lose much of a dinner."

"Indeed, I think he loses a very good dinner," interrupted Scrooge's niece. Everybody else said the same, and they must be allowed to have been competent judges, because they had just had dinner; and, with the dessert upon the table, were clustered round the fire, by lamplight.

"Well, I am very glad to hear it," said Scrooge's nephew, "because I haven't any great faith in these young housekeepers. What do *you* say, Topper?"

Topper clearly had his eye on one of Scrooge's niece's sisters, for he answered that a bachelor was a wretched outcast, who had no right to express an opinion on the subject. Whereat Scrooge's niece's sister—the plump one with the lace tucker; not the one with the roses—blushed.

After tea they had some music. For they were a musical family, and knew what they were about, when they sung a Glee or Catch, I can assure you,—especially Topper, who could growl away in the bass like a good one, and never swell the large veins in his forehead, or get red in the face over it.

But they didn't devote the whole evening to music. After a while they played at forfeits; for it is good to be children sometimes, and never better than at Christmas, when its mighty Founder was a child himself. There was first a game at blind man's-buff though. And I no more believe Topper was really blinded than I believe he had eyes in his boots. Because the way in which he went after that plump sister in the lace tucker was an outrage on the credulity of human nature. Knocking down the fire-irons, tumbling over the chairs, bumping up against the piano, smothering himself among the curtains, wherever she went there went he! He always knew where the plump sister was. He wouldn't catch anybody else. If you had

fallen up against him, as some of them did, and stood there, he would have made a feint of endeavoring to seize you, which would have been an affront to your understanding, and would instantly have sidled off in the direction of the plump sister.

"Here is a new game," said Scrooge. "One half-hour, Spirit, only one!"

It was a Game called Yes and No, where Scrooge's nephew had to think of something, and the rest must find out what; he only answering to their questions yes or no, as the case was. The fire of questioning to which he was exposed elicited from him that he was thinking of an animal, a live animal, rather a disagreeable animal, a savage animal, an animal that growled and grunted sometimes, and talked sometimes, and lived in London, and walked about the streets, and wasn't made a show of, and wasn't led by anybody, and didn't live in a menagerie, and was never killed in a market, and was not a horse, or an ass, or a cow, or a bull, or a tiger, or a dog, or a pig, or a cat, or a bear. At every new question put to him, this nephew burst into a fresh roar of laughter; and was so inexpressibly tickled, that he was obliged to get up off the sofa and stamp. At last the plump sister cried out:—

"I have found it out! I know what it is, Fred! I know what it is!"

"What is it?" cried Fred.

"It's your uncle Scro-o-o-o-oge!"

Which it certainly was. Admiration was the universal sentiment, though some objected that the reply to "Is it a bear?" ought to have been "Yes."

Uncle Scrooge had imperceptibly become so gay and light of heart, that he would have drunk to the unconscious company in an inaudible speech. But the whole scene passed off in the breath of the last word spoken by his nephew; and he and the Spirit were again upon their travels.

Much they saw, and far they went, and many homes they visited, but always with a happy end. The Spirit stood beside sick-beds, and they were cheerful; on foreign lands, and they were close at home; by struggling men, and they were patient in their greater hope; by poverty, and it was rich. In almshouse, hospital, and jail, in misery's every refuge, where vain man in his little brief authority had not made fast the door, and barred the Spirit out, he left his blessing, and taught Scrooge his precepts. Suddenly, as they stood together in an open place, the bell struck twelve.

Scrooge looked about him for the Ghost, and saw it no more. As the last stroke ceased to vibrate, he remembered the prediction of old Jacob Marley, and, lifting up his eyes, beheld a solemn Phantom, draped and hooded, coming like a mist along the ground towards him.

THE LAST OF THE SPIRITS

The Phantom slowly, gravely, silently approached. When it came near him, Scrooge bent down upon his knee; for in the air through which this Spirit moved it seemed to scatter gloom and mystery.

It was shrouded in a deep black garment, which concealed its head, its face, its form, and left nothing of it visible save one outstretched hand. He knew no more, for the Spirit neither spoke nor moved.

"I am in the presence of the Ghost of Christmas Yet To Come? Ghost of the Future! I fear you more than any spectre I have seen. But as I know your purpose is to do me good, and as I hope to live to be another man from what I was, I am prepared to bear you company, and do it with a thankful heart. Will you not speak to me?"

It gave him no reply. The hand was pointed straight before them.

"Lead on! Lead on! The night is waning fast, and it is precious time to me, I know. Lead on, Spirit!"

They scarcely seemed to enter the city; for the city rather seemed to spring up about them. But there they were in the heart of it; on 'Change, amongst the merchants.

The Spirit stopped beside one little knot of business men. Observing that the hand was pointed to them, Scrooge advanced to listen to their talk.

"No," said a great fat man with a monstrous chin, "I don't know much about it either way. I only know he's dead."

"When did he die?" inquired another.

"Last night, I believe."

"Why, what was the matter with him? I thought he'd never die."

"God knows," said the first, with a yawn.

"What has he done with his money?" asked a red-faced gentleman.

"I haven't heard," said the man with the large chin. "Company, perhaps. He hasn't left it to me. That's all I know. By, by!"

Scrooge was at first inclined to be surprised that the Spirit should attach importance to conversation apparently so trivial; but feeling assured that it must have some hidden purpose, he set himself to consider what it was likely to be. It could scarcely be supposed to have any bearing on the death of Jacob, his old partner, for that was Past, and this Ghost's province was the Future.

He looked about in that very place for his own image; but another man stood in his accustomed corner, and though the clock pointed to his usual time of day for being there, he saw no likeness of himself among the multitudes that poured in through the Porch. It gave him little surprise, however; for he had been revolving in his mind a change of life, and he thought and hoped he saw his new-born resolutions carried out in this.

They left this busy scene, and went into an obscure part of the town, to a low shop where iron, old rags, bottles, bones, and greasy offal were bought. A gray-haired rascal, of great age, sat smoking his pipe.

Scrooge and the Phantom came into the presence of this man, just as a woman with a heavy bundle slunk into the shop. But she had scarcely entered, when another woman, similarly laden, came in too; and she was closely followed by a man in faded black. After a short period of blank astonishment, in which the old man with the pipe had joined them, they all three burst into a laugh.

"Let the charwoman alone to be the first!" cried she who had entered first. "Let the laundress alone to be the second; and let the undertaker's man alone to be the third. Look here, old Joe, here's a chance! If we haven't all three met here without meaning it!"

"You couldn't have met in a better place. You were made free of it long ago, you know; and the other two ain't strangers. What have you got to sell? What have you got to sell?"

"Half a minute's patience, Joe, and you shall see."

"What odds then! What odds, Mrs. Dilber?" said the woman. "Every person has a right to take care of themselves.

He always did! Who's the worse for the loss of a few things like these? Not a dead man, I suppose."

Mrs. Dilber, whose manner was remarkable for general propitiation, said, "No, indeed, ma'am."

"If he wanted to keep 'em after he was dead, a wicked old screw, why wasn't he natural in his life-time? If he had been, he'd have had somebody to look after him when he was struck with Death, instead of lying gasping out his last there, alone by himself."

"It's the truest word that ever was spoke, it's a judgment on him."

"I wish it was a little heavier judgment, and it should have been, you may depend upon it, if I could have laid my hands on anything else. Open that bundle, old Joe, and let me know the value of it. Speak out plain. I'm not afraid to be the first, nor afraid for them to see it."

Joe went down on his knees for the greater convenience of opening the bundle, and dragged out a large and heavy roll of some dark stuff.

"What do you call this? Bed-curtains!"

"Ah! Bed-curtains! Don't drop that oil upon the blankets, now."

"*His* blankets?"

"Whose else's do you think? He isn't likely to take cold without 'em, I dare say. Ah! You may look through that shirt till your eyes ache; but you won't find a hole in it, nor a thread-bare place. It's the best he had, and a fine one too. They'd have wasted it by dressing him up in it, if it hadn't been for me."

Scrooge listened to this dialogue in horror.

"Spirit! I see, I see. The case of this unhappy man might be my own. My life tends that way, now. Merciful Heaven, what is this!"

The scene had changed, and now he almost touched a bare, uncurtained bed. A pale light, rising in the outer air, fell straight upon this bed; and on it, unwatched, unwept, uncared for, was the body of this plundered unknown man.

"Spirit, let me see some tenderness connected with a death, or this dark chamber, Spirit, will be forever present to me."

The Ghost conducted him to poor Bob Cratchit's house, —the dwelling he had visited before,—and found the mother and the children seated round the fire.

Quiet. Very quiet. The noisy little Cratchits were as still as statues in one corner, and sat looking up at Peter, who had a book before him. The mother and her daughters were engaged in needle-work. But surely they were very quiet!

" 'And he took a child, and set him in the midst of them.' "

Where had Scrooge heard those words? He had not dreamed them. The boy must have read them out, as he and the Spirit crossed the threshold. Why did he not go on?

The mother laid her work upon the table, and put her hand up to her face.

"The color hurts my eyes," she said.

The color? Ah, poor Tiny Tim!

"They're better now again. It makes them weak by candle-light; and I wouldn't show weak eyes to your father when he comes home, for the world. It must be near his time."

"Past it rather," Peter answered, shutting up his book. "But I think he has walked a little slower than he used, these few last evenings, mother."

"I have known him walk with—I have known him walk with Tiny Tim upon his shoulder, very fast indeed."

"And so have I," cried Peter. "Often."

"And so have I," exclaimed another. So had all.

"But he was very light to carry, and his father loved him so, that it was no trouble,—no trouble. And there is your father at the door!"

She hurried out to meet him; and little Bob in his com-forter—he had need of it, poor fellow—came in. His tea was ready for him on the hob, and they all tried who should help him to it most. Then the two young Cratchits got upon his knees and laid, each child, a little cheek against his face, as if they said, "Don't mind it, father. Don't be grieved!"

Bob was very cheerful with them, and spoke pleasantly to all the family. He looked at the work upon the table, and praised the industry and speed of Mrs. Cratchit and the girls. They would be done long before Sunday, he said.

"Sunday! You went to-day, then, Robert?"

"Yes, my dear," returned Bob. "I wish you could have gone. It would have done you good to see how green a place it is. But you'll see it often. I promised him that I would walk there on a Sunday. My little, little child! My little child!"

He broke down all at once. He couldn't help it. If he could have helped it, he and his child would have been farther apart, perhaps, than they were.

"Spectre," said Scrooge, "something informs me that our parting moment is at hand. I know it, but I know not how. Tell me what man that was, with the covered face, whom we saw lying dead?"

The Ghost of Christmas Yet To Come conveyed him to a dismal, wretched, ruinous churchyard.

The Spirit stood among the graves, and pointed down to one.

"Before I draw nearer to that stone to which you point, answer me one question. Are these the shadows of the things that Will be, or are they shadows of the things that May be only?"

Still the Ghost pointed downward to the grave by which it stood.

"Men's courses will foreshadow certain ends, to which, if persevered in, they must lead. But if the courses be departed from, the ends will change. Say it is thus with what you show me!"

The Spirit was immovable as ever.

Scrooge crept towards it, trembling as he went; and, following the finger, read upon the stone of the neglected grave his own name,—Ebenezer Scrooge.

"Am *I* that man who lay upon the bed? No, Spirit! O no, no! Spirit! hear me! I am not the man I was. I will not be the man I must have been but for this intercourse. Why show me this, if I am past all hope? Assure me that I yet may change these shadows you have shown me by an altered life."

For the first time the kind hand faltered.

"I will honor Christmas in my heart, and try to keep it all the year. I will live in the Past, the Present, and the Future. The Spirits of all three shall strive within me. I will not shut out the lessons that they teach. O, tell me I may sponge away the writing on this stone!"

Holding up his hands in one last prayer to have his fate reversed, he saw an alteration in the Phantom's hood and dress. It shrunk, collapsed, and dwindled down into a bedpost.

Yes, and the bedpost was his own. The bed was his own, the room was his own. Best and happiest of all, the Time before him was his own, to make amends in!

He was checked in his transports by the churches ringing out the lustiest peals he had ever heard.

Running to the window, he opened it, and put out his head. No fog, no mist, no night; clear, bright, stirring, golden day.

"What's to-day?" cried Scrooge, calling downward to a boy in Sunday clothes, who perhaps had loitered in to look about him.

"Eh?"

"What's to-day, my fine fellow?"

"To-day! Why, Christmas day."

"It's Christmas day! I haven't missed it. Hallo, my fine fellow!"

"Hallo!"

"Do you know the Poulterer's, in the next street but one,

at the corner?"

"I should hope I did."

"An intelligent boy! A remarkable boy! Do you know whether they've sold the prize Turkey that was hanging up there? Not the little prize Turkey,—the big one?"

"What, the one as big as me?"

"What a delightful boy! It's a pleasure to talk to him. Yes, my buck!"

"It's hanging there now."

"Is it? Go and buy it."

"Walk-ER!" exclaimed the boy.

"No, no, I am in earnest. Go and buy it, and tell 'em to bring it here, that I may give them the direction where to take it. Come back with the man, and I'll give you a shilling. Come back with him in less than five minutes, and I'll give you half a crown!"

The boy was off like a shot.

"I'll send it to Bob Cratchit's! He sha'n't know who sends it. It's twice the size of Tiny Tim. Joe Miller never made such a joke as sending it to Bob's will be!"

The hand in which he wrote the address was not a steady one; but write it he did, somehow, and went down stairs to open the street door, ready for the coming of the poulterer's man.

It *was* a Turkey! He never could have stood upon his legs, that bird. He would have snapped 'em short off in a minute, like sticks of sealing-wax.

Scrooge dressed himself "all in his best," and at last got out into the streets. The people were by this time pouring forth, as he had seen them with the Ghost of Christmas Present; and, walking with his hands behind him, Scrooge regarded every one with a delighted smile. He looked so irresistibly pleasant, in a word, that three or four good-humored fellows said, "Good morning, sir! A merry Christmas to you!" And Scrooge said often afterwards, that, of all the blithe sounds he had ever heard, those were the blithest in his ears.

In the afternoon, he turned his steps towards his nephew's house.

He passed the door a dozen times, before he had the courage to go up and knock. But he made a dash, and did it.

"Is your master at home, my dear?" said Scrooge to the girl. Nice girl! Very.

"Yes, sir."

"Where is he, my love?"

"He's in the dining-room, sir, along with mistress."

"He knows me," said Scrooge, with his hand already on the dining-room lock. "I'll go in here, my dear."

"Fred!"

"Why, bless my soul!" cried Fred, "who's that?"

"It's I. Your uncle Scrooge. I have come to dinner. Will you let me in, Fred?"

Let him in! It is a mercy he didn't shake his arm off. He was at home in five minutes. Nothing could be heartier. His niece looked just the same. So did Topper when *he* came. So did the plump sister, when *she* came. So did every one when *they* came. Wonderful party, wonderful games, wonderful unanimity, won-der-ful happiness!

But he was early at the office next morning. O, he was early there. If he could only be there first, and catch Bob Cratchit coming late! That was the thing he had set his heart upon.

And he did it. The clock struck nine. No Bob. A quarter past. No Bob. Bob was full eighteen minutes and a half behind his time. Scrooge sat with his door wide open, that he might see him come into the tank.

Bob's hat was off, before he opened the door; his comforter too. He was on his stool in a jiffy; driving away with his pen, as if he were trying to overtake nine o'clock.

"Hallo!" growled Scrooge, in his accustomed voice, as near as he could feign it. "What do you mean by coming here at this time of day?"

"I am very sorry, sir. I *am* behind my time."

"You are? Yes. I think you are. Step this way, if you please."

"It's only once a year, sir. It shall not be repeated. I was making rather merry yesterday, sir."

"Now, I'll tell you what, my friend. I am not going to stand this sort of thing any longer. And therefore," Scrooge continued, leaping from his stool, and giving Bob such a dig in the waist coat that he staggered back into the tank again,—

"and therefore I am about to raise your salary!"

Bob trembled, and got a little nearer to the ruler.

"A merry Christmas, Bob!" said Scrooge, with an earnestness that could not be mistaken, as he clapped him on the back. "A merrier Christmas, Bob, my good fellow, than I have given you for many a year! I'll raise your salary, and endeavor to assist your struggling family, and we will discuss your affairs this very afternoon, over a Christmas bowl of smoking bishop, Bob! Make up the fires, and buy a second coal-scuttle before you dot another i, Bob Cratchit!"

Scrooge was better than his word. He did it all, and infinitely more; and to Tiny Tim, who did NOT die, he was a second father. He became as good a friend, as good a master, and as good a man as the good old city knew, or any other good old city, town, or borough in the good old world. Some people laughed to see the alteration in him; but his own heart laughed, and that was quite enough for him.

He had no further intercourse with Spirits, but lived in that respect upon the Total-Abstinence Principle ever afterwards; and it was always said of him, that he knew how to keep Christmas well, if any man alive possessed the knowledge. May that be truly said of us, and all of us! And so, as Tiny Tim observed, God Bless Us, Every One!

THE FIR-TREE

Hans Christian Andersen

FAR DOWN IN the forest, where the warm sun and the fresh air made a sweet resting-place, grew a pretty little fir-tree; and yet it was not so happy, it wished so much to be tall like its companions—the pines and firs which grew around it. The sun shone, and the soft air fluttered its leaves, and the little peasant children passed by, prattling merrily, but the fir-tree heeded them not. Sometimes the children would bring a large basket of raspberries or strawberries, wreathed on a straw, and seat themselves near the fir-tree, and say, "Is it not a pretty little tree?" which made it feel more unhappy than before. And yet all this while the tree grew a notch or joint taller every year; for by the number of joints in the stem of a fir-tree we can discover its age. Still, as it grew, it complained, "Oh! how I wish I were as tall as the other trees, then I would spread out my branches on every side, and my top would overlook the wide world. I should have the birds building their nests on my boughs, and when the wind blew, I should bow with stately dignity like my tall companions." The tree was so discontented, that it took no pleasure in the warm sunshine, the birds or the rosy clouds that floated over it morning and evening. Sometimes, in winter, when the snow lay white and glittering on the ground, a hare would come springing along, and would jump right over the little tree; and then how mortified it would feel! Two winters passed, and when the third arrived, the tree had grown so tall the hare was obliged to run round it. Yet it remained unsatisfied, and would exclaim,

Lighting the Yule Log, lithograph by Alice Barber, 1890

Christmas Morning in Old New York, lithograph by Howard Pyle, 1880

The Yule Log in India—Bringing in the Ice, English lithograph from the drawing by Adrien Marie, 1889

Holiday Greens—A Scene in Washington Market, New York, American lithograph, 1874

"Oh, if I could but keep on growing tall and old! There is nothing else worth caring for in the world!" In the autumn, as usual, the woodcutters came and cut down several of the tallest trees, and the young fir-tree, which was now grown to its full height, shuddered as the noble trees fell to the earth with a crash. After the branches were lopped off, the trunks looked so slender and bare, that they could scarcely be recognized. Then they were placed upon wagons, and drawn by horses out of the forest. "Where were they going? What would become of them?" The young fir-tree wished very much to know; so in the spring, when the swallows and the storks came, it asked, "Do you know where those trees were taken? Did you meet them?"

The swallows knew nothing; but the stork, after a little reflection, nodded his head, and said, "Yes, I think I do. I met several new ships when I flew from Egypt, and they had fine masts that smelt like fir. I think these must have been the trees; I assure you they were stately, very stately."

"Oh, how I wish I were tall enough to go on the sea," said the fir-tree. "What is this sea, and what does it look like?"

"It would take too much time to explain," said the stork, flying quickly away.

"Rejoice in thy youth," said the sunbeam; "rejoice in thy fresh growth, and the young life that is in thee."

And the wind kissed the tree, and the dew watered it with tears; but the fir-tree regarded them not.

Christmas-time drew near, and many young trees were cut down, some even smaller and younger than the fir-tree who enjoyed neither rest nor peace with longing to leave its forest home. These young trees, which were chosen for their beauty, kept their branches, and were also laid on wagons and drawn by horses out of the forest.

"Where are they going?" asked the fir-tree. "They are not taller than I am: indeed, one is much less; and why are the branches not cut off? Where are they going?"

"We know, we know," sang the sparrows; "we have looked in at the windows of the houses in town, and we know what is done with them. They are dressed up in the most splendid manner. We have seen them standing in the middle of a warm room, and adorned with all sorts of beautiful things,—honey cakes, gilded apples, and many hundreds of wax tapers."

"And then," asked the fir-tree, trembling through all its branches, "and then what happens?"

"We did not see any more," said the sparrows; "but this was enough for us."

"I wonder whether anything so brilliant will ever happen to me," thought the fir-tree. "It would be much better than crossing the sea. I long for it almost with pain. Oh! when will Christmas be here? I am now as tall and well grown as those which were taken away last year. Oh! that I were now laid on the wagon, or standing in the warm room, with all that brightness and splendor around me! Something better and more beautiful is to come after, or the trees would not be so decked out. Yes, what follows will be grander and more splendid. What can it be? I am weary with longing. I scarcely know how I feel."

"Rejoice with us," said the air and the sunlight. "Enjoy thine own bright life in the fresh air."

But the tree would not rejoice, though it grew taller every day; and, winter and summer, its dark-green foliage might be seen in the forest, while passers-by would say, "What a beautiful tree!"

A short time before Christmas, the discontented fir-tree was the first to fall. As the ax cut through the stem, and divided the pith, the tree fell with a groan to the earth, conscious of pain and faintness, and forgetting all its anticipations of happiness, in sorrow at leaving its home in the forest. It knew that it should never again see its dear old companions, the trees, nor the little bushes and many-colored flowers that had grown by its side; perhaps not even the birds. Neither was the journey at all pleasant. The tree first recovered itself while being unpacked in the courtyard of a house, with several other trees; and it heard a man say, "We only want one, and this is the prettiest."

Then came two servants in grand livery, and carried the fir-tree into a large and beautiful apartment. On the walls hung pictures, and near the great stove stood great china vases, with lions on the lids. There were rocking-chairs, silken sofas, large tables, covered with pictures, books, and playthings, worth a great deal of money,—at least, the children said so. Then the fir-tree was placed in a large tub, full of sand; but

green baize hung all around it, so that no one could see it was
a tub, and it stood on a very handsome carpet. How the fir-
tree trembled! "What was going to happen to him now?"
Some young ladies came, and the servants helped them to
adorn the tree. On one branch they hung little bags cut out
of colored paper, and each bag was filled with sweetmeats;
from other branches hung gilded apples and walnuts, as if they
had grown there; and above, and all round, were hundreds
of red, blue, and white tapers, which were fastened on the
branches. Dolls, exactly like real babies, were placed under
the green leaves,—the tree had never seen such things before,
—and at the very top was fastened a glittering star made of
tinsel. Oh, it was very beautiful!

"This evening," they all exclaimed, "how bright it will
be!" "Oh, that the evening were come," thought the tree, "and
the tapers lighted! then I shall know what else is going to happen. Will the trees of the forest come to see me? I wonder if
the sparrows will peep in at the windows as they fly? shall I
grow faster here, and keep on all these ornaments during
summer and winter?" But guessing was of very little use; it
made his bark ache, and this pain is as bad for a slender fir-
tree, as headache is for us. At last the tapers were lighted, and
then what a glistening blaze of light the tree presented! It
trembled so with joy in all its branches, that one of the candles
fell among the green leaves and burnt some of them. "Help!
help!" exclaimed the young ladies, but there was no danger,
for they quickly extinguished the fire. After this, the tree tried
not to tremble at all, though the fire frightened him; he was
so anxious not to hurt any of the beautiful ornaments, even
while their brilliancy dazzled him. And now the folding doors
were thrown open, and a troop of children rushed in as if they
intended to upset the tree; they were followed more slowly by
their elders. For a moment the little ones stood silent with
astonishment, and then they shouted for joy, till the room rang,
and they danced merrily round the tree, while one present after
another was taken from it.

"What are they doing? What will happen next?" thought
the fir. At last the candles burnt down to the branches and were
put out. Then the children received permission to plunder the
tree.

Oh, how they rushed upon it, till the branches cracked, and had it not been fastened with the glistening star to the ceiling, it must have been thrown down. The children then danced about with their pretty toys, and no one noticed the tree, except the children's maid, who came and peeped among the branches to see if an apple or a fig had been forgotten.

"A story, a story," cried the children, pulling a little fat man towards the tree.

"Now we shall be in the green shade," said the man as he seated himself under it, "and the tree will have the pleasure of hearing also, but I shall only relate one story; what shall it be? Ivede-Avede, or Humpty Dumpty, who fell downstairs, but soon got up again, and at last married a princess."

"Ivede-Avede," cried some. "Humpty Dumpty," cried others, and there was a fine shouting and crying out. But the fir-tree remained quite still, and thought to himself, "Shall I have anything to do with all this?" but he had already amused them as much as they wished. Then the old man told them the story of "Humpty Dumpty," how he fell downstairs, and was raised up again, and married a princess. And the children clapped their hands, and cried, "Tell another, tell another," for they wanted to hear the story of "Ivede-Avede"; but they only had "Humpty Dumpty." After this the fir-tree became quite silent and thoughtful; never had the birds in the forest told such tales as "Humpty Dumpty," who fell downstairs, and yet married a princess.

"Ah! yes, so it happens in the world," thought the fir-tree; he believed it all, because it was related by such a nice man. "Ah! well," he thought, "who knows? perhaps I may fall down too, and marry a princess"; and he looked forward joyfully to the next evening, expecting to be again decked out with lights and playthings, gold and fruit. "To-morrow I will not tremble," thought he; "I will enjoy all my splendor, and I shall hear the story of Humpty Dumpty again, and perhaps Ivede-Avede." And the tree remained quiet and thoughtful all night. In the morning the servants and the housemaid came in. "Now," thought the fir, "all my splendor is going to begin again." But they dragged him out of the room and upstairs to the garret, and threw him on the floor, and in a dark corner, where no daylight shone, and there they left him. "What does this mean?" thought the tree. "What am I to do here? I can hear nothing in a place like this," and he leant against the wall, and thought and thought. And he had time enough to think, for days and nights passed and no one came near him, and when at last somebody did come, it was only to put away large boxes in a corner. So the tree was completely hidden from sight as if it had never existed. "It is winter now," thought the tree, "the ground is hard and covered with snow, so that people cannot plant me. I shall be sheltered here, I dare say, until spring comes. How thoughtful and kind everybody is to me! Still I wish this place were not so dark, as well as lonely, with not even a little hare to look at. How pleasant it was out in the forest while the snow lay on the ground, when the hare would run by, yes, and jump over me too, although I did not like it then. Oh! it is terribly lonely here."

"Squeak, squeak," said a little mouse, creeping cautiously towards the tree; then came another, and they both sniffed at the fir-tree and crept between the branches.

"Oh, it is very cold," said the little mouse; "or else we should be so comfortable here, shouldn't we, you old fir-tree?"

"I am not old," said the fir-tree; "there are many who are older than I am."

"Where do you come from? and what do you know?" asked the mice, who were full of curiosity. "Have you seen the most beautiful places in the world, and can you tell us all about them? and have you been in the storeroom, where cheeses lie on the shelf, and hams hang from the ceiling? One can run about on tallow candles there, and go in thin and come out fat."

"I know nothing of that place," said the fir-tree, "but I know the wood where the sun shines and all the birds sing." And then the tree told the little mice all about its youth. They had never heard such an account in their lives; and after they had listened to it attentively, they said, "What a number of things you have seen! you must have been very happy."

"Happy!" exclaimed the fir-tree, and then as he reflected upon what he had been telling them, he said, "Ah, yes! after all, those were happy days." But when he went on and related all about Christmas-eve, and how he had been dressed up with cakes and lights, the mice said, "How happy you must have been, you old fir-tree!"

"I am not old at all," replied the tree, "I only came from the forest this winter; I am now checked in my growth."

"What splendid stories you can relate!" said the little mice. And the next night four other mice came with them to hear what the tree had to tell. The more he talked the more he remembered, and then he thought to himself, "Those were happy days, but they may come again. Humpty Dumpty fell downstairs, and yet he married the princess; perhaps I may marry a princess too." And the fir-tree thought of the pretty little birch tree that grew in the forest, which was to him a real beautiful princess.

"Who is Humpty Dumpty?" asked the little mice. And then the tree related the whole story; he could remember every single word, and the little mice were so delighted with it, that they were ready to jump to the top of the tree. The next night a great many more mice made their appearance, and on Sunday two rats came with them; but they said, it was not a pretty story at all, and the little mice were very sorry, for it made them also think less of it.

"Do you know only one story?" asked the rats.

"Only one," replied the fir-tree; "I heard it on the happiest evening in my life; but I did not know I was so happy at that time."

"We think it is a very miserable story," said the rats. Don't you know any story about bacon, or tallow in the storeroom?"

"No," replied the tree.

"Many thanks to you then," replied the rats, and they marched off.

The little mice also kept away after this, and the tree sighed and said, "It was very pleasant when the merry little mice sat round me and listened while I talked. Now that is all past too. However, I shall consider myself happy when some one comes to take me out of this place." But would this ever happen? Yes; one morning people came to clear out the garret, the boxes were packed away, and the tree was pulled out of the corner, and thrown roughly on the garret floor; then the servant dragged it out upon the staircase where the daylight shone. "Now life is beginning again," said the tree, rejoicing in the sunshine and fresh air. Then it was carried downstairs

and taken into the courtyard so quickly, that it forgot to think
of itself, and could only look about, there was so much to be
seen. The court was close to a garden, where everything looked
blooming. Fresh and fragrant roses hung over the little palings.
The lindentrees were in blossom; while the swallows flew here
and there, crying, "Twit, twit, twit, my mate is coming," but
it was not the fir-tree they meant. "Now I shall live," cried the
tree, joyfully spreading out its branches; but alas! they were
all withered and yellow, and it lay in a corner amongst weeds
and nettles. The star of gold paper still stuck in the top of the
tree and glittered in the sunshine. In the same courtyard two
of the merry children were playing who had danced round the
tree at Christmas, and had been so happy. The youngest saw
the gilded star, and ran and pulled it off the tree. "Look what
is sticking to the old ugly fir-tree," said the child, treading on
the branches till they crackled under his boots. And the tree
saw all the fresh bright flowers in the garden, and then looked
at itself, and wished it had remained in the dark corner of the
garret. It thought of its fresh youth in the forest, of the merry
Christmas evening, and of the little mice who had listened to
the story of "Humpty Dumpty." "Past! past!" said the old tree.
"Oh, had I but enjoyed myself while I could have done so! but
now it is too late." Then a lad came and chopped the tree into
small pieces, till a large bundle lay in a heap on the ground.
The pieces were placed in a fire under the copper, and they
quickly blazed up brightly, while the tree sighed so deeply
that each sigh was like a little pistol-shot. Then the children,
who were at play, came and seated themselves in front of the
fire, and looked at it, and cried, "Pop, pop." But at each "pop,"
which was a deep sigh, the tree was thinking of a summer day
in the forest, or of some winter night there, when the stars
shone brightly; and of Christmas evening, and of "Humpty
Dumpty," the only story it had ever heard or knew how to
relate, till at last it was consumed. The boys still played in the
garden, and the youngest wore the golden star on his breast,
with which the tree had been adorned during the happiest
evening of its existence. Now all was past; the tree's life was
past, and the story also,—for all stories must come to an end
at last.

THE PETERKINS' CHRISTMAS-TREE

Lucretia P. Hale

EARLY IN THE autumn the Peterkins began to prepare for their Christmas-tree. Everything was done in great privacy, as it was to be a surprise to the neighbors, as well as to the rest of the family. Mr. Peterkin had been up to Mr. Bromwick's wood-lot, and, with his consent, selected the tree. Agamemnon went to look at it occasionally after dark, and Solomon John made frequent visits to it mornings, just after sunrise. Mr. Peterkin drove Elizabeth Eliza and her mother that way, and pointed furtively to it with his whip; but none of them ever spoke of it aloud to each other. It was suspected that the little boys had been to see it Wednesday and Saturday afternoons. But they came home with their pockets full of chestnuts, and said nothing about it.

At length Mr. Peterkin had it cut down and brought secretly into the Larkins' barn. A week or two before Christmas a measurement was made of it with Elizabeth Eliza's yard-measure. To Mr. Peterkin's great dismay it was discovered that it was too high to stand in the back parlor.

This fact was brought out at a secret council of Mr. and Mrs. Peterkin, Elizabeth Eliza, and Agamemnon.

Agamemnon suggested that it might be set up slanting; but Mrs. Peterkin was very sure it would make her dizzy, and the candles would drip.

But a brilliant idea came to Mr. Peterkin. He proposed that the ceiling of the parlor should be raised to make room for the top of the tree.

Elizabeth Eliza thought the space would need to be quite large. It must not be like a small box, or you could not see the tree.

"Yes," said Mr. Peterkin, "I should have the ceiling lifted all across the room; the effect would be finer."

Elizabeth Eliza objected to having the whole ceiling raised, because her room was over the back parlor, and she would have no floor while the alteration was going on, which would be very awkward. Besides, her room was not very high now, and, if the floor were raised, perhaps she could not walk in it upright.

Mr. Peterkin explained that he didn't propose altering the whole ceiling, but to lift up a ridge across the room at the back part where the tree was to stand. This would make a hump, to be sure, in Elizabeth Eliza's room; but it would go across the whole room.

Elizabeth Eliza said she would not mind that. It would be like the cuddy thing that comes up on the deck of a ship, that you sit against, only here you would not have the sea-sickness. She thought she should like it, for a rarity. She might use it for a divan.

Mrs. Peterkin thought it would come in the worn place of the carpet, and might be a convenience in making the carpet over.

Agamemnon was afraid there would be trouble in keeping the matter secret, for it would be a long piece of work for a carpenter; but Mr. Peterkin proposed having the carpenter for a day or two, for a number of other jobs.

One of them was to make all the chairs in the house of the same height, for Mrs. Peterkin had nearly broken her spine by sitting down in a chair that she had supposed was her own rocking-chair, and it had proved to be two inches lower. The little boys were now large enough to sit in any chair; so a medium was fixed upon to satisfy all the family, and the chairs were made uniformly of the same height.

On consulting the carpenter, however, he insisted that the tree could be cut off at the lower end to suit the height of the parlor, and demurred at so great a change as altering the ceiling. But Mr. Peterkin had set his mind upon the improvement, and Elizabeth Eliza had cut her carpet in preparation.

So the folding-doors into the back parlor were closed, and for nearly a fortnight before Christmas there was great litter of fallen plastering, and laths, and chips, and shavings; and Elizabeth Eliza's carpet was taken up, and the furniture had to be changed, and one night she had to sleep at the Bromwicks', for there was a long hole in her floor that might be dangerous.

All this delighted the little boys. They could not understand what was going on. Perhaps they suspected a Christmas-tree, but they did not know why a Christmas-tree should have so many chips, and were still more astonished at the hump that appeared in Elizabeth Eliza's room. It must be a Christmas present, or else the tree in a box.

Some aunts and uncles, too, arrived a day or two before Christmas, with some small cousins. These cousins occupied the attention of the little boys, and there was a great deal of whispering and mystery, behind doors, and under the stairs, and in the corners of the entry.

Solomon John was busy, privately making some candles for the tree. He had been collecting some bayberries, as he understood they made very nice candles, so that it would not be necessary to buy any.

The elders of the family never all went into the back parlor together, and all tried not to see what was going on. Mrs. Peterkin would go in with Solomon John, or Mr. Peterkin with Elizabeth Eliza, or Elizabeth Eliza and Agamemnon and Solomon John. The little boys and the small cousins were never allowed even to look inside the room.

Elizabeth Eliza meanwhile went into town a number of times. She wanted to consult Amanda as to how much ice-cream they should need, and whether they could make it at home, as they had cream and ice. She was pretty busy in her own room; the furniture had to be changed, and the carpet altered. The "hump" was higher than she expected. There was danger of bumping her own head whenever she crossed it. She had to nail some padding on the ceiling for fear of accidents.

The afternoon before Christmas, Elizabeth Eliza, Solomon John, and their father collected in the back parlor for a council. The carpenters had done their work, and the tree stood at its full height at the back of the room, the top stretching up into the space arranged for it. All the chips and shavings were cleared away, and it stood on a neat box.

But what were they to put upon the tree?

Solomon John had brought in his supply of candles; but they proved to be very "stringy" and very few of them. It was strange how many bayberries it took to make a few candles! The little boys had helped him, and he had gathered as much as a bushel of bayberries. He had put them in water, and skimmed off the wax, according to the directions; but there was so little wax!

Solomon John had given the little boys some of the bits sawed off from the legs of the chairs. He had suggested that they should cover them with gilt paper, to answer for gilt apples, without telling them what they were for.

These apples, a little blunt at the end, and the candles, were all they had for the tree!

After all her trips into town Elizabeth Eliza had forgotten to bring anything for it.

"I thought of candies and sugar-plums," she said; "but I concluded if we made caramels ourselves we should not need them. But, then, we have not made caramels. The fact is, that day my head was full of my carpet. I had bumped it pretty badly, too."

Mr. Peterkin wished he had taken, instead of a fir-tree, an apple-tree he had seen in October, full of red fruit.

"But the leaves would have fallen off by this time," said Elizabeth Eliza.

"And the apples, too," said Solomon John.

"It is odd I should have forgotten, that day I went in on purpose to get the things," said Elizabeth Eliza, musingly. "But I went from shop to shop, and didn't know exactly what to get. I saw a great many gilt things for Christmas-trees; but I knew the little boys were making the gilt apples; there were plenty of candles in the shops, but I knew Solomon John was making the candles."

Mr. Peterkin thought it was quite natural.

Solomon John wondered if it were too late for them to go into town now.

Elizabeth Eliza could not go in the next morning, for there

was to be a grand Christmas dinner, and Mr. Peterkin could not be spared, and Solomon John was sure he and Agamemnon would not know what to buy. Besides, they would want to try the candles to-night.

Mr. Peterkin asked if the presents everybody had been preparing would not answer. But Elizabeth Eliza knew they would be too heavy.

A gloom came over the room. There was only a flickering gleam from one of Solomon John's candles that he had lighted by way of trial.

Solomon John again proposed going into town. He lighted a match to examine the newspaper about the trains. There were plenty of trains coming out at that hour, but none going in except a very late one. That would not leave time to do anything and come back.

"We could go in, Elizabeth Eliza and I," said Solomon John, "but we should not have time to buy anything."

Agamemnon was summoned in. Mrs. Peterkin was entertaining the uncles and aunts in the front parlor. Agamemnon wished there was time to study up something about electric lights. If they could only have a calcium light! Solomon John's candle sputtered and went out.

At this moment there was a loud knocking at the front door. The little boys, and the small cousins, and the uncles and aunts, and Mrs. Peterkin, hastened to see what was the matter.

The uncles and aunts thought somebody's house must be on fire. The door was opened, and there was a man, white with flakes, for it was beginning to snow, and he was pulling in a large box.

Mrs. Peterkin supposed it contained some of Elizabeth Eliza's purchases, so she ordered it to be pushed into the back parlor, and hastily called back her guests and the little boys into the other room. The little boys and the small cousins were sure they had seen Santa Claus himself.

Mr. Peterkin lighted the gas. The box was addressed to Elizabeth Eliza. It was from the lady from Philadelphia! She had gathered a hint from Elizabeth Eliza's letters that there was to be a Christmas-tree, and had filled this box with all that would be needed.

It was opened directly. There was every kind of gilt hanging-thing, from gilt pea-pods to butterflies on springs. There were shining flags and lanterns, and birdcages, and nests with birds sitting on them, baskets of fruit, gilt apples and bunches of grapes, and, at the bottom of the whole, a large box of candles and a box of Philadelphia bonbons!

Elizabeth Eliza and Solomon John could scarcely keep from screaming. The little boys and the small cousins knocked on the folding-doors to ask what was the matter.

Hastily Mr. Peterkin and the rest took out the things and hung them on the tree, and put on the candles.

When all was done, it looked so well that Mr. Peterkin exclaimed:—

"Let us light the candles now, and send to invite all the neighbors to-night, and have the tree on Christmas Eve!"

And so it was that the Peterkins had their Christmas-tree the day before, and on Christmas night could go and visit their neighbors.

A STAR FOR HANSI

Marguerite Vance

SOPHIE IS A friendly name. You cannot think that a little girl to whom it belonged would sulk, or refuse to answer to "How do you do?" or take the largest currant muffin.

Sophie Ebbert, who lived in the large, lemon-colored house behind the very high green hedge, was just the little girl to be called by a friendly name. Her eyes were gray, and a dimple near the corner of the left one gave to her face when she smiled what Grossmutter called her "twinkly look." When Sophie smiled—and she did very often—you thought of hidden fairy lights shining from those merry twinkly eyes. Sophie's cheeks were red and round as snow apples, and her brown hair, in two neat, short pigtails, bobbed across her shoulders.

Sometimes they were tied with blue ribbons, and sometimes with red, but on important days, or when there were guests, plaid ribbons, red and blue and gold all together, finished the ends of the fat brown braids.

One of the things that always made Sophie happy was that her birthday—and this time it had been her eighth—came just a week before Christmas when one was growing a little impatient for the great day itself to come. A birthday, though not so important, did a great deal to make a pleasant break in the time of waiting.

Today, however, was one of the very rare times when the "twinkly look" was gone and even the brave plaid bows on her braids drooped.

It was Sunday afternoon. Snow drifted softly down on the

238

garden. The bushes looked like huge white frosted cakes, the
pine trees like the sugar trees in the candy shops, which would
stand on Christmas dinner tables next week. Inside, the lamps
had not been lighted, but from the hearth a pink warm light
stole out to touch the edges of things. Sophie watched the
white snowflakes lose themselves in the gray twilight, and
sighed. Grossmutter closed her book and lighted the lamp—
the one with the pink china shade. Then she came and stood
beside Sophie.

"What is it, Liebchen?" she asked. "You are quiet today
and just now you sighed much too deeply for a little girl just
halfway between her birthday party and Christmas. What is
it?"

"Nothing—" began Sophie, and then, before she could stop
them, big tears were sliding down her cheeks and Grossmutter
was wiping them with her handkerchief, which smelled of
lavender and spice.

"Come, come, tell me what is troubling you, little child.
Maybe I can help. Here on my lap—come."

She drew Sophie onto her lap and listened while the little
story was told.

"I had saved my allowance to buy Mother and Father,
and you and Peter, Christmas gifts," she began. "I got Peter's
boat, and Father's pencil, and—and your gift. The man in the
perfume shop has a little bottle shaped like a green lantern.
It is filled with the cologne Mother likes. He is saving it for
me. I had enough money to buy it, and Father was going to
take me to town tomorrow afternoon to get it—and now—"
Sophie's voice trailed off and stopped.

"And now what?"

"Well—you see, when Karen came for my party last week
we went to the village and—I—I spent all I had left for gingerbread men, and now—" Again the big tears began to slip down
Sophie's cheeks.

Grossmutter looked grave, even with the pink lamp and
the firelight making everything so warm and friendly.

"So you spent all your money on gingerbread men," she
said. "Ach, that is bad, little Sophie, very bad. Now, now,
don't cry so!" for now the tears were coming faster and faster.
"See, I shall tell you the story of the applewood box. Would

you like that?"

Sophie nodded.

"What did it look like?" she asked.

"It was round—round as a chestnut, and just that color. Now listen well.

"Once long ago there stood on the edge of the great Black Forest a beautiful castle. Around it spread its parks where deer and antelope walked softly through the speckled shadows. Beyond the park was the hamlet where lived the people who served the baron of the castle. In their little cottages they lived—woodcutters, shepherds, farmers, the blacksmith, shopkeepers, the schoolteacher, the pastor, the bürgermeister.

"In the little house of the bürgermeister, besides himself there lived his wife and their three children, Tomas, little Hans, and a little girl about your age. And what do you suppose her name was?"

Sophie shook her head, and almost the dimple peeped out.

"I don't know. What was it?"

"Sophie."

"Sophie—like me?"

"Yes, Liebchen, very much like you. I think that other Sophie looked just a little like you too. Tomas was two years older than his sister and four years older than little Hans.

"In all the Black Forest region there was no child just like little Hans. His hair was like pale sunshine caught and rolled into soft curls all over his head. His dark eyes seemed to see faraway places; and when little Hans laughed Tomas put down his whittling and Sophie stopped her knitting the better to listen to so sweet a sound. Little Hans did not play their games, nor did he go with them to tend geese in the swamp. He sat and played quietly in a sunny spot where his chair was placed. Sometimes his father carried him into the woods and he called to the birds in his high sweet voice, by little names he made up for them.

"Sophie and Tomas and their parents all loved one another dearly, but their love for little Hans was quite different. It was as though there must be enough love for Hansi to remember forever and ever.

"Now, though the bürgermeister had his snug cottage, and though his family was clothed and fed, still he was not a rich

A *New England Fireside*, 19th-century American lithograph

Christmas Contrasts, American lithograph by W. St. John Harper, 1884

Roast Goose with Fruit Stuffing, page 288
Whipped Potatoes in Orange Cups, page 291

man, and his children earned whatever they could to buy the little extra things that girls and boys like. Tomas helped the woodcutter gather the lighter branches as they fell under his ax and saw, and tied them in neat, tight bundles. On baking days, when his mother's loaves were ready to be carried to the village oven for baking, he stopped at the cottage of the blacksmith, the tailor, and the doctor, and carried the loaves their wives had set too, and later returned each golden loaf, crusty and hot from the oven, to its owner.

"Sophie crocheted fine lace for the linen pillowcases in the castle and knitted worsted caps and mufflers for the children of the baron. Each morning when she drove her mother's geese to the swamp, she drove the geese of the miller and of the storekeeper too.

"For these little tasks the children received a few coppers. That is how Tomas came to own his jackknife for whittling, and how Sophie had the white knitting needles with tiny roses and violets painted on them.

"One day in early autumn the schoolteacher called Sophie to him and said:

" 'I have something here for you, Sophie, which I hope you will always treasure. Look, it was given me by my teacher when I was your age.'

"He put into Sophie's hands a small round box."

"Was it the applewood box, Grossmutter?"

"Yes, exactly, and this is what he said: 'This little box is only for a careful child, and I believe you are that. There is a coin in it now. See that there is at least one coin, however small, in it at all times. There is only one exception to this rule. When your heart quite plainly says, "Now, now is the time to spend the last coin," then spend it gladly. Otherwise, remember, always keep at least one coin in the box. It will call in others. When you have grown to be an old lady, search well for another careful child and pass the box on to him or her with this same advice.'

"So he gave the applewood box to the happy little girl, and—"

"And did it have a coin in it?"

"Yes, a pfennig; and Sophie promised that she would never let the little box be empty unless her heart quite plainly said,

'Now, now is the time to spend the last coin.'

"She was so proud of her new prize that she ran home through the woods and burst in on her mother, who was spinning beside the fire."

"What did Tomas and little Hans say?"

"Tomas was away in the woods with the woodcutter, but little Hans held the box against his cheek and laughed softly and said, 'It is smooth and cool like the moon.'

"The days flew and Sophie worked very diligently at all the tasks at home, at school, and at those other tasks which brought coins to the little box.

"One day a peddler came to the village with strange and beautiful toys from across the Russian border—little carved squirrels that climbed a string, small tops of many colors, music boxes that played wild, sweet tunes that seemed to come from faraway lovely places behind the snowy sunset. Tomas selected a set of tops, spent his last coin, and grieved when evening came and his tops were broken. Sophie knew that little Hans would have loved a music box, but as he had not seen ANY of the toys, she carried the prettiest brown squirrel home to him instead and shared his fun as he watched it run up and down the string. In the applewood box there was still the last coin to begin fresh saving for the other useful and amusing things.

"Again, when the family all went to the fair in the early winter, Sophie was tempted. There was the man selling cardamon cakes, another selling chocolate and herb tea delicately spiced. In one tent a big black bear danced and boxed with his trainer; in another a troupe of dwarfs tumbled and did amusing tricks. Tomas spent his last coin, poor lad, yet saw only half that he wanted. Sophie chose a cardamon cake and saw the dancing bear, and went home happy, with a cake for little Hans, and a coin still rattling in the applewood box. More lace to be crocheted, more cold mornings helping with the geese and chickens, and soon there would be more coins to make a gay tinkling in the box.

"Soon it was time for the lovely Christmas festival. Mother baked pfeffernüsse and springerle until the little cottage was sweet with spicy fragrance. Father brought in fresh wood and laid pine cones between the kindling to make a more snapping

Christmas fire while he told the children stories of other Christmases in the Black Forest.

"One evening he told the story of the first Christmas and how a great, beautiful, silver star had led the way to the baby Jesus. Little Hans was in his arms, listening to the story. His sunny hair made a great splash of gold against his father's coat.

" 'Did they find him, Father?' he asked.

" 'Of course,' Father answered; 'they just followed where the star led, and there at last they found the Child, and he held out his little arms to them.'

"The other children did not say anything, but little Hans smiled.

" 'That was nice,' he said, 'nice.'

"The next day was Christmas Eve, so Sophie and Tomas took their coins and went to the village, and what fun they had! A bit of beeswax for Mother's ironingboard, a new goose quill for Father's writing pad, a jumping jack and a stick of candy for little Hans. For each other they chose a collection of small things which, of course, they would not show until the tree was lighted after sunset. Hugging their packages, they ran home through the twilight, hoping Mother had not finished trimming the tree and placing the little manger beneath it."

"But, was it really, truly, a manger, Grossmutter?"

"Yes, a tiny stable, and just inside, a manger filled with real hay for the child Jesus to lie upon. And then grouped all around were the figures of Mary and Joseph and the Wise Men and shepherds—all made of wax.

"Tomas ran to hide his packages and Sophie threw off her hood and cape and went to little Hans. He was not in his chair by the window this evening, but in his little bed, for he was tired. So Sophie put the lumpy jumping jack in its brown wrapping on the bed beside him.

" 'Guess what Sophie brought for you, Hansi,' she said, and waited while his fingers moved over the stiff paper. Never, never would he guess!

" 'Is it—Sophie, is it—a star?' he whispered at last, and his own dark eyes were like stars.

"Sophie's heart sank. A jumping jack! and he had wanted a star! For a few pfennigs a beautiful star, all shimmering and

silvery white, could be had in a shop at the other end of the village! But she had spent all her money—all but—! Suddenly Sophie straightened up. There was that last coin which must never be touched unless quite plainly her heart said, 'Now, now is the time to spend the last coin,' and now her heart spoke.

"She smiled down at little Hans, and he smiled happily back.

" 'Is it—is it truly a star?' he asked again; very softly.

"Sophie kissed his fingers resting on the package.

" 'Just you wait, Hansi, until Sophie comes back,' she whispered, and taking the jumping jack, she ran to the wood-shed, where Tomas was helping Father with the little tree for which Mother was clearing a space on the table.

" 'Hide this with your other things, Tomas,' she said. 'I'm going to run back to the village. I'll not be gone long—I'll hurry.'

"She threw on her cape, and holding the applewood box tightly, ran through the woods to the village, thinking she never had heard anything more comforting than the sound of the coin rattling away merrily in the little box as she ran. The shopkeeper smiled at her serious face.

" 'A star for little Hansi, eh?' he exclaimed. Together they looked over the rows of beautiful white-and-silver stars hanging like a sparkling girdle around the shop walls, and at last the shopkeeper took down the shiniest one he had and held it out to her.

" 'There,' he said, 'there is the brightest star in the shop, and little Hans is just the child it was meant to shine for. Be sure to wish him a good Christmas for me, eh?'

"Sophie gave him her last coin happily, and holding the star carefully under her cape, sped back over the snow to the cottage at the edge of the wood.

"Now the sun had set and from the windows of the bürger-meister's little house a warm welcoming light streamed out, making a gay pattern on the snow.

" 'The whole house seems to glow,' thought Sophie, hurry-ing toward it, 'as though it were full of lovely stars!'

"Softly she opened the door, and softly—not knowing why—hurried through the passage. At the door of the family room she stopped. There was a hush in the room—as when a bird stops singing or a bubbling fountain ceases to play.

"The little tree standing on the table shone quietly in the soft white light of its candles. Before it, all together, was the family—Mother, Father, Tomas, and in Father's arms little Hans. Mother knelt beside Father's chair, with her cheek against Hansi's curls, and Sophie could see that she had forgotten Father and Tomas and even Christmas—everything but little Hans. Father was telling the Christmas story again, very slowly, very carefully, so that even if one were tired and drowsy, still one could hear and understand.

" 'They followed where the star led,' Father said, 'and there at last—'

"Little Hans opened his eyes. He saw Sophie. He smiled all over his little face.

" 'Look, Hansi,' she whispered, and slid to her knees before Father's chair and held up the great quivering silver star.

" 'For me! For me!' the little boy said softly, and held out his hands and laughed; and looking at his Christmas star, he fell asleep there before the baby Christ in the manger, who held out his little arms to him. And Sophie knew she had done well to take the last coin from the applewood box. And that is the end of the story, Liebchen."

Sophie stirred.

"Tell some more," she begged. "Did little Hans wake up after awhile and see his star again? and did Sophie grow up? and what did she do with the box?"

Grossmutter smiled gently.

"Little Hans woke up—yes, and never was tired any more. Sophie grew up, and what do you suppose she did with the applewood box? Jump down, dear; I am going to show you something."

Grossmutter went to her room, and in a moment she was back, carrying a small object in her hands.

"This is from one Sophie to another," she said, smiling— "to you."

Sophie could not believe her eyes, for there in her hands was a small, round, dark box of polished wood!

"Is it—oh, Grossmutter, IS IT THE APPLEWOOD BOX?" Sophie's dimple was back and so was the "twinkly look."

Grossmutter nodded.

"Then are you—were you—that Sophie?"

Again Grossmutter nodded, or tried to, because Sophie's arms were around her neck in a bear hug, and her flushed round cheek pressed so tightly to Grossmutter's that she scarcely could move.

"Oh, it was the loveliest, LOVELIEST story, Grossmutter!" she said, "and I'll be so proud of my box!"

"Then see, child; let us open it."

Carefully Sophie took off the polished lid. The box was quite filled with coins.

"Now then," Grossmutter asked, "how much shall we need to buy the lantern filled with cologne?"

Sophie's dimple disappeared.

"Fifty cents," she answered, and just saying it made it sound twice as much.

Grossmutter emptied the coins on the table and together they counted them.

"Just exactly fifty pennies!" Grossmutter beamed. Sophie shrieked with glee.

"Goody! Goody!" she cried. "Now in the morning the first thing Father and I can go to town and buy the lantern! Fifty cents is exactly what I needed and now I have it! I'm so happy! So happy!" She danced around the room. Then suddenly she noticed that Grossmutter was looking at her a little strangely, a little sadly.

"I am afraid," she said, "that my little Sophie does not remember the most important part of all in the story of the box. What about the last coin?"

Sophie stopped short in her dance.

"Oh—I forgot," she said. "I forgot."

"When does Father give you your next allowance?"

"Tomorrow. Peter and I get it every Monday morning."

"Well, then—?"

"Oh, I see!" The dimple came twinkling out again. "I see! Look, Grossmutter, I'll leave five pennies instead of only one in the box. That will leave forty-five pennies I can keep out. Then tomorrow I'll add five pennies from my allowance, and that will give me enough to buy the lantern and still leave coins in the box to 'call in others,' as the schoolteacher said when he gave the box to So—I mean to you."

Grossmutter patted her cheek.

"That is my little Sophie," she said. "That is being a 'careful child,' a worthy owner of the applewood box."

So on Christmas Eve, tucked in her snug bed, Sophie thought happily of Mother's cologne lantern hanging bravely on the tree downstairs. Above, the Christmas stars shone softly down, and one larger, brighter than the others, she thought must look very like the one the other Sophie had brought to little Hans on that long-ago Christmas Eve in the Black Forest. As she drifted into happy Christmas dreams she made a solemn promise always to guard her last coin carefully, but to spend it gladly, thankfully, when her heart quite plainly said, "Now, now is the time."

A CHRISTMAS CAROL

The Christ Child lay on Mary's lap,
His hair was like a light.
(O weary, weary were the world,
But here is all aright.)

The Christ Child lay on Mary's breast,
His hair was like a star.
(O stern and cunning are the Kings,
But here the true hearts are.)

The Christ Child lay on Mary's heart,
His hair was like a fire.
(O weary, weary is the world,
But here the world's desire.)

The Christ Child stood at Mary's knee,
His hair was like a crown,
And all the flowers looked up at Him
And all the stars looked down.

G. K. CHESTERTON

THE SMALL ONE

Charles Tazewell

THE SAME WINTER sun that dances on the northern snow
sprawls indolently at ease in the thick white dust of El
Camino del Norte, Old Mexico. This is the hour of siesta, and
the road belongs to the dust devils and the little brown lizards,
and lying here in the shade of a pepper tree, a man, and in
this case, an old padre, can drowse and dream the strangest
stories ever dreamed.

If only that bee would stop buzzing! Or is it a hornet?

"Estúpido!"

Oh, no! It's only a small boy berating a disreputable-
looking donkey.

"A donkey! A donkey, you call yourself, Estúpido! A fine
animal with a stout leg on each corner, a handsome, service-
able tail to shoo off the flies and two beautiful ears to point
the way you are going, and what do you do with these things
the good God has given you? Nothing at all!"

"Pablo!" called the padre.

"You are a disgrace to all the donkeys of Mexico!"

"Pablo!"

"¿Sí ¡Oh, buenos días, padre! I did not see you, I—"

"Look, it's much too hot for all that commotion."

"But this donkey—"

"What's he done?"

"He has done nothing, but nothing!"

"Nothing?"

"Nothing is all he ever wants to do! Here it is but two

248

days before Christmas, when a load of wood could be sold in the village to buy gifts and a candle, but does he care? *No.*"

"Well, there's no use getting upset about it. A donkey's a donkey. They're all alike."

"*Sí*, ungrateful and stubborn."

"Oh, no—oh, no! You're wrong there, Pablo."

"Yes, but—"

"I know, yes, everybody says they are, and they beat them and curse them and call them stupid. The trouble is, they don't know the truth about little donkeys."

"No? And what is the truth?"

"Why, it's not stubbornness at all! No, sir! Why, it's pride that makes donkeys so—well, kind of aloof."

"Aloof?"

"That's right. Sun, rain, good luck, bad luck, what does it matter? Their pride is a shield against anything that man or the elements can do to them."

"I don't see what a donkey has to be proud of."

"Oh, he has! Yes, indeed! You see a long, long time ago, a great honor came to one of them, an honor so great that it lifted him and all the other donkeys to a place that you or I or all the world might envy."

"I do not envy this donkey."

"Well, you should. Do you know why?"

"Why?"

"Because of all animals and of all men, he's already fulfilled his destiny."

"What is destiny?"

"Well—it's the reason for people being born—or a thing created. Come on, bring your donkey over here in the shade and I'll tell you about it."

"*Sí, sí, señor.* Come on, Cupido!" Pablo tugged on the rope.

"Listen! Listen, Pablo! Do you hear that? Only a small donkey can make that sound with his hoofs on the stones of the road! Sit down, and I will tell you why that is!

"You see, Pablo, once upon a Christmas Eve there was a small donkey. He was fourteen unhappy years old. He'd worked hard and long for at least fourteen masters."

"He was a valuable animal, *señor?*"

"Oh, no, he wasn't much to look at. He was battered and scarred, and his tail was like a piece of rope, unraveled down at the end. Yes—and one of his ears stood straight up like a cactus plant, but the other hung down like a wilted cabbage leaf. And on top of that, his off hind leg had a limp."

"What was his name?" asked Pablo.

"They just called him the Small One."

"Small One?"

"That's right. His latest master was a woodcutter who also owned four younger, and therefore stronger, donkeys."

"Was the woodcutter kind to him?"

"His son was. It was this boy who took care of Small One; made sure there was straw for his bed, and that the loads weren't too heavy for Small One's back."

"I guess the boy and the old donkey were what we call *amigos.*"

"Very close *amigos!* But one morning the woodcutter called his son to him and he said: 'Son, I want you to take this donkey, the one you call Small One, to a shop just inside the town gates. They'll give you a piece of silver in exchange for the animal.'"

"'Do you mean?' said the boy in horror—'You don't mean —you're going to sell Small One?'

"'He can no longer do his share of the work.'

"'Yes, but—'

"'Even when carrying half the load of the other donkeys, his worn-out legs tremble and his sides heave like a bellows.'

"'But he'll be strong as the others soon,' pleaded the boy. 'Just give him a few weeks!'

"'An old donkey is of no use! One day he'll drop dead on us up in the hills, a total loss.'

"'Yes, but he's mine—'

"'The shop you will take him to is the second on the left as you pass through the town gates.'

"'But—but the second shop is the tanner's—'

"'His hide may be old, but it'll make good leather,' growled the father.

"'But you can't do that to him!' wept the boy. 'He's worked hard! He's been faithful!'

"'Come now, no crying over a miserable, old donkey!'

ordered the father. 'Hurry now, be off with you! Yes, and take good care not to lose that piece of silver on the way home!'

"Well, that small boy and his small donkey made a pretty sorrowful picture as they traveled along the road to town. People along the way wondered why the boy was crying. You see, they couldn't know that the Small One's hoofs on the road were beating out the words,

"'Going to the tanner's,'

"'Going to the tanner's.'

"It was early afternoon when the small boy and the small donkey went through the great town gates. It was market day and all at once the boy remembered there was a horse market in the square! Why, if he could sell Small One to some new and kind master, the little donkey wouldn't be killed and yet his father would still have the piece of silver!

"Holding tight to Small One's rope, and with his face streaked with dust and tears, the boy hurried to the horse market and pushed his way to the platform of the sweating, shouting auctioneer.

"'Seventy is the bid! Seventy for a mare so fine that naught but princes ever sat on her back. Strong of limb, sound of wind. Who'll make it seventy-one? Look at that proud head. See that flowing mane. Do I hear seventy-one? Seventy once, seventy twice, sold for seventy pieces of silver! A fine bargain, my friend! Now, who has the next animal? Step up, please.'

"'Please, sir,' the boy tugged on his rope, 'would you try to sell this small donkey?'

"'Go 'way, boy,' growled the auctioneer.

"'He's a very fine animal,' insisted the boy, 'and not nearly as old as he looks!'

"'I told you to go away!'

"'He's terribly strong, and eats very little!'

"'This is a horse market! We've no time to waste on donkeys!'

"'But—' the boy's eyes pleaded—'but a small donkey would take such a small time!'

"'All right!' laughed the auctioneer, 'all right, my boy, if you insist! My friends, a great bargain I have to offer you! The proud owner terms it a donkey, but being truthful, I would call it an animated pile of shaking bones!'

"The crowd roared with laughter.

" 'No, he isn't!' cried the boy. 'He's strong!'

" 'Observe how the moths have been at the hide, and the tail—*is* it a tail? I think it's the stub of a broom, worn out from sweeping the courtyard!'

" 'Don't say those things about him!' protested the boy over the howls of the crowd.

" 'Yes, a true museum piece, my friends, moldy with age and loose in the joints!'

" 'He's not!' cried the boy over the jeering laughter, 'he's not like that at all!'

" 'Ah, but we mustn't laugh, my friends, because its owner assures me that this—animal—is fine enough to share a stall with the king's horses.'

" 'You can't make fun of him like that!' wept the boy. 'He's a fine donkey, and he does belong in a king's stable! Yes, and maybe someday, that's where he'll be!'

" 'All right, all right, boy,' said the auctioneer, 'take your donkey and move along! We've got business to attend to! And now, my friends, that we've had our fun and disposed of the king's donkey, I have another animal here—'

"The little boy and the little donkey left the market place. The afternoon was slipping by and the long shadows on the

street told him that before long he'd have to start for home, and when he got there he must have the piece of silver to give to his father.

"He tried stopping people along the street. He went from door to door, but no one in all the town seemed to want to buy a small, tired donkey. The sun was going down when he got back to the great town gates. His hot tears fell on the Small One's back, and the little donkey's head drooped so low that his limp ear almost touched the ground. And then, just as the boy was leading Small One up the path to the tanner's door, a voice spoke to him.

" 'My son—'

" 'Yes? Yes, sir?' The boy turned a tear-stained face toward a poorly dressed traveler.

" 'I have a great favor to ask of you.' The man laid a hand on Small One's back. 'Are you the owner of this small donkey?'

" 'Oh, yes, sir!' said the boy anxiously.

" 'I have a long journey to make. My wife is not well. I have great need of a strong and gentle animal to carry her safely.'

" 'Oh, Small One is very strong and very trustworthy!' the boy said eagerly.

" 'I can see that,' smiled the man. 'Would you sell him to me?'

" 'Oh, yes, sir, and the price is only one piece of silver!'

" 'One piece of silver?'

" 'Is—is that too much?' the boy asked fearfully.

" 'Oh, no,' smiled the man, 'a very reasonable price for such a beautiful animal.'

" 'Well,' the boy looked at his friend, 'I—I guess he's not really beautiful, but he's *good*.'

" 'Yes, I believe you.' The man drew a very flat purse from his robe. 'I'll be kind to him, I promise you. Here's your piece of silver. Come, Small One.'

" 'Do you mind'—the boy's voice was choked with the tears of parting. 'Do you mind if I come as far as the town gate? You see, Small One and I—'

" 'Not at all. You'll want to say good-by to him, of course. Come along—you can do that while I see my wife safely on his back.' The man led the little donkey to where a woman

waited in the shadow of the great town gates.

" 'Good-by, Small One,' whispered the boy. 'It isn't forever, you know. When I grow up and earn many pieces of silver, I'll buy you back. Won't that be wonderful, Small One?'

" 'All right, my son,' said the man softly. 'Come, Small One—'

" 'Wait, traveler!' called the guard of the town gate.

" 'Yes, soldier?' the man and the small donkey with the woman on his back halted.

" 'I must make out the record before you can pass through the town gates. Who are you?'

" 'My name is Joseph.'

" 'And your wife?'

" 'They call her Mary.'

" 'Your destination?'

" 'Bethlehem.'

" 'Pass, traveler.'

" 'Come, Small One.' The man, the woman, and the small donkey moved onward into the gathering twilight.

" 'Good-by, Small One,' called the boy. 'Be very gentle and sure of foot and carry her safely to Bethlehem.'

"And so, the Small One passed through the town gates and plodded the many weary miles to Bethlehem, and there in a stable, which became a King's stable, he saw a King born, a King of men, of centuries, of life, of death. Yes, and the Small One's tired old eyes saw the shepherds and the Wise Men, who came to pay homage to his small Master, and he heard the voices of angels rejoicing, and the notes that they sang were the very same ones his own hoofs had rung out on the stones of the road.

"And then it came to pass, that all those who had laughed at his ragged coat and his limping gait, and his drooping ear—they all envied the Small One—for he had become a part of a great miracle.

"Oh, this was a long, long time ago, but even today, all small donkeys stand and dream—especially at Christmas time—dream of the Small One—the Small One of Bethlehem!"

And so, this reiterates the ancient Christmas theme: that humble service may reap rich reward, and that in strange ways, the meek do inherit the earth.

CHRISTMAS AMONG THE ANIMALS

Old Dutch Tale

MARY HELD HER newborn baby in her arms. She was happy, but troubled too. It was cold in the stable, and there was a nasty draft. She pressed her little son against her heart and wished that her love for him could warm his cold little body.

Worried, she glanced at the big holes in the roof. Through the largest of these a beautiful flickering star looked down, the star which later was to show the way to the shepherds and the Three Magi. But Mary did not know about this yet. She was a mother, worried about her little baby, and waiting for Joseph, who had gone out to borrow some fire.

Tenderly cradling her little son in her arms, she looked around at the animals whose home she shared: an ox, a mule, a horse, and a goat. It was obvious that the animals regarded her as an intruder, except perhaps for the ox: he looked kind of friendly, sometimes glancing behind him to a corner where his sister, the cow, was giving birth to a little calf.

Mary was looking for a tiny place in which to put her son to sleep, but all she saw was the hard, rough ground, the heavy beams and dark corners full of spider webs. Maybe she could use the animals' manger. She filled it with some hay and laid her baby down. Then she tore off part of her dress to cover him and sat down quietly beside him, now and then reaching for his little feet, to see if they were still warm.

The animals had been watching this for some time and the goat was working herself into a rage. Loudly bleating, she tried to set the others against the human beings. Such manners!

255

Intruding upon their privacy, and taking their manger and their food too! Pretty soon the horse and the mule began to agree with the goat; they pounded the floor with their hoofs and cast malicious glances at the little group of humans. Mary noticed it and felt the animals were justified. She got up and began to gather the hay which lay all over the stable floor. It was a difficult task but she felt that it was her duty, and finally she had assembled a whole lot of it.

But the big hungry horse thought that it wasn't enough. Full of contempt, he stamped his hoofs on the heap of hay, snorted indignantly, and tossed his mane and tail in anger. What he wanted was that delicious bit of hay right under the little boy in the manger. He pushed the mule out of his way and began to nibble greedily.

Poor Mary was desperate. She took her baby in her arms again and began to pray. Suddenly she heard a sound on the roof, and when she looked up—lo!—there was a beautiful angel looking down at her through the biggest hole in the roof. He addressed the horse: "You greedy and intolerant animal! Henceforth you and your offspring shall serve and carry human beings. You are larger and more powerful than they are, but you will be their humble servant." And so it came to pass.

Meanwhile the ox felt sorry for Mary and her infant, and he also wanted to make up for what his friend had done. With his heavy hoofs he scraped some hay together for a bed and blew his warm breath comfortingly over the cold little body. He whispered in Mary's ear that his sister, the cow, wished to give her little calf to her son for a playmate.

Oh, how grateful was Mary! She looked up and—lo!— there was the angel again, this time peering at the ox through the biggest hole in the roof. "Henceforth," he said, "you and your sister shall eat in peace, and even digest your food four times. And your sister shall have a calf each year and always have plenty of milk." And so it came to pass.

The mule had listened to all these prophecies but didn't really know whether to believe them or not. It was all rather silly, he thought. He had his own opinion, and very bad manners. Suddenly he began to bray stupidly. When Mary was thanking the ox for his kindness, he snatched the hay away from under the baby and began to eat rapidly, while moving

Sugar Cookies, page 299

Gingerbread Cookies, page 298

his long ears up and down.

But before Mary could do anything to prevent him—lo!—there was the angel shaking a menacing finger at the mule through the biggest hole in the roof. "Mule," he said, "just for this you and your kind will never have any babies as from this day." And so it came to pass.

One would think that by this time the goat might have learned her lesson and behaved herself. But no, she was stupid and brazen. Still bleating loudly, she rushed through the stable, kicking up her heels and generally making a fool of herself. The little boy began to cry, and Mary didn't know what to do next. And when she looked up at the star shining through the roof—lo!—there was the angel sticking his head through the biggest hole. To this day the goat and her offspring have kept their silly laugh, and their milk has lost its good flavor, so that people don't like to drink it. And so it came to pass.

At long last, peace returned to the stable—wonderful, comforting peace. Joseph returned and brought some fire, the animals stood in awe, and a great and heavenly light shone through the biggest hole in the roof. The little infant fell into an untroubled sleep, and Mary folded her hands in prayer.

This is what happened during the holy night—at least, many people believe it, or at least that is what people in Holland tell one another.

THE GIFT OF THE MAGI

O. Henry

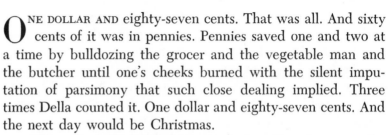

ONE DOLLAR AND eighty-seven cents. That was all. And sixty cents of it was in pennies. Pennies saved one and two at a time by bulldozing the grocer and the vegetable man and the butcher until one's cheeks burned with the silent imputation of parsimony that such close dealing implied. Three times Della counted it. One dollar and eighty-seven cents. And the next day would be Christmas.

There was clearly nothing to do but flop down on the shabby little couch and howl. So Della did it. Which instigates the moral reflection that life is made up of sobs, sniffles, and smiles, with sniffles predominating.

While the mistress of the home is gradually subsiding from the first stage to the second, take a look at the home. A furnished flat at $8 per week. It did not exactly beggar description, but it certainly had that word on the lookout for the mendicancy squad.

In the vestibule below was a letter-box into which no letter would go, and an electric button from which no mortal finger could coax a ring. Also appertaining thereunto was a card bearing the name "Mr. James Dillingham Young."

The "Dillingham" had been flung to the breeze during a former period of prosperity when its possessor was being paid $30 per week. Now, when the income was shrunk to $20, the letters of "Dillingham" looked blurred, as though they were thinking seriously of contracting to a modest and unassuming D. But whenever Mr. James Dillingham Young came home and reached his flat above he was called "Jim" and greatly hugged by Mrs. James Dillingham Young, already introduced to you as Della. Which is all very good.

Della finished her cry and attended to her cheeks with the powder rag. She stood by the window and looked out dully at a gray cat walking a gray fence in a gray backyard. To-morrow would be Christmas Day, and she had only $1.87 with which to buy Jim a present. She had been saving every penny she could for months, with this result. Twenty dollars a week doesn't go far. Expenses had been greater than she had calculated. They always are. Only $1.87 to buy a present for Jim. Her Jim. Many a happy hour she had spent planning for something nice for him. Something fine and rare and sterling —something just a little bit near to being worthy of the honor of being owned by Jim.

There was a pier-glass between the windows of the room. Perhaps you have seen a pier-glass in an $8 flat. A very thin and very agile person may, by observing his reflection in a rapid sequence of longitudinal strips, obtain a fairly accurate conception of his looks. Della, being slender, had mastered the art.

Suddenly she whirled from the window and stood before the glass. Her eyes were shining brilliantly, but her face had lost its color within twenty seconds. Rapidly she pulled down her hair and let it fall to its full length.

Now, there were two possessions of the James Dillingham Youngs in which they both took a mighty pride. One was Jim's gold watch that had been his father's and his grandfather's. The other was Della's hair. Had the Queen of Sheba lived in the flat across the airshaft, Della would have let her hair hang out the window some day to dry just to depreciate Her Majesty's jewels and gifts. Had King Solomon been the janitor, with all his treasures piled up in the basement, Jim would have pulled out his watch every time he passed, just to see him pluck at his beard from envy.

So now Della's beautiful hair fell about her, rippling and shining like a cascade of brown waters. It reached below her knee and made itself almost a garment for her. And then she did it up again nervously and quickly. Once she faltered for a minute and stood still while a tear or two splashed on the worn red carpet.

On went her old brown jacket; on went her old brown hat. With a whirl of skirts and with the brilliant sparkle still in her eyes, she fluttered out the door and down the stairs to the street.

Where she stopped the sign read: "Mme. Sofronie. Hair Goods of All Kinds." One flight up Della ran, and collected herself, panting. Madame, large, too white, chilly, hardly looked the "Sofronie."

"Will you buy my hair?" asked Della.

"I buy hair," said Madame. "Take yer hat off and let's have a sight at the looks of it."

Down rippled the brown cascade.

"Twenty dollars," said Madame, lifting the mass with a practiced hand.

"Give it to me quick," said Della.

Oh, and the next two hours tripped by on rosy wings. Forget the hashed metaphor. She was ransacking the stores for Jim's present.

She found it at last. It surely had been made for Jim and no one else. There was no other like it in any of the stores, and she had turned all of them inside out. It was a platinum fob chain simple and chaste in design, properly proclaiming its value by substance alone and not by meretricious ornamentation—as all good things should do. It was even worthy of The Watch. As soon as she saw it she knew that it must be Jim's. It was like him. Quietness and value—the description applied to both. Twenty-one dollars they took from her for it, and she hurried home with the 87 cents. With that chain on his watch Jim might be properly anxious about the time in any company. Grand as the watch was, he sometimes looked at it on the sly on account of the old leather strap that he used in place of a chain.

When Della reached home her intoxication gave way a little to prudence and reason. She got out her curling irons and lighted the gas and went to work repairing the ravages made by generosity added to love. Which is always a tremendous task, dear friends—a mammoth task.

Within forty minutes her head was covered with tiny, close-lying curls that made her look wonderfully like a truant schoolboy. She looked at her reflection in the mirror long, carefully, and critically.

"If Jim doesn't kill me," she said to herself, "before he takes a second look at me, he'll say I look like a Coney Island chorus girl. But what could I do—oh! what could I do with a dollar and eighty-seven cents?"

At 7 o'clock the coffee was made and the frying-pan was on the back of the stove hot and ready to cook the chops.

Jim was never late. Della doubled the fob chain in her hand and sat on the corner of the table near the door that he always entered. Then she heard his step on the stair away down on the first flight, and she turned white for just a moment. She had a habit of saying little silent prayers about the simplest everyday things, and now she whispered: "Please God, make him think I am still pretty."

The door opened and Jim stepped in and closed it. He looked thin and very serious. Poor fellow, he was only twenty-two—and to be burdened with a family! He needed a new overcoat and he was without gloves.

Jim stopped inside the door, as immovable as a setter at the scent of quail. His eyes were fixed upon Della, and there was an expression in them that she could not read, and it terrified her. It was not anger, nor surprise, nor disapproval, nor horror, nor any of the sentiments that she had been prepared for. He simply stared at her fixedly with that peculiar expression on his face.

Della wriggled off the table and went for him.

"Jim, darling," she cried, "don't look at me that way. I had my hair cut off and sold it because I couldn't have lived through Christmas without giving you a present. It'll grow out again—you won't mind, will you? I just had to do it. My hair grows awfully fast. Say 'Merry Christmas!' Jim, and let's be happy. You don't know what a nice—what a beautiful, nice gift I've got for you."

"You've cut off your hair?" asked Jim, laboriously, as if he had not arrived at that patent fact yet even after the hardest mental labor.

"Cut it off and sold it," said Della. "Don't you like me just as well, anyhow? I'm me without my hair, ain't I?"

Jim looked about the room curiously.

"You say your hair is gone?" he said, with an air almost

of idiocy.

"You needn't look for it," said Della. "It's sold, I tell you —sold and gone, too. It's Christmas Eve, boy. Be good to me, for it went for you. Maybe the hairs of my head were numbered," she went on with a sudden serious sweetness, "but nobody could ever count my love for you. Shall I put the chops on, Jim?"

Out of his trance Jim seemed quickly to wake. He enfolded his Della. For ten seconds let us regard with discreet scrutiny some inconsequential object in the other direction. Eight dollars a week or a million a year—what is the difference? A mathematician or a wit would give you the wrong answer. The magi brought valuable gifts, but that was not among them. This dark assertion will be illuminated later on.

Jim drew a package from his overcoat pocket and threw it upon the table.

"Don't make any mistake, Dell," he said, "about me. I don't think there's anything in the way of a haircut or a shave or a shampoo that could make me like my girl any less. But if you'll unwrap that package you may see why you had me going a while at first."

White fingers and nimble tore at the string and paper. And then an ecstatic scream of joy; and then, alas! a quick feminine change to hysterical tears and wails, necessitating the immediate employment of all the comforting powers of the lord of the flat.

For there lay The Combs—the set of combs, side and back, that Della had worshipped for long in a Broadway window. Beautiful combs, pure tortoiseshell, with jeweled rims —just the shade to wear in the beautiful vanished hair. They were expensive combs, she knew, and her heart had simply craved and yearned over them without the least hope of possession. And now, they were hers, but the tresses that should have adorned the coveted adornments were gone.

But she hugged them to her bosom, and at length she was able to look up with dim eyes and a smile and say: "My hair grows so fast, Jim!"

And then Della leaped up like a little singed cat and cried, "Oh, oh!"

Jim had not yet seen his beautiful present. She held it

out to him eagerly upon her open palm. The dull precious metal seemed to flash with a reflection of her bright and ardent spirit.

"Isn't it a dandy, Jim? I hunted all over town to find it. You'll have to look at the time a hundred times a day now. Give me your watch. I want to see how it looks on it."

Instead of obeying, Jim tumbled down on the couch and put his hands under the back of his head and smiled.

"Dell," said he, "let's put our Christmas presents away and keep 'em a while. They're too nice to use just at present. I sold the watch to get the money to buy your combs. And now suppose you put the chops on."

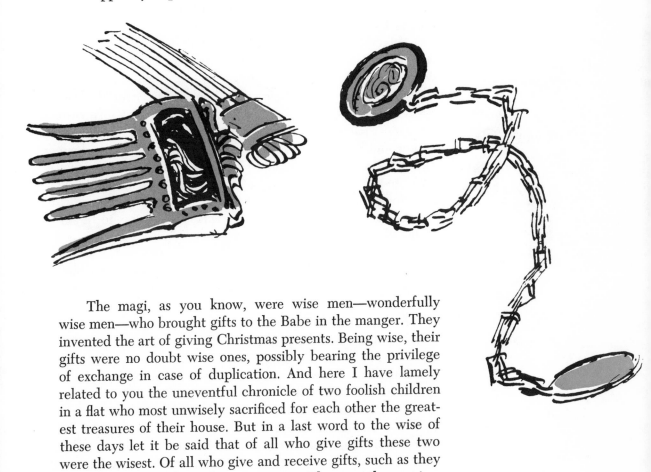

The magi, as you know, were wise men—wonderfully wise men—who brought gifts to the Babe in the manger. They invented the art of giving Christmas presents. Being wise, their gifts were no doubt wise ones, possibly bearing the privilege of exchange in case of duplication. And here I have lamely related to you the uneventful chronicle of two foolish children in a flat who most unwisely sacrificed for each other the greatest treasures of their house. But in a last word to the wise of these days let it be said that of all who give gifts these two were the wisest. Of all who give and receive gifts, such as they are wisest. Everywhere they are wisest. They are the magi.

THE LEGEND
OF BABOUSCHKA

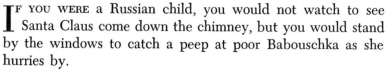

Old Russian Tale

IF YOU WERE a Russian child, you would not watch to see
Santa Claus come down the chimney, but you would stand
by the windows to catch a peep at poor Babouschka as she
hurries by.

Who is Babouschka? Is she Santa Claus's wife?

No, indeed. She is only a poor little crooked wrinkled old
woman, who comes at Christmas time into everybody's house,
who peeps into every cradle, turns back every coverlid, drops
a tear on the baby's white pillow, and goes away very sorrowful.

And not only at Christmas time, but through all the cold
winter and especially in March, when the wind blows loud,
and whistles and howls and dies away like a sigh, the Russian
children hear the rustling step of the Babouschka. She is always
in a hurry. One hears her running fast along the crowded
streets and over the quiet country fields. She seems to be out
of breath and tired, yet she hurries on.

Whom is she trying to overtake?

She scarcely looks at the little children as they press their
rosy faces against the windowpane and whisper to each other,
"Is the Babouschka looking for us?"

No, she will not stop; only on Christmas Eve will she
come upstairs into the nursery and give each little one a
present. You must not think she leaves handsome gifts such
as Santa Claus brings for you. She does not bring bicycles to
the boys or French dolls to the girls. She does not come in a
gay little sleigh drawn by reindeer, but hobbling along on
foot, and she leans on a crutch. She has her old apron filled
with candy and cheap toys, and the children all love her
dearly. They watch to see her come, and when one hears a
rustling, he cries, "Lo! the Babouschka!" then all others look,
but one must turn one's head very quickly or she vanishes.

I never saw her myself.

Best of all, she loves little babies, and often when the tired mothers sleep, she bends over their cradles, puts her brown, wrinkled face close down to the pillow and looks very sharply.

What is she looking for?

Ah, that you can't guess unless you know her sad story.

Long, long ago, a great many yesterdays ago, the Babouschka, who was even then an old woman, was busy sweeping her little hut. She lived in the coldest corner of cold Russia, and she lived alone in a lonely place where four wide roads met. These roads were at this time white with snow, for it was wintertime. In the summer, when the fields were full of flowers and the air full of sunshine and singing birds, Babouschka's home did not seem so very quiet; but in the winter, with only the snowflakes and the shy snowbirds and the loud wind for company, the little old woman felt very cheerless. But she was a busy old woman, and as it was already twilight, and her home but half swept, she felt in a great hurry to finish her work before bedtime. You must know the Babouschka was poor and could not afford to do her work by candlelight.

Presently, down the widest and the lonesomest of the white roads, there appeared a long train of people coming. They were walking slowly, and seemed to be asking each other questions as to which way they should take. As the procession came nearer, and finally stopped outside the little hut, Babouschka was frightened at the splendor. There were three kings, with crowns on their heads, and the jewels on the kings' breastplates sparkled like sunlight. Their heavy fur cloaks were white with the falling snowflakes, and the queer humpy camels on which they rode looked white as milk in the snowstorm. The harness on the camels was decorated with gold, and plates of silver adorned the saddles. The saddlecloths were of the richest Eastern stuffs, and all the servants had the dark eyes and hair of an Eastern people.

The slaves carried heavy loads on their backs, and each of the three kings carried a present. One carried a beautiful transparent jar, and in the fading light Babouschka could see in it a golden liquid which she knew from its color must be myrrh. Another had in his hand a richly woven bag, and it seemed to be heavy, as indeed it was, for it was full of gold. The third had a stone vase in his hand, and from the rich perfume which

filled the snowy air, one could guess the vase to have been filled with incense.

Babouschka was terribly frightened, so she hid herself in her hut, and let the servants knock a long time at her door before she dared open it and answer their questions as to the road they should take to a faraway town. You know she had never studied a geography lesson in her life, was old and stupid and scared. She knew the way across the fields to the nearest village, but she knew nothing else of all the wide world full of cities. The servants scolded, but the three kings spoke kindly to her, and asked her to accompany them on their journey that she might show them the way as far as she knew it. They told her, in words so simple that she could not fail to understand, that they had seen a star in the sky and were following it to a little town where a young child lay. The snow was in the sky now, and the star was lost out of sight.

"Who is the child?" asked the old woman.

"He is a King, and we go to worship him," they answered. "These presents of gold, frankincense, and myrrh are for him. When we find him we will take the crowns off our heads and lay them at his feet. Come with us, Babouschka!"

What do you suppose? Shouldn't you have thought the poor little woman would have been glad to leave her desolate home on the plains to accompany these kings on their journey?

But the foolish woman shook her head. No, the night was dark and cheerless, and her little home was warm and cozy. She looked up into the sky, and the star was nowhere to be seen. Besides, she wanted to put her hut in order—perhaps she would be ready to go tomorrow. But the three kings could not wait; so when tomorrow's sun rose they were far ahead on their journey. It seemed like a dream to poor Babouschka, for even the tracks of the camels' feet were covered by the deep white snow. Everything was the same as usual; and to make sure that the night's visitors had not been a fancy, she found her old broom hanging on a peg behind the door, where she had put it when the servants knocked.

Now that the sun was shining, and she remembered the glitter of the gold and the smell of sweet gums and myrrh, she wished she had gone with the travelers.

And she thought a great deal about the little baby the three kings had gone to worship. She had no children of her own—nobody loved her—ah, if she had only gone! The more she brooded on the thought, the more miserable she grew, till the very sight of her home became hateful to her.

It is a dreadful feeling to realize that one has lost a chance of happiness. There is a feeling called remorse that can gnaw like a sharp little tooth. Babouschka felt this little tooth cut into her heart every time she remembered the visit of the three kings.

After a while the thought of the little child became her first thought at waking and her last at night. One day she shut the door of her house forever and set out on a long journey. She had no hope of overtaking the three kings, but she longed to find the child, that she too might love and worship him. She asked everyone she met, and some people thought her crazy, but others gave her kind answers. Have you perhaps guessed that the young child whom the three kings sought was our Lord himself?

People told Babouschka how he was born in a manger, and many other things which you children have learned long ago. These answers puzzled the old lady mightily. She had but one idea in her ignorant head. The three kings had gone to seek a baby. She would, if not too late, seek him too.

She forgot, I am sure, how many long years had gone by. She looked in vain for the Christ-child in his manger-cradle. She spent all her savings in toys and candy so as to make friends with little children, that they might not run away when she came hobbling into their nurseries.

Now you know for whom she is sadly seeking when she pushes back the bed curtains and bends down over each baby's pillow. Sometimes, when the old grandmother sits nodding by the fire, and the bigger children sleep in their beds, old Babouschka comes hobbling into the room, and whispers softly, "Is the young child here?"

Ah, no; she has come too late, too late. But the little children know her and love her. Two thousand years ago she lost the chance of finding him. Crooked, wrinkled, old, sick and sorry, she yet lives on, looking into each baby's face—always disappointed, always seeking. Will she find him at last?

THE OLD STORY IN A NEW LAND

Grace W. McGavran

FATHER ANTOINE SHIVERED slightly, even in the shelter of the log hut. He was cold with the bitter chill of the Canadian northland. But he was colder with loneliness and longing for home. Home, to Father Antoine, was the ordered peace of his monastery, back on the sunny slopes of the southern French hills. Home was the sweet ringing of the chapel bell, the solemn songs of the deep-voiced choir, the conversation about high and holy things.

Father Antoine raised homesick eyes to his surroundings. Outside were the huge pine trees hung with gleaming snow; the dead stillness of the forest; the snowshoes piled beside the low door of the nearby hunter's lodge. Around and about moved the tall forms of Indians, members of an unfriendly tribe camped nearby for a few days. Their presence made Father Antoine feel that he was indeed a stranger in a foreign land. For it was Christmas Eve! Christmas Eve, and not a soul but faithful Pierre the fur trapper, his guide and companion, to join with him in the Christmas service tomorrow.

Yes, it was Christmas Eve, and all about him were the people of this unfriendly tribe. He had not expected to find them here, near the lonely hut of Pierre, where he had come to rest for a few days. Yet for the sake of just such people he had left the peace and order of the monastery and braved danger and hardship in an unfriendly, new world. Now was his chance to help.

As the thought took hold of his mind, Father Antoine's heart began to glow once more. Christmas Eve, and here were those who had never heard the most glorious story of all the world. Christmas Eve, and here was he, knowing their language and able, though haltingly, to tell them of that story.

The loneliness and cold vanished from the heart of Father Antoine. The wintry woods at which he had shivered not so many minutes ago seemed to sparkle with light and joy.

Father Antoine went hurrying into the woods, filled with the delight of a new idea. He would cut boughs of pine and hemlock and the graceful balsam. He would deck the cabin door and window. Pierre would bring logs and build a mighty fire before the door. They would invite the Indians to come and listen to the Christmas story. As he worked busily to get the greens, Father Antoine began to repeat to himself the story of the angels and the shepherds and the Wise Men. In what words should he tell the story to these Indians?

Father Antoine came to a sudden pause as he worked. He remembered that he did not know the Indian word for "sheep"; nor for "shepherd"; nor for "camels," as far as that went. I must ask Pierre, he thought. Then he laughed aloud in the still forest. There would be no such words in the language of the people of the far north woods. They had never seen any sheep. Nor any shepherds! And most certainly no camels!

Father Antoine went slowly on with his work. His mind was busy planning the story in a way which could be understood by the Indians. "Perhaps it is not needful for these forest folk to hear of the beasts that live in Palestine," he said to himself. "I think not. For it is about the wonder and beauty of that first Christmas night that I want to tell them."

Pierre was delighted when he heard Father Antoine's plan. He carried the invitation to the Indian camp. He helped to deck the lodge with pine and spruce and balsam and dark hemlock. He heaped high a pile of logs near the door. Then, when the hour had come, he carried embers from the fire within and lighted the Christmas logs.

It was a strange sight that firelight showed—the keen, bronzed faces, and lean and hardy forms of chiefs and braves, the slender figures and the deep dark eyes of squaws and maidens. Among them were the children, eager to know the news this pale-faced man might bring.

Father Antoine stood upon the threshold of the lodge. He raised his hand. Then in words that sometimes faltered, but with voice strong and clear, he told the Christmas story. And in these words he spoke it.

"It was a night like this," said Father Antoine. "The woods

were dark and full of snow. The moon shone bright upon the hills and valleys. Through the woods, traveling to join a gathering of their tribes, there came a man and woman, worn with cold, weary of the trail.

"Night had fallen before they reached the camp. The place was already full. There was no room for them within the wigwams of their friends. No room in any lodge! But she, the squaw, had bitter need of shelter. So at length a place was found, beneath the spreading branches of a mighty pine. There had been heaped the poles on which the wigwam coverings were dragged in travel. There, a sort of shelter was devised where she might rest."

The Indian folk leaned forward to hear better. They knew well how weary one could be from winter travel.

Father Antoine went on. " 'Twas on that very night, within that shelter, that her child was born. There was no bed in which to lay the babe. They placed him on a deerskin, soft as moss, laid in a cradle of soft evergreen. Her brave kept a fire blazing in the open place between the trees. He dared not have the flaming logs beneath the pine tree. But he carried hot coals so as to bring their warmth to the mother and to the child."

Father Antoine paused. This next part of the story was not easy to make clear to those who listened.

"Out on the forest trails," he said, "the hunters of the tribe followed the deer in search of food for their people. When the hunt was over and they had started home, their feet came to a sudden stop upon the trail. They listened. From somewhere there came sounds such as they had never in their lives heard before. It was the music of sweet voices singing. Sweeter than the voice of wind among the treetops; fairer than the sound of rain upon parched forest; softer than the sound of waves lapping upon the lake shore, came the music. Suddenly, before them on the trail, in garments whiter than the snow itself, with great white wings that reached as high as the tallest pine tree, stood a messenger with arms outstretched. The hunters feared not man nor beast, but now they were filled with fearsome wonder. As they stood in awe, the messenger spoke and said: 'In a forest shelter near, a child is just now born. That child is sent by the Great Spirit, for your people's good. Beneath a pine tree, cradled in a deerskin, you will find him.'

"His message given, with quivering wings the messenger floated out of sight. Suddenly all the sky was filled with brightness. Praise to the Great Spirit filled the air."

Father Antoine's very voice was full of wonder as he pictured the scene. He went on with the story. "When the song was finished, and the forest once again lay silent, the hunters hurried to their camp. Beneath the ancient tree they found the child, as the messenger had said, all wrapped in deerskin. Such a tiny babe! So deep and cold the snow! The youngest hunter stripped away the wolfskin he was wearing and wrapped it around the child."

Listening carefully to the story, the squaws nodded their heads. They knew how warm a wolfskin was. The baby in the story would lie snug that night, they knew.

Father Antoine continued. "In those days, three chiefs appeared, striding along the forest trails as if in search of something. They were unarmed and carried gifts. The hunters of the tribe met them along the trails and took them before their leader. All the braves of the tribe gathered to hear what strange errand brought them here.

"The strangers had a curious tale to tell. 'Listen to how the voice of the Great Spirit came to us, in our distant hunting fields,' they said. 'It spoke to us from a glorious star whose light outshone the moon. It told us to seek a child newborn, who later would be the mightiest chief the world will ever know!'

"There were many little Indian babies in the winter camp. How could the strangers know which one was the child they had come to see? They waited for their star. When darkness fell, the waning moon had not yet risen to give light. But a great star's brightness shone in the sky. It seemed to move, then came to quiet rest above the topmost branches of the tree beneath which lay the newborn child.

"Softly through the snow the strangers strode. They came beneath the sheltering branches of the ancient tree. They looked and saw the child. One by one, in silence, each brought out his gift and laid it before the cradleboard on which the child was bound. Rich pelts of beaver were the gift of one.

The second brought long strings of wampum. But the third laid by the cradleboard an eagle feather.

"So," said Father Antoine, "was full welcome given to the Son of the Great Spirit who should save his people and the people of the world. When that child became a man, he taught his people of the Great Spirit and how to live in his ways. These ways I have come to teach to you that you also may know."

Father Antoine paused as he finished his story. Then he lifted high his arms above the listening folk. "Great Spirit, Father, God," he prayed, "be here, within this forest and among these folk. Enter their hearts that they may then come to know thy love which sent thy Son to us to teach us of thee."

When the Indians had gone, old Pierre smiled. "Father, I had forgotten it could be Christmas in such a wilderness. But as you talked I felt the same springing joy I used to know at home."

"Christmas is in the heart, Pierre," said Father Antoine. "And I pray that the good God may someday have the love of these wild children of the forest. May their hearts someday be full of Christmas love and of the love of God."

The embers of the fire cooled and blackened. Within the close-barred lodge, Father Antoine and old Pierre wrapped themselves in their skins of wolf and otter and lay down to sleep. Their loneliness was gone. They were happy in the memory of the Christmas story spread.

SNOW DOUGH

Christmas Eve cookies
 Baked for the great day,
I start making snow;
 Cut out each flake from snow dough
  On my kitchen table;
 Toss them out my window,
And lean over the sill
 To watch them fly down the air
  To Christmas.

EMILIE GLEN

Old-fashioned Plum Pudding, page 305

Ice Cream Bombe, page 309

SAINT FRANCIS AND THE CHRISTMAS STORY

THE ITALIAN SUNSHINE was warm and bright as Saint Francis walked in the woods near the village of Greccio (GRAY-chee-oh). The year was 1223 and the month December.

Saint Francis moved slowly, head bowed. "It's almost here, Il Natale (Eel Nah-TAH-le), the birth of Jesus, the season of good will. But the people here in Greccio seem to have forgotten Jesus. They constantly hurt each other by their cruel and selfish ways. If only I could help them think about that first Christmas night and about the baby Jesus, who, when he became a man, 'went about doing good.'"

Saint Francis continued to ponder as he walked. Then he stopped suddenly, a light glowing in his eyes. "I know! I know what I can do!"

With that he quickened his steps until he reached the home of his friend, Giovanni (Joh-VAHN-nee), to whom he unfolded his plan. Giovanni was enthusiastic too.

If you had been in the Greccio Woods the next afternoon, you would have seen a procession of Giovanni's servants making their way to the big cave. Some carried boughs of pine and cypress, others lumber and a bale of straw. Two more brought from Giovanni's stable a manger filled with hay. A neighboring farmer arrived with three white cows, sheep, and lambs.

Meanwhile, word had spread around the village that Saint Francis was inviting everyone to come to the cave that night.

When it grew dark, men, women, and children approached the cave, bearing torches and candles. Upon entering, they

stood transfixed with awe and wonder. There, before their very eyes they *saw* the Christmas story—the stable spread with clean straw and the walls covered with sweet-smelling greens. The white cows chewed their cud and a little gray donkey looked quietly into the hay-filled manger, while sheep and lambs crouched close.

At the appointed time, a young father and mother came forward and gently laid their sleeping baby in the manger. When the picture was thus completed, Saint Francis stepped from the shadowed corner where he had been standing.

Looking into the faces of the hushed and reverent worshipers, he told the Bethlehem story of Mary and Joseph, of the shepherds and the Wise Men. He spoke not only of the baby Jesus, but also of Jesus, the man, and implored his listeners to follows Jesus' way of loving-kindness.

Later that evening when the villagers left the cave to return to their homes the winter stars were shining brightly in the dark sky.

"See!" exclaimed a child, pointing to one star which was especially large and bright. "It's the star of Bethlehem!"

Saint Francis heard it and his heart sang with joy. He knew that Christmas—the real Christmas—had come that night to the village of Greccio, Italy.

ABOUT TO BE

Lambs about to be
    White as kitchen enamel,
About to be
    White as Christmas snow,
Lambs for the Nativity,
    About to shine the star of Bethlehem,
Scent the winds of winter with pine boughs,
    Street boys tenderly set the lambs
        In the gutter,
Hose them white,
    White as Christmas snow.

EMILIE GLEN

Santa Claus and His Presents, from HARPER'S WEEKLY, 1858

Christmas Belles, by Winslow Homer from HARPER'S WEEKLY, 1869

A VISIT FROM ST. NICHOLAS

'Twas the night before Christmas, when all through the house
Not a creature was stirring, not even a mouse;
The stockings were hung by the chimney with care,
In hopes that St. Nicholas soon would be there;
The children were nestled all snug in their beds,
While visions of sugar-plums danced in their heads;
And mamma in her 'kerchief, and I in my cap,
Had just settled our brains for a long winter's nap,
When out on the lawn there arose such a clatter,
I sprang from the bed to see what was the matter.
Away to the window I flew like a flash,
Tore open the shutters and threw up the sash.
The moon on the breast of the new-fallen snow
Gave the lustre of mid-day to objects below,
When, what to my wondering eyes should appear,
But a miniature sleigh, and eight tiny reindeer,
With a little old driver, so lively and quick,
I knew in a moment it must be St. Nick.
More rapid than eagles his coursers they came,
And he whistled, and shouted, and called them by name:
"Now, Dasher! now, Dancer! now, Prancer and Vixen!
On, Comet! on, Cupid! on, Donder and Blitzen!

To the top of the porch! to the top of the wall!
Now dash away! dash away! dash away all!"
As dry leaves that before the wild hurricane fly,
When they meet with an obstacle, mount to the sky,
So up to the house-top the coursers they flew,
With the sleigh full of toys, and St. Nicholas too.
And then, in a twinkling, I heard on the roof
The prancing and pawing of each little hoof.
As I drew in my head, and was turning around,
Down the chimney St. Nicholas came with a bound.
He was dressed all in fur, from his head to his foot,
And his clothes were all tarnished with ashes and soot;
A bundle of toys he had flung on his back,
And he looked like a peddler just opening his pack.
His eyes—how they twinkled! his dimples how merry!
His cheeks were like roses, his nose like a cherry!
His droll little mouth was drawn up like a bow,
And the beard of his chin was as white as the snow;
The stump of a pipe he held tight in his teeth,
And the smoke, it encircled his head like a wreath;
He had a broad face and a little round belly,
That shook, when he laughed, like a bowlful of jelly.
He was chubby and plump, a right jolly old elf,
And I laughed when I saw him, in spite of myself;
A wink of his eye and a twist of his head,
Soon gave me to know I had nothing to dread;
He spoke not a word, but went straight to his work,
And filled all the stockings; then turned with a jerk,
And laying his finger aside of his nose,
And giving a nod, up the chimney he rose;
He sprang to his sleigh, to his team gave a whistle,
And away they all flew like the down of a thistle.
But I heard him exclaim, ere he drove out of sight,
"Happy Christmas to all, and to all a good-night."

CLEMENT CLARKE MOORE

CHRISTMAS COOKERY

THE TRADITIONAL CHRISTMAS dinner has changed somewhat over the years. We have moved away from the elaborate sit-down affair with many courses and a serving of sherbet in between to refresh the palate before going on to the remainder of the meal. Today we can break away and have just a few of the traditional dishes with the help of modern convenience foods. Or we can take the time, as our ancestors did, to make special breads, cookies, fruitcake, and plum pudding. Whatever the family's mealtime preferences, enough of the special preparations should be made in every home to show the children what fun it was—and still is—to mark the holidays in the traditional ways. The youngster who has not known the mouth-watering aroma of the Christmas kitchen, had a hand in the mixing and mincing and stirring, and enjoyed the delicious anticipation of the goodies to come out of the oven has missed a delightful part of the American holiday tradition. Many of the customary Christmas specialties are sweet, and the preparation of them lends a festive air to the occasion, particularly for children.

The menus given are based on the foods of our forefathers from the five major regions of the country and show the foreign influences of many of our early settlers. They are the foods of our land today, as they were when our country was being settled. Particular combinations of foods are traditional at Christmas time and through association make a meal a festive one. Family favorites may be substituted for certain dishes suggested in the menus, some may be subtracted, or more may be added.

Almost all the dishes called for in the menus are included among the recipes. Those that are not included are identified with an asterisk, and any favorite recipe for the dish in question can be used.

The reader will note that no recipe has been given for preparing turkey—although there is an excellent recipe for Oyster Stuffing for Turkey. The omission is intentional. Turkeys are marketed in a variety of ways—some are specially fed, some are prelarded—and there are a number of equally good methods of cooking. Some authorities recommend roasting the turkey uncovered. Others suggest covering with greased brown paper or cheesecloth or with aluminum foil. The reader should use the method she prefers and that is best suited to the type of turkey she buys.

Generally speaking, the American pioneers tended to settle and make their homes where they found terrain, climate, and available foods that were akin to those of their homelands.

In the North Central states—particularly Minnesota, the Dakotas, Montana, and Iowa—settlers from Denmark, Sweden, and Norway found the fauna to which they were accustomed, including fish, goose, and game birds. They brought with them their recipes for cookies, sweet breads, and puddings, and to this day the cuisine of the region has a distinctly Scandinavian flavor.

Pumpkin Soup
or
Kringle Salad - Horseradish Cream Dressing
Fruit-Stuffed Roast Goose
Whipped Potatoes in Orange Cups
Glazed Turnips* - Baked Onions*
Christmas Twist
Cranberry Cider Pie
or
Tray of Christmas Cookies

In the Midwest—Wisconsin, Indiana, Ohio, Nebraska, and Pennsylvania—the German and Dutch settlers found their familiar Christmas staples: rabbit, duck, and game birds. They brought with them their recipes for braised vegetables, dumplings, and puddings and carried on their homeland traditions.

Split Pea Soup*

or

Whitefish Stew*

Roast Pheasant   -   Rice-Mushroom Stuffing

Cranberry-Onion Sauce

Spiced Squash   -   Braised Celery*

Dinner Rolls

Old-fashioned Plum Pudding   -   Brandy Sauce

or

Compote of Dried Fruit Stewed in Cider*

Sand Tarts

In the Southern states, the cuisine of Virginia, Delaware, and Georgia was strongly influenced by the English settlers. In the Carolinas, the French Huguenots influenced the food specialties. The French also left their mark on the cuisine of Louisiana. Mixed with influences from the West Indies, it developed into the Creole style of cooking. Florida received significant Spanish influence, with emphasis on the use of pork and the readily available fish from the coastal areas.

Crab Creole*

or

Broiled Shrimp in White Wine*

Baked Country Ham*

or

Standing Rib Roast of Beef*

Christmas Corn Medley   -   Minted Peas*

Dinner Rolls

Mincemeat Royal Pie

or

White Fruitcake   -   Brandy Sauce

Pralines

New England was heavily influenced by the customs of the English settlers, and later the Irish. The ubiquitous "Irish potato," so important a feature of New England meals, actually is a native American. It was taken to Europe in the seventeenth century and introduced to Ireland, where it became the staple food. In the mid-nineteenth century, so dependent had the people become on the potato that a failure of the crop resulted in widespread famine and wholesale emigration, principally to the United States. Understandably, the emigrants brought their liking for potatoes with them and thus gave potato dishes a popularity they had never before enjoyed in the New World.

Deviled Clams

or

Consommé Noël

Turkey with Oyster Stuffing - Giblet Gravy*

Roast Potatoes*

Brussels Sprouts and Chestnuts - Glazed Baby Carrots*

Celery - Olives

Cranberry Sauce*

Crescent Rolls

Pilgrim Pie

or

English Fruitcake - Hard Sauce

Glacéed Nuts

On the West Coast, Spanish influence was strong all up and down the Pacific region. In California, Italians and Germans settled in the rich Napa Valley, and many fine Spanish vintners settled in the Sonoma Valley. Washington had a heavy influx of Swedish settlers, and in Oregon and other coastal areas, German and Swiss farmers found their favorite foods—quail, pheasant, fish, and fruits.

The cuisine of Hawaii is a mixture of Polynesian cooking and dishes originating in the Orient—Japan, China, and Korea. The Oriental recipes have found greater favor than the Polynesian, largely because they employ a greater variety of foods and are more attuned to the average Western taste. There were no recipes to be handed down from one Hawaiian generation to the next—except those introduced by the missionaries—because few of the foods of the islands needed cooking. Mangoes, papayas, coconuts, avocados, and raw fish were the staples of the Hawaiian diet. The roasting of a pig in a stone pit was generally reserved for ceremonial occasions and festivals.

In the Southwest, Arizona, New Mexico, and Texas were

influenced by Mexican and Spanish fare, the holiday menus tending to feature specialties adopted from other areas.

Oyster Bisque
or
Island Salad   -   Paradise Dressing
Roast Suckling Pig*
or
Crown Roast of Pork
Roast Sweet Potatoes*
Artichokes in Lemon Butter Sauce*
and/or
Green Beans with Ground Macadamia Nuts*
Cloverleaf Rolls
Ice Cream Bombe
or
Fresh Fruit
Candied Orange Peel

All around the country, the holiday season is a time for entertaining. The spirit of Christmas Present and the anticipation and hope that come with the New Year bring with them a wish to be close to our families and friends.

Both Christmas and New Year's lend themselves especially well to the open house, when friends can come and go and be replaced by others throughout the afternoon or evening. The following suggestions for refreshments provide three widely differing beverages and an assortment of snacks, both of the appetizer type and sweets to please all tastes.

Holiday Punch
or
Hot Cranberry Snap
or
Fruit Punch
Curried Chicken Nuggets
Cheese Puffs
Sand Tarts
White Fruitcake, cubed
Highland Shortbread
Meringues
Sugar Cookies
Pfeffernüsse

A very special holiday party can be built around the traditional eggnog. Hearty and rich as the eggnog is, however, guests will want something to munch, and the following suggestion of refreshments is varied enough to make the buffet the center of attraction.

Southern Eggnog
Cheese Puffs
Cranberry Bread and Butter Sandwiches
Quick Miniature Fruitcakes
Sand Tarts
Glacéed Nuts
Meringues
Candied Orange Peel

The dishes suggested in the menus, as well as others given in the Christmas recipe section, lend themselves equally well to enjoyment on other special occasions throughout the year, or just to spark up a quiet dinner at home. A dish that is decorated or served with a touch of elegance provides a festive touch for foods that otherwise are ordinary daily fare.

A few suggestions follow for especially effective uses of some of the recipes:

For summer meals, Island Salad served with hot Cloverleaf Rolls makes an excellent luncheon. Dieters will applaud Kringle Salad with cottage cheese. For a cool opener to a summer dinner, try Oyster Bisque served icy cold, or Consommé Noël transformed into a jellied soup by the addition of a little gelatin.

For a special luncheon or tea, Candied Fruit Peel and Glacéed Nuts add an attractive touch, and Meringues can be filled with ice cream or with fresh fruits of the season.

A child's lunchbox can be made a special treat if topped off with Gingerbread Cookies, Sugar Cookies, or Quick Miniature Fruitcakes.

Fruit Punch, nonalcoholic, topped with a sprig of mint, makes a delicious tall summer cooler, and Holiday Punch is festive enough to grace a wedding reception.

And for gift giving at any season, make a gay or ingenious package of Highland Shortbread, Quick Miniature Fruitcakes, Candied Fruit Peel, or Glacéed Nuts.

CHEESE PUFFS

¾ cup sifted all-purpose flour
¼ teaspoon salt
½ cup shortening
2 cups grated Swiss cheese
1 cup finely grated Parmesan cheese
¼ teaspoon salt
½ teaspoon hot pepper sauce
1 tablespoon Worcestershire sauce
1 egg, beaten with 1 teaspoon water

In a mixing bowl, combine flour, salt, and shortening. With a pastry blender, mix together until it resembles coarse cornmeal. Mix in the next 5 ingredients. Form into a ball. Cut in half and cut each half into 16 pieces. Roll each piece into a little ball. Place on an ungreased baking sheet 1 inch apart and press the tops slightly with a fork. Brush with beaten egg and bake in a preheated 400° F. oven for 8 to 10 minutes or until golden. Makes 32 puffs.

DEVILED CLAMS

24 unopened cherrystone clams
½ cup minced green onions
½ cup minced celery
5 tablespoons butter or margarine
1 cup finely grated bread crumbs made from firm-type bread
2 tablespoons finely chopped parsley
⅛ teaspoon hot pepper sauce or more to taste
½ teaspoon Worcestershire sauce

Wash and scrub clams. Place in a baking pan in a preheated 450° F. oven until shells open wide and edges of clams become slightly crinkled. Remove from oven; when cool, shell, mince, and drain the clams. Reserve half of the shells. Sauté onion and celery in 4 tablespoons of the butter until tender but not brown. In a small bowl, combine the sautéed vegetables, clams, bread crumbs, parsley, and seasonings. Lightly fill 24 shells. Dot the tops with the remaining butter. Place in a shallow pan and cover with foil; bake 15 minutes in a preheated 375° F. oven. Serve 4 to a person. Makes 6 servings.

CURRIED CHICKEN NUGGETS

1   can (3½ ounces) flaked coconut
1½ teaspoons curry powder
¼   cup finely minced onion
½   teaspoon finely minced garlic
2   tablespoons butter or margarine
1   cup cooked ground chicken
½   teaspoon Worcestershire sauce
½   teaspoon soy sauce
⅛   teaspoon hot pepper sauce
     mayonnaise
     salt and pepper

Toss the coconut and curry powder together and spread on a baking sheet. Toast in a preheated 250° F. oven until golden, stirring frequently; cool. Sauté onion and garlic in butter until tender but not brown. In a medium-sized bowl, combine the chicken with the Worcestershire, soy, and hot pepper sauces. Add ¾ cup of the toasted coconut and mix well. Add enough mayonnaise to make a moist but firm mixture, and salt and pepper to taste. Refrigerate for 1 hour or longer. With a ½-teaspoon measuring spoon, scoop up rounded amounts of the mixture and shape into little balls. Roll in the remaining coconut. Chill until ready to serve. These appetizers may be speared on picks or eaten with the fingers. Makes about 3 dozen balls.

CONSOMMÉ NOËL

6   cups chicken or turkey broth
¾   cup canned beet liquid
3   teaspoons onion juice
     salt
3   tablespoons dry sherry
2   limes, sliced

Remove all fat from broth. Combine broth, beet liquid, and onion juice. For a clear consommé, strain through a piece of flannel. Bring to a boil. Remove from heat and salt to taste. Stir in sherry. Serve in bouillon cups or festive mugs with a slice of lime. Makes 6 to 8 servings.

PUMPKIN SOUP

1   large onion, finely minced
3   tablespoons butter or margarine
3   tablespoons flour
2   cups milk
2   cups chicken stock
1¾   cups cooked pumpkin, fresh or canned
2   teaspoons sugar
½   teaspoon freshly ground nutmeg
2   teaspoons salt
¼   teaspoon white pepper
½   cup heavy cream
3   tablespoons sherry

In a 3-quart saucepan, sauté onion in butter until tender. Blend in flour and cook 1 minute. Stir in milk and chicken stock and cook, stirring occasionally, until slightly thickened. Press pumpkin through a strainer and add to liquid. Stir in sugar, nutmeg, salt, and pepper. Bring to a boil; adjust the seasoning to taste. Before serving, add heated cream and sherry. Pour into a warm soup tureen. Serves 6 to 8.

OYSTER BISQUE

1   quart milk
1   quart medium cream
¼   cup all-purpose flour
¼   cup water
2   teaspoons celery salt
2   teaspoons salt
¼   teaspoon white pepper
⅛   teaspoon cayenne
1½   tablespoons Worcestershire Sauce
2   cups shucked oysters and liquid
3   tablespoons butter or margarine

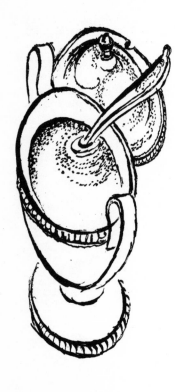

In a 4-quart saucepan, heat the milk and cream, but do not boil. In a small saucepan, combine the flour with the next 6 ingredients, mixing to a paste. Stir in the liquid from the oysters and add the oysters and 1 cup of the milk mixture. Cook gently until the edges of the oysters curl. Put into a blender or food mill and purée. Empty into the remainder of the hot milk mixture. Cover and let stand 10 minutes. Reheat if necessary, and add butter or margarine. Serve in a heated tureen or individual bowls. Makes 8 to 10 servings.

ROAST PHEASANTS

2 pheasants about 2½ pounds each, ready to cook
½ cup butter or margarine
1½ cups chopped onions
1½ cups chopped celery
½ pound fresh mushrooms, chopped
2 teaspoons salt
¼ teaspoon pepper
½ teaspoon marjoram
1 teaspoon thyme
1 cup chopped walnuts
2 cups cooked rice
1 recipe Cranberry-Onion Sauce

Wipe pheasants inside and out with a damp paper towel. Sauté onions and celery in ¼ cup of the butter. Add mushrooms and cook about 3 minutes more. Add seasonings and walnuts and toss with the rice; cool. Stuff birds loosely with rice mixture and fasten with poultry pins; truss and place in a roasting pan. Brush breasts, legs, and wings thoroughly with the remaining butter. Place in a preheated 325° F. oven and roast for 1 hour, basting twice during the hour. Coat pheasants thoroughly with Cranberry-Onion Sauce and roast another 30 minutes or until tender. Remove to a heated platter and serve with the remaining sauce. Makes 4 to 6 servings.

CRANBERRY-ONION SAUCE

4 cups cranberries
2 cups water
2 cups light brown sugar
3 tablespoons lemon juice
1 teaspoon ground ginger
1½ cups chopped onions
¼ cup butter or margarine

In a medium-sized saucepan, combine the first 5 ingredients. Bring to a boil and cook about 5 minutes until cranberries pop open. Sauté onions in butter until tender. Add to cranberries and purée in a blender or food mill. Coat game birds or poultry with the sauce in the last half hour of roasting. Warm the remaining sauce and serve in a sauceboat. Makes about 4½ cups.

ROAST GOOSE WITH FRUIT STUFFING

1   12- to 14-pound goose, ready to cook
1½ cups chopped onions
6   tablespoons butter or margarine
2   quarts small bread cubes, lightly toasted
2½ cups peeled, cored, and coarsely chopped tart apples
¾   pound pitted prunes, cut into small pieces
2   teaspoons sage
1   teaspoon basil
2¼ teaspoons salt
¼   teaspoon freshly ground pepper
1   cup apple juice
    Whipped Potatoes in Orange Cups
    giblet gravy
    green leaves

Remove any loose fat from inside the goose. Sauté onions in butter until tender. In a large mixing bowl, toss the bread cubes with the onions, apples, prunes, seasonings, and apple juice. Stuff goose loosely and fasten with poultry pins. Truss and place goose on a rack in a roasting pan. Roast in a preheated 325° F. oven (20 to 25 minutes per pound). Remove fat from pan as it accumulates during cooking. When goose is tender and crisp, place on a warm platter. Garnish with Whipped Potatoes in Orange Cups and decorate with green leaves. Serve with giblet gravy. Makes 8 to 10 servings.

This stuffing can also be used in capon, turkey, or other poultry.

OYSTER STUFFING FOR TURKEY

4   quarts toasted bread cubes from firm-type sliced loaf (about 32 slices)
1   cup butter or margarine
1   cup chopped celery
1½ cups chopped onion
½   cup finely chopped green pepper
1   quart fresh oysters (including 1½ cups oyster liquid) or equivalent frozen
½   cup light cream
¼   cup chopped parsley
2   teaspoons salt
½   teaspoon pepper
1   teaspoon each thyme and marjoram

Crown Roast of Pork, page 289

Sand Tarts, page 300
Highland Shortbread, page 301

Remove crust from bread and cut into ⅜-inch cubes. Spread cubes on a baking sheet and dry out in a preheated 350° F. oven until very lightly toasted. In a 10-inch skillet, melt butter and sauté celery, onion, and green pepper until tender. Pick over oysters and remove any pieces of shell; chop coarsely. Add the oysters, liquid, cream, parsley, and seasonings. Bring to a boil over medium heat and cook for 2 minutes. Add to bread cubes in a large bowl and toss together lightly. Let cool before stuffing turkey. Makes enough for a 16- to 18-pound turkey.

This stuffing may also be put in a casserole, covered with foil, and baked in a preheated 350° F. oven for 1 hour. It can also be served with ham or roast beef.

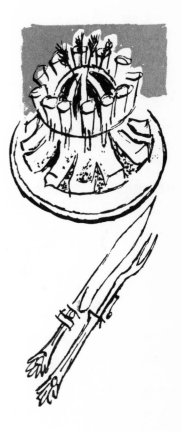

CROWN ROAST OF PORK

crown roast of pork weighing from 9 to 10 pounds (20 ribs)
1   large clove garlic
1   pound ground veal
½   pound ground pork
½   cup ¼-inch bread cubes, lightly toasted
¼   teaspoon marjoram
¼   teaspoon thyme
2   tablespoons minced green onions
1   teaspoon salt
2   tablespoons milk
2   tablespoons chopped parsley
    gravy

Wipe roast with a damp paper towel. Rub meat and ribs with cut garlic. Mix together the veal, pork, and the next 7 ingredients. Fill the center of the roast with the dressing and cover that with foil. Wrap each rib tip with a piece of foil to prevent burning, leaving the rest of the roast exposed. Place in an open pan on a piece of foil and protect bottom of bones with turned-up foil. Roast in a preheated 325° F. oven about 3½ to 4 hours. Remove all foil and place on a heated platter. Garnish upper ends of ribs with paper frills if desired. Serve with gravy. Makes 10 to 12 servings.

SPICED SQUASH

3   cups cooked butternut or Hubbard squash
3   tablespoons butter or margarine
½   teaspoon cinnamon
¼   teaspoon nutmeg
$\frac{1}{16}$ teaspoon ground clove
1½   tablespoons light brown sugar
     salt and pepper to taste

Cook, drain, and mash the squash, discarding the peel. Combine squash and remaining ingredients in a saucepan over low heat for 3 or 4 minutes, stirring to prevent burning. Serve in a warm vegetable dish. Makes 6 servings.

CHRISTMAS CORN MEDLEY

½   pound small white whole onions (peeled), either fresh or
     frozen
2   10-ounce packages frozen corn
1   cup chopped green pepper
¼   cup chopped pimiento
3   tablespoons melted butter or margarine
     salt and pepper

Cook onions in boiling salted water until tender. Cook corn according to package instructions. Drain vegetables and combine with green pepper and pimiento. Toss with butter; add salt and pepper to taste. Serve in a warm vegetable dish. Makes 8 servings.

BRUSSELS SPROUTS AND CHESTNUTS

1 pound fresh chestnuts
1½ pounds fresh or 2 10-ounce packages frozen Brussels
　　sprouts
½ cup butter or margarine
　　salt and pepper

With a sharp knife, cut a gash in the flat side of the chestnuts. Cover with water and boil 20 minutes. Remove shells and inner skins. Cook Brussels sprouts in salted water until tender. Simmer chestnuts in butter for 5 minutes, add the drained Brussels sprouts, and toss together. Salt and pepper to taste. Serve in a warm vegetable dish. Makes 8 to 10 servings.

WHIPPED POTATOES IN ORANGE CUPS

4 oranges
¼ cup melted butter or margarine
½ cup orange juice
1 tablespoon grated orange peel
6 cups cooked whipped potatoes
　　salt and pepper

Cut oranges in half and remove the pulp. Scallop edges of orange cups if desired. Mix the butter, orange juice, and peel into the potatoes. Salt and pepper to taste. Fill each orange cup with potatoes and keep warm until ready to serve. Makes 8 servings.

BRANDIED WHIPPED SWEET POTATOES

2 pounds sweet potatoes
2 eggs
¼ cup melted butter or margarine
¼ cup heavy cream
2 tablespoons brandy
　　salt and pepper

Boil potatoes; when slightly cool, peel and mash. Beat eggs until very thick and lemon-colored. Beat in potatoes. Add butter, cream, and brandy and whip until light. Salt and pepper to taste. Pile in a 2-quart soufflé dish or casserole and bake in a preheated 350° F. oven for 30 minutes. Do not brown the top. Makes 6 servings.

KRINGLE SALAD

1 head of lettuce or a variety of greens
  French dressing
1 1-pound can julienne beets, drained
1 hard-cooked egg
  Horseradish Cream Dressing

Wash lettuce and pat dry with a paper towel. Tear lettuce into bite-sized pieces and toss with just enough French dressing to coat the leaves. Place in a glass serving bowl. Toss beets in French dressing in the same way and arrange across the middle of the lettuce. Sprinkle grated egg white on the beets and top with grated yolk. Serve with Horseradish Cream Dressing. Makes 8 servings.

HORSERADISH CREAM DRESSING

1 cup sour cream
2 teaspoons horseradish
2 tablespoons chopped green pepper

Combine all ingredients and chill.

ISLAND SALAD

2 small pineapples
2 medium avocados
  lemon juice
  Paradise Dressing
  chopped Macadamia nuts

With a large sharp knife, cut pineapples in fourths lengthwise through the tops. Be careful to keep the tops intact. Slice out the core, leaving a flat surface. Cut just above the inside of the skin to loosen the edible pulp. Make cuts every half inch crosswise and lengthwise through the pulp while still retaining the shape. Cut avocados in half and remove the pit. Do not peel. Cut each avocado into fourths. With a ¾-inch melon scoop, cut 3 balls from each fourth, scooping down to the skin to obtain the greener part, and place the avocado balls on top of each wedge of pineapple, green side up. Squeeze a little lemon juice on each. Cover with plastic wrap and chill. Serve on individual plates, or, for a buffet, place the 8 wedges on a large round platter radiating from the center. Serve with Paradise Dressing and a bowl of chopped Macadamia nuts to sprinkle on top. Makes 8 servings.

PARADISE DRESSING

½ cup mashed avocado
2   tablespoons lemon juice
2   tablespoons light cream
½ cup mayonnaise

Combine avocado, lemon juice, and light cream. Whip in the mayonnaise. If a smoother dressing is desired, put into the blender for 5 seconds. Makes about 1 cup.

SWEET DOUGH

3½ to 4½ cups all-purpose flour
⅓ cup granulated sugar
2   packages active dry yeast
1½ teaspoons salt
½ cup milk
¼ cup water
¼ cup butter or margarine
2   eggs at room temperature

In a large mixing bowl, combine 1½ cups flour and the sugar, undissolved yeast, and salt; mix together. In a small saucepan, heat milk, water, and butter until just warm, about 110° F. Stir into flour-sugar mixture and beat until smooth. Beat in eggs one at a time. Gradually add flour until batter becomes too stiff to mix with a spoon or beater. Turn onto a lightly floured cloth and work in enough flour to make a soft but firm dough. Knead until smooth and elastic, about 8 to 10 minutes. Place in a large greased bowl and lightly grease the top. Cover with a cloth and let rise in a warm (80° to 85° F.) place until doubled in bulk, about 1½ hours. The dough is now ready to be used in making Stollen, Panettone, Swedish Tea Ring, Christmas Twist, or dinner rolls.

PANETTONE
Christmas Bread

½ recipe Sweet Dough
2 tablespoons chopped candied orange peel
¼ cup chopped citron
¼ cup golden raisins
2 tablespoons each slivered almonds, chopped walnuts, and piñon nuts
1½ teaspoons flour
melted butter or margarine

Prepare the half-recipe of Sweet Dough and reserve. Combine candied peel, citron, raisins, and nuts in a bowl; add flour and toss to coat. On a lightly floured cloth, knead fruits and nuts into the Sweet Dough until evenly distributed. Place dough in a greased 6-inch springform pan. Cover with a cloth and let rise in a warm (80° to 85° F.) place until double in bulk. Brush top of dough with melted butter. Bake in a preheated 350° F. oven for 20 to 30 minutes, or until the bread is golden and sounds hollow when the top is tapped with the fingers.

STOLLEN

½ recipe Sweet Dough
⅓ cup raisins
⅓ cup toasted slivered almonds
⅓ cup cut-up candied cherries
1½ teaspoons flour
confectioners' sugar

Prepare the half-recipe of Sweet Dough and reserve. Combine raisins, almonds, and cherries in a bowl; add flour and toss to coat. On a lightly floured cloth, knead the almonds and fruits into the Sweet Dough until evenly distributed. Roll dough into a 7 x 12-inch oval, then fold in half lengthwise. Place on a greased baking sheet. Cover with a cloth and let rise in a warm (80° to 85° F.) place until almost double in bulk. Bake in a preheated 350° F. oven about 25 minutes, until Stollen is golden and sounds hollow when the top is tapped with the fingers. Cool on a wire rack. Sprinkle with confectioners' sugar.

SWEDISH TEA RING

½ recipe Sweet Dough
2 tablespoons softened butter or margarine
½ cup light brown sugar, firmly packed
2 teaspoons cinnamon
½ cup broken walnuts
½ cup raisins
½ recipe Fondant Frosting
    candied cherries

Roll Sweet Dough into a rectangle 7 x 15 inches. Spread with butter and sprinkle sugar, cinnamon, walnuts, and raisins on top. Starting with the long edge, roll tightly as for a jelly-roll. Shape into a ring on a greased baking sheet, sealed edge down. Pinch ends together. With scissors make cuts ⅔ of the way through the ring at 1-inch intervals. Twist each cut section slightly to separate. Cover with a cloth and let rise in a warm (80° to 85° F.) place until almost double in bulk. Bake in a preheated 375° F. oven about 20 to 25 minutes or until golden. Frost with Fondant Frosting and decorate with cherries.

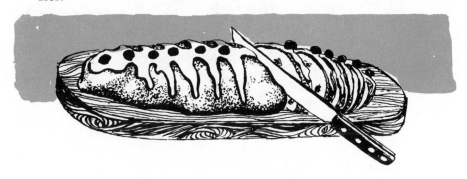

FONDANT FROSTING

2 cups sifted confectioners' sugar
1½ teaspoons lemon juice or vanilla
2 to 3 tablespoons water

In a medium-sized bowl, mix sugar, lemon juice, and enough water for desired consistency. Stir until smooth. Store the Fondant Frosting in a covered jar in refrigerator. Remove one hour before using to soften. Spread over slightly warm breads, or use for decorating or frosting cookies. Makes about ¾ cup.

CLOVERLEAF DINNER ROLLS

1 recipe Sweet Dough
1 egg, beaten with 1 teaspoon water

Form bits of Sweet Dough into balls 1 inch in diameter. In a greased muffin pan, place three balls in each cup. Cover with a cloth and let rise in a warm (80° to 85° F.) place until light in color and almost double in bulk. Brush with beaten egg. Bake in a preheated 400° F. oven about 10 to 12 minutes or until golden. Makes 12 rolls.

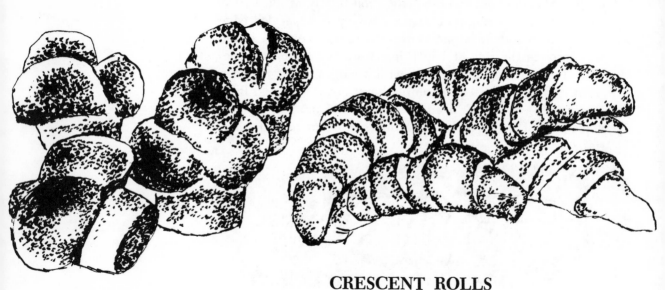

CRESCENT ROLLS

1 recipe Sweet Dough
2 tablespoons soft butter or margarine
1 egg, beaten with 1 teaspoon water

Roll Sweet Dough into a 12-inch circle, spread with butter, and cut into 16 pie-shaped pieces. Starting at the curved edge of each piece, roll toward the point and form into the shape of a crescent. Place on a greased baking sheet, point underneath. Cover with a cloth and let rise in a warm (80° to 85° F.) place until light in color and almost double in bulk. Brush with beaten egg. Bake in a preheated 400° F. oven about 10 to 12 minutes or until golden. Makes 16 rolls.

CRANBERRY BREAD

3   cups all-purpose flour
1½   cups sugar
1   tablespoon double-acting baking powder
½   teaspoon baking soda
¾   teaspoon salt
1   teaspoon freshly ground nutmeg
2   eggs
1½   cups apple juice
½   cup melted butter or margarine
1   cup broken walnuts
1½   cups coarsely chopped fresh cranberries

In a large mixing bowl, sift together the first 6 ingredients. Beat the eggs, and then add the apple juice and the melted butter. Stir into the dry ingredients. Fold in the walnuts and cranberries. Pour into a greased and floured loaf pan 9 x 5 x 3 inches. Bake in a preheated 350° F. oven for 1½ hours or until loaf is lightly browned and tests done with a wooden pick. Cool 15 minutes in the pan before turning out on a rack. This loaf will slice better the day after baking.

CHRISTMAS TWIST

½ recipe Sweet Dough
½ cup golden raisins
½ cup chopped citron
½ cup cut-up candied cherries
1 teaspoon cinnamon
¼ teaspoon mace
1 teaspoon flour
1 egg, beaten with 1 tablespoon water

Prepare the half-recipe of Sweet Dough and reserve. Mix the next 6 ingredients in a bowl. On a lightly floured cloth, knead the fruit mixture into the Sweet Dough until evenly distributed. Divide dough in half and roll each half into a rope 15 inches long. Place on a greased baking sheet and twist one over the other to form a two-strand braid, pinching the ends together. Cover with a cloth and let rise in a warm (80° to 85° F.) place until almost double in bulk. Brush top and sides with egg and bake in a preheated 350° F. oven for about 20 to 30 minutes, until the twist is golden and sounds hollow when tapped with the fingers.

GINGERBREAD COOKIES

⅓ cup brown sugar, firmly packed
⅓ cup butter, margarine, or shortening
⅔ cup molasses
1 egg, unbeaten
3 cups sifted all-purpose flour
1 tablespoon baking powder
1½ teaspoons ground ginger
½ teaspoon salt

Cream sugar and shortening until light and fluffy. Beat in molasses and egg. Sift in flour, baking powder, ginger, and salt; blend well. Chill 2 or more hours until firm enough to roll. Divide dough into fourths; work with one fourth at a time, refrigerating the remainder. Roll out to desired thickness for various sizes and shapes of cookies. Place on a greased cookie sheet and bake in a preheated 350° F. oven until firm, about 5 to 7 minutes. Cool slightly before removing to a wire rack. Makes about 2 dozen 4- to 6-inch cookies.

SUGAR COOKIES

1½ cups sugar
1   cup shortening
2   eggs, well beaten
1½ teaspoons vanilla
3½ cups sifted all-purpose flour
1   teaspoon baking powder
½   teaspoon salt
     tinted frosting, Fondant Frosting, raisins, colored sugar
     (optional)

Cream sugar and shortening until light and fluffy; beat in eggs and vanilla. Sift in flour, baking powder, and salt; blend well. Pat into a ball, wrap in foil, and chill until firm. Divide the dough into fourths; work with one fourth at a time, refrigerating the remainder. Roll out to desired thickness for various sizes and shapes of cookies. Place on a greased cookie sheet and bake in a preheated 375° F. oven until the edges are golden, about 5 to 7 minutes. Cool slightly before removing to a wire rack.

Decorate as desired with tinted frosting, raisins, or colored sugar. Dough may be cut with cookie cutters or with a knife from cardboard patterns. Picture cutouts may be "pasted" on with Fondant Frosting. Makes about 4 dozen cookies.

SAND TARTS
Sandbakelser

¾ cup butter or margarine
¾ cup sugar
1 egg, unbeaten
⅓ cup pulverized almonds
1¾ cups sifted all-purpose flour

In a medium bowl, cream butter and sugar. Add egg and beat until creamy; stir in the nuts. Add the flour, a little at a time, and mix well. Chill dough several hours or overnight. Press dough into tiny greased molds, or roll out the dough ⅛ inch thick and cut into rectangles 1¾ x 2¾ inches. Place the molds on a baking sheet or the cut dough on a greased cookie sheet and bake in a preheated 350° F. oven for about 10 minutes or until a light golden color. Makes about 3 dozen tarts or about 20 cookies.

PFEFFERNÜSSE

3 eggs
1 cup sugar
3 cups all-purpose flour
½ teaspoon baking powder
½ teaspoon baking soda
¼ teaspoon salt
¼ teaspoon freshly ground pepper
½ teaspoon ground cloves
1½ teaspoons cinnamon
¼ cup finely ground blanched almonds
   confectioners' sugar or frosting (optional)

Beat eggs until light and thick. Gradually add sugar while continuing to beat. Sift together the next 7 ingredients and add, a little at a time, to the egg mixture. Beat in the almonds. Chill dough for 1 hour or more for easier handling. Form a rounded teaspoon of dough and roll between floured palms into a ball about 1¼ inches in diameter. Place on a greased cookie sheet 1 inch apart. Bake in a preheated 350° F. oven for about 12 minutes, or until lightly browned on bottom. Do not overcook, because Pfeffernüsse harden after removal from the oven. They may be rolled in sugar while warm, or frosted if desired. Store in an airtight container with a slice of apple for at least a week. Makes about 4 dozen Pfeffernüsse.

HIGHLAND SHORTBREAD

1   cup softened butter
½   cup sugar
2½ cups sifted all-purpose flour

Cream butter and sugar until light and fluffy. Gradually work the flour into the butter and sugar until the dough is well mixed. Form dough into a ball and divide in half. Press into two 8-inch greased and floured cake pans or into a wooden Scotch shortbread mold prepared in the same way. Press around the edges with a fork to make the dough fluted, and prick it all over. Bake in a preheated 375° F. oven for 10 minutes; reduce heat to 300° F. and bake about 30 minutes more, or until golden. Let cool slightly before removing from pans, and cut into 8 wedges. If wooden mold is used, baking time will be somewhat longer.

PASTRY FOR TWO-CRUST PIE

2¼ cups sifted all-purpose flour
1   teaspoon salt
¾   cup shortening
⅓   cup (about) cold water

In a medium-sized bowl, combine flour, salt, and shortening. Cut shortening into flour with a pastry blender or two knives until it resembles corn meal. Sprinkle in water, 1 tablespoon at a time, and toss until all particles stick together. Form into 2 balls. Wrap in waxed paper and chill. Makes one 8- or 9-inch two-crust pie, or two 8- or 9-inch pie shells, or ten medium-sized tarts.

CRANBERRY CIDER PIE

1   recipe Pastry for Two-Crust Pie
1   cup apple cider
2   cups light brown sugar, firmly packed
5   tablespoons flour
¼   teaspoon salt
4   cups cranberries
1   tablespoon brandy (optional)

Prepare the Pastry for Two-Crust Pie, divide in two, and cool in refrigerator. Boil cider over high heat and reduce to ½ cup. Combine and stir in the sugar, flour, and salt and mix well. Add cranberries and boil 3 minutes, stirring constantly. Remove from heat and blend in brandy, if used; cool. Pour into a 9-inch pie pan lined with half the pastry. Bake in a preheated 425° F. oven until crust is golden, about 30 minutes. Roll out remainder of dough ⅛ inch thick and cut into any desired shapes, such as bells, Christmas trees, or stars. Place cutouts on an ungreased cookie sheet and bake until golden. Arrange on top of the baked pie before serving. Makes 8 servings.

MINCEMEAT ROYAL PIE

½   recipe Pastry for Two-Crust Pie
3   tablespoons butter
¼   cup light brown sugar, firmly packed
1   teaspoon salt
2   tablespoons flour
¾   cup light corn syrup
¼   cup brandy
3   eggs, separated
1½   cups mincemeat
½   cup broken nut meats
½   pint heavy cream, whipped (optional)

　　　Line a 9-inch pie plate with the half-recipe of pastry rolled
⅛ inch thick; flute a standing rim. Cream together butter,
sugar, salt, and flour. Mix in corn syrup and brandy. Whip egg
yolks until thick and add to sugar mixture; blend well. Stir in
mincemeat and nuts. Fold in stiffly beaten egg whites. Spoon
into the unbaked pastry shell. Bake in a preheated 325° F.
oven for about 50 minutes. Serve warm, with whipped cream
if desired. Makes 8 servings.

PILGRIM PIE

½ recipe Pastry for Two-Crust Pie
2 cups pumpkin, fresh or canned
¾ cup light brown sugar, firmly packed
½ teaspoon salt
1 teaspoon cinnamon
½ teaspoon each ginger and nutmeg
¼ teaspoon each ground allspice and cloves
2 eggs
1 cup heavy cream
6 tablespoons rum, cider, or applejack

Prepare the half-recipe of pastry and shape it into a 9-inch pie shell; place it in the refrigerator, uncooked, to chill. In a medium-sized saucepan, heat pumpkin and cook about 5 minutes to dry out, stirring to prevent burning. Stir in the sugar, salt, and the 5 spices. In a medium-sized bowl, beat the eggs until thick and lemon-colored; add cream and rum. Stir into the pumpkin mixture. Strain through a fine strainer and pour into the chilled unbaked shell. Bake in a preheated 450° F. oven for 15 minutes. If necessary, cover edges with strips of foil to keep from browning too rapidly. Reduce heat to 300° F. and bake 30 to 40 minutes more or until pie is set.

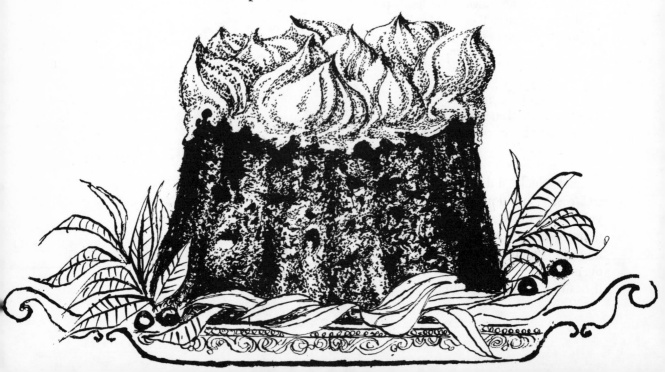

Hot Cranberry Snap, page 314

Quick Miniature Fruitcakes, page 308
Southern Eggnog, page 315

OLD-FASHIONED PLUM PUDDING

¼   cup butter or margarine
½   cup sugar
1   egg
½   cup milk
1   teaspoon allspice
1   teaspoon cinnamon
½   teaspoon salt
2½ cups toasted bread crumbs from firm-type bread
1½ cups chopped apples
1   cup chopped dates
1   cup mixed candied fruits and peels
½   cup chopped walnuts
4   tablespoons rum
    Brandy Sauce or Hard Sauce

Cream butter and sugar together. Add egg and beat well. Stir in milk and add the next 9 ingredients. Turn into a greased 1½-quart mold. Cover with a greased tightly fitting lid or with foil held in place with string. Place mold on a rack in a large deep pan. Pour in enough water to cover bottom half of the mold; cover. Simmer over low heat 4 hours, adding more water to pan as needed. Serve with Brandy Sauce or Hard Sauce. Makes 10 to 12 servings.

BRANDY SAUCE

½   cup butter or margarine
2   cups sifted confectioners' sugar
2   egg yolks
½   cup heavy cream
2   tablespoons brandy or bourbon

Cream butter and sugar and beat until light. Add egg yolks and beat until thick and lemon-colored; beat in cream. Cook over simmering water for 6 minutes, stirring constantly. Add brandy or bourbon and serve warm. Makes 2½ cups.

HARD SAUCE

½   cup butter
2   cups sifted confectioners' sugar
1   tablespoon brandy, bourbon, or vanilla

Cream butter and add sugar gradually, beating until light and fluffy. Beat in flavoring. Makes 1½ cups.

ENGLISH FRUITCAKE

1	cup golden raisins
1	cup chopped figs
¾	cup chopped citron
½	cup red candied cherries, cut in halves
½	cup green candied cherries, cut in halves
¾	cup candied pineapple, cut in pieces
½	cup chopped candied lemon peel
1½	cups walnuts, broken
1	cup shortening
1¼	cups sugar
4	eggs
2¼	cups all-purpose flour
1½	teaspoons double-acting baking powder
¾	teaspoon salt
¼	teaspoon ground cardamon
1½	teaspoons ground nutmeg
½	teaspoon cinnamon
1	teaspoon mace
1	teaspoon allspice
¾	cup orange marmalade
¼	cup brandy or orange juice

In a medium bowl, combine fruits and nuts. Cream shortening and sugar until fluffy. Add eggs, one at a time, beating well after each addition. Sift flour, baking powder, salt, and spices over the fruits and nuts and mix together until well coated. Combine with the egg mixture. Stir marmalade and brandy or orange juice together and add to batter. Mix thoroughly. Pour into a tube cake pan (8¼-inch bottom diameter by 4¼-inch high) that has been lined with 2 thicknesses of greased brown paper. Bake in a preheated 275° F. oven for about 3 hours. After the first 2 hours of baking, place foil over the top. Test for doneness before removing from oven. Cool in the pan for 30 minutes. Turn out and remove paper. May be served when cool. Or, wrap in cheesecloth that has been dampened in sherry or brandy and age the cake for a month in a tightly covered container.

WHITE FRUITCAKE

⅓ cup golden raisins
⅓ cup currants
¾ cup finely chopped figs
⅓ cup finely chopped dates
½ cup broken walnuts
4 eggs, separated
¾ cup sugar
1¾ cups sifted all-purpose flour
½ cup melted butter or margarine
1 tablespoon brandy
Fruitcake Glaze (optional)

In a medium-sized bowl, combine fruits and walnuts. In a mixing bowl, beat egg yolks and gradually add sugar, beating until thick. Beat egg whites until stiff but not dry; fold into the egg yolks. Sift flour over fruits and nuts and mix thoroughly; stir into egg mixture. Add butter, a little at a time, folding in lightly. Mix in brandy. Turn into a greased, waxed paper-lined loaf pan 8½ x 4½ x 2½ inches. Bake in a preheated 300° F. oven. Cover top of cake with foil after the first 45 minutes; then bake an additional 45 minutes, or until cake tests done. Cool in pan for 30 minutes. Remove from pan and peel off the paper. Glaze and decorate if desired.

QUICK MINIATURE FRUITCAKES

24   miniature-sized fluted foil baking cups
1   pound or 2 cups mixed chopped candied fruits
¾   cup golden raisins
1   cup broken walnuts
1½ cups sifted all-purpose flour
1   teaspoon double-acting baking powder
¼   teaspoon salt
¼   teaspoon each (ground) nutmeg, clove, allspice, cinnamon, ginger
½   cup sugar
½   cup cooking oil
2   eggs, unbeaten
3   tablespoons sherry or orange juice
    Fruitcake Glaze (optional)
    candied cherries (optional)

Remove paper liners from foil cups and place cups on a baking sheet. Put candied fruits, raisins, and walnuts in a bowl. Add flour, baking powder, salt, and spices. Toss thoroughly to coat all fruits and nuts. Add sugar, oil, eggs, and sherry or orange juice, and stir to blend well. Spoon into the foil cups. Bake in a preheated 275° F. oven for 1 hour. If desired, decorate the cakes with Fruitcake Glaze and candied cherries. Store in an airtight container. Makes 24 cakes.

FRUITCAKE GLAZE

1 tablespoon corn syrup
2 tablespoons light brown sugar
2 tablespoons water
2 tablespoons brandy or orange juice

In a small saucepan, combine syrup, sugar, and water; bring to a boil and cook until sugar is dissolved. Cool slightly and add brandy or orange juice. Brush over top of cake and repeat two or more times, waiting 5 minutes or more between each brushing. Decorate top of cake as desired and brush again.

ICE CREAM BOMBE

1 quart vanilla ice cream
¾ cup chopped mixed candied fruits
3 tablespoons rum
1 quart pistachio ice cream
   red candies or any desired decoration
1 pint heavy cream, whipped

Put two 1½-quart bowls in the freezer for at least 1 hour. Working with one bowl at a time, line bottom and sides of bowl with vanilla ice cream, using 1 pint for each bowl. Crush ice cream against side of bowl with the back of a large spoon, forming a shell about ½ inch thick. Return to freezer until ice cream is very firm. Combine candied fruit and rum, mixing and tossing to coat each piece. Refrigerate for at least an hour. In a large bowl break up the pistachio ice cream and work in the candied fruits. Do not let ice cream become mushy. Return to freezer until firm again. Fill the center of each ice cream shell with the fruited pistachio ice cream and return to freezer until firm.

To unmold: Run a pointed knife around edge of one bowl. Place a hot damp dishcloth about the bowl for a few seconds. Invert onto a chilled plate. With the help of a wide spatula, flip it over so that it is resting with the open side up. Return to freezer to firm up; then unmold the other half on top, to form a ball. Smooth the seam and return to freezer until firm. Cover bombe with whipped cream rosettes and decorate with red candies or as desired. Makes 8 servings.

MARZIPAN

1 can (8 ounces) almond paste
2 tablespoons slightly beaten egg white
1 cup sifted confectioners' sugar

In a medium-sized bowl, break up almond paste with a fork. Add egg white and work in well. Knead in the sugar until the mixture is stiff enough to form into desired shapes.

Fruits and vegetables may be modeled from marzipan and tinted with food coloring. Marzipan may be used to stuff dried apricots, figs, and dates; or it may be rolled into candies, spread with Fondant Frosting and topped with an almond, pecan, or walnut. Makes about 1½ dozen candies 1½ x ¾ x ¾ inches, or about 36 fillings for dried fruits.

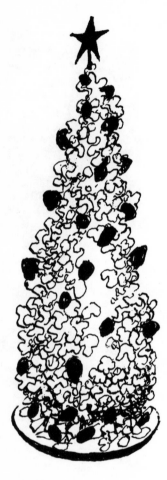

POPCORN TREE

     butter or margarine
8   cups popped popcorn
1   cup sugar
⅓   cup light corn syrup
⅓   cup water
     styrofoam cone 12 inches high with a 3½-inch base
     wood picks
     small gumdrops
     green foliage (optional)

Place the popcorn in a large greased bowl. Combine sugar, corn syrup, and water in a 1-quart saucepan. Cook over medium heat, without stirring, until syrup reaches 240° F. on a candy thermometer, or forms a soft ball when a small amount is dropped into a cup of cold water. Pour hot syrup over popcorn. Immediately mix and toss the popcorn with two forks until well coated. Working rapidly, pull off small amounts and form into balls of graduated sizes, placing them on waxed paper. When ready to assemble, place a pick in each ball and stick into the styrofoam cone to form the tree, using smaller balls for the top. Place gumdrops on picks and insert to resemble ornaments. Decorate with green foliage if desired.

Popcorn may also be made into 12 popcorn balls or 3 balls of graduated size to form a snowman.

CANDIED CITRUS PEEL

3   large oranges
3   large grapefruit
1½   cups water
3   cups granulated sugar
3   tablespoons honey
⅛   teaspoon salt
1   teaspoon unflavored gelatin

Cut oranges into fourths and grapefruit into eighths. Remove pulp and scrape away all the white part. Cut peel into ½-inch strips. Place peel in a 2-quart saucepan, cover with water, and simmer 15 minutes; drain and discard the water. Pour over the peel 1¼ cups of the measured water, 2 cups of the sugar, the honey, and the salt. Cook 45 minutes over low heat, stirring occasionally. Just before removing from heat, soften gelatin in remaining ¼ cup of water and add to hot mixture. Stir to dissolve. Let cool, and drain well in a colander.

Roll the strips of peel in the remaining 1 cup of sugar, and let dry overnight on a baking sheet lined with waxed paper. Store in a tightly covered container. The peel will keep moist for several weeks. Makes about 12 ounces.

PRALINES

2 cups sugar
¾ teaspoon baking soda
1 cup light cream
1½ tablespoons butter or margarine
2 cups pecan halves

Combine sugar and soda in a 3-quart saucepan. Add cream and stir to dissolve sugar. Bring to a boil over medium heat, stirring occasionally. When mixture starts to boil, reduce heat. The mixture will gradually turn golden as it cooks. Boil until syrup forms a soft ball when a small amount is dropped into a cup of cold water, or reaches 234° F. on a candy thermometer. Remove pan from heat and add butter. Stir in pecans and beat just until thick enough to drop from a metal spoon. Drop candy on waxed paper placed on a cookie sheet. If necessary, add a tablespoon or so of hot water to keep candy at the right consistency for dropping from spoon. Cool until firm before removing. Makes about 1 dozen 2½-inch pralines.

GLACÉED NUTS

2 cups granulated sugar
⅛ teaspoon cream of tartar
½ cup water
⅓ cup each almonds, pecan halves, and cashews

Combine sugar, cream of tartar, and water in a small heavy saucepan. Place over medium heat and stir constantly until sugar is dissolved. Wipe crystals from sides of pan. Boil, without stirring, to 240° F. on a candy thermometer, or until syrup forms a soft ball when dropped in cold water. Add nuts and continue to boil to 300° F., the hard-crack stage, when a small amount tested in cold water forms a brittle thread. Pour into a large sieve; drain. Turn onto a buttered cookie sheet and separate the nuts quickly with two forks. When cool, store in an airtight container.

Do not attempt to glacé more than 1 cup of nuts at a time unless someone is available to help separate the nuts before they harden.

MERINGUES

6   egg whites at room temperature
⅛   teaspoon cream of tartar
1½   cups granulated sugar
½   teaspoon vanilla
       candy decorations

In a large bowl with an electric mixer at high speed, beat egg whites until frothy. Add cream of tartar and continue to beat until soft peaks form. Very slowly add sugar while beating, about 12 minutes. Add vanilla and beat until meringue looks glossy and holds stiff peaks. Line a baking sheet with ungreased brown paper. Scoop meringue onto the paper, forming desired shapes with a spoon, or pipe with a pastry tube. Decorate with colored sugar crystals, spangles, or silver shot. Bake in a preheated 200° F. oven for about 2 hours or until very dry but still white. Makes about 2 dozen 2-inch meringues.

HOLIDAY PUNCH

1 quart bourbon whiskey
1 bottle (1 pint 8 ounces) dry white wine
1 pint light rum
1 pint brandy
4 ounces curaçao
1 quart orange juice
1 pint grenadine syrup
1 quart soda water
   Sugar Syrup (optional)

Combine all ingredients except soda water and chill thoroughly. If a sweeter punch is desired, add Sugar Syrup according to taste. Pour over a block of ice in a large punchbowl. Add soda water just before serving. Makes about 5 quarts.

SUGAR SYRUP

½ cup sugar
1 cup water

Bring sugar and water to a boil. Cover and simmer 3 minutes. Chill. Makes about 1¼ cups.

Christmas Boxes in Camp—Christmas, 1861, from HARPER'S WEEKLY, 1862

FRUIT PUNCH
(Nonalcoholic)

1 can (6 ounces) frozen lemonade, reconstituted
1 can (6 ounces) frozen orange juice, reconstituted
1 can (12 ounces) pineapple juice
  ginger ale (optional)
  sliced fruit for garnish (optional)
  Sugar Syrup (optional)

Combine lemonade, orange juice, and pineapple juice. Chill thoroughly. Pour over a block of ice in a punch bowl, or serve in a pitcher with ice cubes. Ginger ale may be added just before serving. Garnish with sliced fruit if desired. For a sweeter punch, add Sugar Syrup to taste. Makes 2 quarts.

HOT CRANBERRY SNAP

4 cups cranberries
2 quarts water
4 cups sugar
  peel from 1 orange
2 pieces cinnamon stick, 1 inch long
2 teaspoons whole cloves
2 teaspoons whole allspice
2 quarts apple juice
1 quart applejack
  whole apples (optional)

Pick over cranberries and put in a large saucepan. Add water, sugar, and orange peel. Tie the spices up in a piece of cheesecloth and add. Bring slowly to a boil and cook 5 minutes. Crush the cranberries with the back of a large spoon against the side of the pan while cooking. Discard spices and orange peel. Pour through a fine strainer. (The drained cranberries may be refrigerated and served with meat or fowl.) Return cranberry liquid to same pan and add apple juice. Heat to boiling point and add warmed applejack. Pour into a heated silver or china bowl. Float a few roasted apples on top if desired. Makes 5 quarts.

SOUTHERN EGGNOG

12 eggs, separated
¾ cup granulated sugar
1 pint brandy
½ pint light rum
1 pint milk
½ pint heavy cream
    freshly grated nutmeg

Beat egg yolks until lemon-colored. Slowly add sugar and continue to beat until sugar is dissolved. Pour in brandy, a little at a time, and continue to beat. Add the rum and beat until well blended; add the milk and mix well. In another bowl, beat the cream until stiff; fold into the egg-sugar mixture. Beat egg whites until stiff but not dry, and fold in. Pour into a punch bowl or serve in prefilled glasses. Sprinkle a generous amount of nutmeg on top. Makes 12 to 16 servings.

Index to Recipes

General Index

317